W9-ABB-926

Cambridge Studies in Social and Cultural Anthropology

95

PEOPLE OF THE SEA

The Vezo, a fishing people of western Madagascar, are known as 'the people who struggle with the sea'. Dr Astuti explores their identity, showing that it is established through what people do rather than being determined by descent. Vezo identity is a 'way of doing' rather than a 'state of being', performative rather than ethnic. However, her innovative analysis of Vezo kinship also uncovers an opposite form of identity based on descent, which she argues is the identity of the dead. By looking at key mortuary rituals that engage the relationship between the living and the dead, Dr Astuti develops a dual model of the Vezo person: the one defined contextually in the present, the other determined by the past.

Cambridge Studies in Social and Cultural Anthropology publishes analytical ethnographies, comparative works, and contributions to theory. All combine an expert and critical command of ethnography and a sophisticated engagement with current theoretical debates.

Editors: Ernest Gellner, Jack Goody, Stephen Gudeman, Michael Herzfeld Jonathan Parry

A list of books in this series will be found at the end of the volume

PEOPLE OF THE SEA

Identity and descent among the Vezo of Madagascar

RITA ASTUTI

London School of Economics and Political Science

CAMBRIDGE
UNIVERSITY PRESS

Published by the Press Syndicate of the University of Cambridge
The Pitt Building, Trumpington Street, Cambridge CB2 1RP
40 West 20th Street, New York, NY 10011–4211, USA
10 Stamford Road, Oakleigh, Melbourne 3166, Australia

First published 1995

Printed in Great Britain at the University Press, Cambridge

A catalogue record for this book is available from the British Library

Library of Congress cataloguing in publication data

DT
469
M277
V483
1995

ISBN 0 521 43350 9 hardback

To dadilahy Naboy,
Lorenzo and
Sean

Contents

List of illustrations

Plates

Figures

Acknowledgements

This book is the outcome of eighteen months of fieldwork spent among the Vezo of Madagascar. Research was supported by Wenner-Gren Grant-in-Aid (1988), and by grants from the Central Research Fund, University of London; the Centro Nazionale delle Ricerche (CNR), Rome; the Istituto Italo-Africano, Rome; and the University of Siena. The British Academy elected me to a Post-Doctoral Fellowship which has made the writing of this book possible. I thank all these institutions for their support.

I am grateful to Jean-Aimé Rakotoarisoa, director of the Musée d'Art et d'Archéologie, Université d'Antananarivo, for his help in making my research successful; my thanks go also to the staff of the Musée. I wish to thank Mme Pénélope Simon, who first taught me Malagasy in London; Rosa Stevan for her friendship and material support in Antananarivo, and Gion Cabalzar and Shirin Sotoudeh for theirs in Morondava.

From a distance, my parents, Carlo and Fernanda, have provided close support and encouragement throughout my studies, the period of fieldwork, and the upheavals of the last year. I thank them for this and much more.

Janet Carsten, Johnny Parry, Pier Giorgio Solinas, Charles Stafford, Michael Stewart, Marilyn Strathern and Paola Tabet have provided invaluable comments and suggestions at different stages of the writing.

Maurice Bloch introduced me to Madagascar, shared the excitement of practising anthropology, and helped me overcome the frustrations of writing what resisted being written.

Lorenzo Epstein learnt about the Vezo, liked them, and understood my immersion into Vezo-ness. He participated in the efforts and rewards of research, and gave unflagging support from the time when I first began to ask questions about the Vezo to the time when I began to answer some of them.

Those I can find no adequate way of thanking are my friends and relatives in Betania and in Belo; I thank them nonetheless for teaching me, with patience, enthusiasm and tolerance, that I could become Vezo and for showing me how. They know how easy they made my life among them, and how much I enjoyed being with them.

1

Introduction

This is a study of two different forms of identity, one which is achieved through activities performed in the present, the other which is given as an essence inherited from the past; one which is of a recognizable Austronesian character, for it is transformative, non-primordialist and non-essentialist, the other which bears instead a clear African imprint, for it is rooted in, and determined by, the unchangeable order of descent. These two identities are both known to the Vezo, a group of people who live on the western coast of Madagascar. One of the aims of this book is to explore how these two different and apparently incompatible ways of being a person are made to co-exist, and how they are articulated with one another.

In the following pages, I shall introduce the reader to these two identities as I encountered them during my fieldwork among the Vezo. I shall describe how I came to formulate the question that will engage us for the whole of this work; at the same time, I shall begin to provide and to explain the local idiom of identity – the contrast between 'un-kindedness' and 'kindedness'.

A few days after arriving in Betania, a coastal village in western Madagascar, I saw two children, aged about six, playing in the hull of a broken canoe half sunk in the sand. As they paddled with two wooden sticks, they chanted to each other '*ve-zo! ve-zo!*'. *Vezo* is the imperative form of the verb *mive*, which means 'to paddle'; the two children were imitating what one of the persons on a canoe-team chants to beat the rhythm for the others.

The term 'Vezo' also denotes a people. The Vezo often point out that their name means 'paddle',[1] a name which indicates who they are: 'people who struggle with the sea and live on the coast' (*olo mitolo rano, olo mipetsaky andriaky*). This point was reiterated many times in my first weeks

1

in the field. Any attempt on my part to learn new words related to fishing or sailing, for example, prompted my instructors to explain that all the people who fish and sail are Vezo; similarly, when I showed a group of young men a map of the coastal region, they told me that all the people who live along the coast, near the sea, are Vezo. I soon found these comments rather tedious, for they appeared to be stating the obvious, namely that the Vezo are people who base their livelihood on the sea.

What I was being told with such insistence seemed of particularly little consequence since virtually all accounts by early travellers or missionaries, or more recent reports by geographers, anthropologists or historians of the region, had already made the point that the Vezo should be regarded as a fishing and coastal people. For example Koechlin, the author of the most detailed study of the Vezo, defined them as 'semi-nomadic marine people, and predators of the coral reef, of the mangrove swamps and of the forest adjacent to the coast' (Koechlin 1975: 23). Other scholars referred to the Vezo less technically as 'marine people, devoted to fishing, who spend a lot of time at sea and live along the sea-coast' (Grandidier 1971: 9), or as 'people of the coast, who practise navigation and are devoted to fishing' (Poirier 1953: 23).[2] In fact, the prevailing view in the literature has been that the only distinguishing feature of the Vezo is their mode of livelihood.[3] This seems to be confirmed by the oft-mentioned fact that if a person leaves the coast to move to the interior, she ceases to be Vezo and becomes Masikoro, the name of the Vezo's neighbours who are cultivators and cattle raisers.[4] It has thus been concluded that the term 'Vezo' does not indicate a trait of identity that is fixed and immutable, for people can move and change their livelihood accordingly. For this reason also, scholars have agreed that the Vezo are not a 'genuine ethnic group' (*une ethnie veritable*), a 'special race' (*une race spéciale*) or a 'distinct people' (*une peuplade distincte*).[5] In other words, it has been argued that while the term 'Vezo' indicates what the Vezo do and where they live (that they are 'people who struggle with the sea and live on the coast'), it fails to reveal who the Vezo 'genuinely' are. As a result, the Vezo have been considered in need of an alternative identity, which has been found by assigning them to the 'large Sakalava ethnic family'[6] (Koechlin 1975: 26), within which they are said to represent a technologically defined sub-group among others.

I began to appreciate that the statement that the Vezo are people who struggle with the sea and live on the coast was less obvious and less tedious than I first thought, and that it was a 'genuine' statement of identity, when I started to ask questions which were based on mistaken assumptions. For example, I asked why villagers who had migrated from the south and were of Antandroy rather than Vezo origin were said nonetheless to be Vezo; or I expressed surprise that people with a broad and differing range of ancestral customs could nonetheless all be considered to be Vezo. To these questions, my informants would answer simply: 'the Vezo are not a kind of people' (*Vezo tsy karazan'olo*).

The word *karaza* means kind, type, and indicates groups of objects, animals or people that share some essential characteristics (see also Bloch 1971: 42–3). For example, fish is a 'kind' of living thing, and Spanish mackerel is a 'kind' of fish. The word *raza*, from which *karaza* derives, applies in turn to the ancestors, and in particular to the ancestors of a certain 'kind', those who are buried in the same tomb and are referred to as 'one *raza*' (*raza raiky*). Membership of a *karaza*, whether of a class of objects, animals or people, is based on intrinsic and inborn qualities of the individual; neither 'fishness', nor a specific kind of 'fishness', can be acquired, learnt or changed – a fish is born what it is. Similarly, a human being does not acquire, or learn, membership of a particular tomb or of the *raza* contained therein, but obtains it through descent.

Consequently, the statement that 'the Vezo are not a *kind* of people', that they are 'un-kinded', is meant to signify that Vezo people are not *inherently* such – that they are not born Vezo, and are not Vezo by descent. It follows that people of Antandroy or of any other origin can be Vezo, because to be Vezo is not an issue of *origin*; and that people with different ancestral customs can all be Vezo, because Vezo-ness is not determined by ancestry.

When I understood that 'the Vezo are not a kind of people', I also realized that when people told me, with some insistence, that they were people who struggle with the sea and live on the coast, they were offering more than a descriptive statement about their mode of livelihood and about the environment in which they live; by describing what they do and where they live, the Vezo were in fact telling me *who they are*. Both statements – that the Vezo are not a kind of people, and that they are people who struggle with the sea and live on the coast – were informed by the same view, namely that Vezo identity is not determined by birth, by descent, by an essence inherited from the past, but is created contextually in the present through what people do and through the place where they live. 'People are not Vezo because of their stock, but because they go out to sea, they go fishing, they live near the sea' (*tsy Vezo am'raza, fa Vezo satsia mandeha andriva, maminta, mipetsaky amin' sisindriaky*).

When I insist, as I shall do in the first part of this book, that the Vezo are what they do, that Vezo identity is an activity rather than a state of being, and that a Vezo person is not what she is or what she becomes, but what she *does*, I depart from the scholarly consensus on the Vezo found in the literature – I will argue, in other words, that the term 'Vezo' defines who the Vezo 'genuinely' are, precisely because it defines them exclusively by reference to what they do and to the place where they live. And yet, I also agree with the view that the Vezo are *not* a 'genuine ethnic group', a 'special race', a 'distinct people', although I reach this conclusion for different reasons and I use it for very different analytical ends. Those scholars who have argued that the Vezo do not constitute an ethnic group were working on the assumption that a 'genuine' identity must be fixed rather than shifting (if a person is 'genuinely' Vezo, she cannot become Masikoro), inherent rather than contextual, that it must be established through descent rather than be achieved through practice. From this perspective, the Vezo were perceived to be anomalous, for they did not fit the 'western ethnotheory of ethnicity' (Linnekin and Poyer 1990: 2), a theory informed by the view that people's identity is drawn from common origins and, through them, from some sort of biological or cultural trait which is either inherent to the person – like blood or descent – or is 'naturalized' and thereby made to appear inherent – like language, religion or a specific kind of history.[7] Having perceptively recognized the Vezo's anomaly, previous scholars failed nonetheless to perceive the full implications of their own finding; by remaining within the narrow framework of their 'ethnic' theory, they were unable to appreciate the non-essentialist character of the Vezo's own 'ethnotheory' of identity. They stopped, in other words, where the present study begins.

This study of Vezo identity was triggered by the statement that the Vezo are not a kind of people. I heard this statement often at the beginning of my fieldwork, when I still formulated questions and made remarks based on misguided assumptions about the nature of Vezo identity. In due time, as I learnt to ask questions more in tune with the Vezo's own perception of their identity, I also came to perceive the 'un-kindedness' of the Vezo embedded in what people had to say about themselves. Rather than a simple denial, the statement of 'un-kindedness' began to seem like a positive affirmation of how the Vezo come to be what they are through what they do.[8]

The first part of this book aims to elucidate the claim that the Vezo are not a kind of people. A more familiar way of describing 'un-kindedness' is to refer to it as undetermination – the undetermination of Vezo-ness and of the Vezo person by the past. In order to be Vezo, a person must act in the present, for it is only in the present that one can perform one's identity. By contrast, activities performed in the past do not determine what a person is at a certain point in time. The Vezo person can thus be imagined to start from scratch every day in creating its identity through practice.

The Vezo deny that the past impinges on the present; they deny, in other words, that Vezo identity has a history. One of the many ways in which the Vezo assert this is by recounting an act of defiance that happened in the past. They claim that they were never part (i.e. subjects) of the Sakalava kingdoms which, up to the colonial period, ruled over the whole of western Madagascar. They add, proudly, that instead of paying homage to the rulers who came visiting the coast, they would take to their canoes and flee; as we shall see, one of the things they fled from was the determining power of history. Whether this story is historically accurate or not is of little consequence, except for suggesting that the little known history of the Vezo's modes of integration into the Sakalava polities[9] might throw light on the origins of Vezo's current 'un-kindedness'. My aim in this study, however, is not to uncover the historical roots of present-day Vezo-ness, but to analyse the particular configurations of identity as they are experienced by the Vezo in their everyday life – the morphology rather than the genesis of that identity.

Fieldwork among the Vezo can easily turn into the experience of becoming a Vezo person. By this I mean something more specific than the common and often romanticized process of acceptance and gradual assimilation experienced by many anthropologists; as we shall see, the possibility of 'becoming Vezo' is closely linked to the specific nature of Vezo identity.

The Vezo readily apply the two related notions that they are 'un-kinded' people and that they are what they do, to any person who lives among them and performs, more or less skilfully, the things that make people Vezo. As I was once told:

the Vezo do not have a master, Vezo is a collective name for everyone who is able to do things all right, if they like the sea. Vezo-ness doesn't belong to any one person, it doesn't have a master. One can't say that so and so is the master of Vezo-ness. No! Everyone is master of Vezo-ness, if they like it and like to practise it.[10]

My Vezo friends often remarked on the fact that I really liked the sea, that I liked swimming, sailing and fishing; they noted that I had been wise in choosing their place to carry out my research – they seemed to agree that I was well suited to becoming Vezo.

Only at the point in my fieldwork when I spent whole days being Vezo by way of doing – by going out fishing, by smoking fish or by selling shrimp at the market – did I fully grasp what the statement 'the Vezo are not a kind of people' meant. My own transformation into a Vezo, experienced subjectively and through other people's perception of myself, was made possible precisely because of the 'un-kindedness' of the Vezo: it is because the Vezo person is undetermined by the past, that I too could shed my own personal history and acquire a new identity in the present. From this perspective, I consider my own transformation as a minor but significant instance of the process experienced by all Vezo people of becoming what they are through what they do.

In the ethnographic account that follows I sometimes deploy personal experience to exemplify the way in which people learn to do Vezo things and become Vezo as a result. It could be argued that when my hosts told me that I was Vezo because I could swim or because I sailed, they did not mean it literally. In other words, did they ever think that I was 'really' Vezo? The answer, of course, is no; but this is not because I was a distant and unreconstructed foreigner, but because no Vezo person is 'really' Vezo in so far as no one can claim to be so inherently. My friends were well aware that once I left them, I would resume a very different identity; but they liked to think that this did not affect my new way of doing, hence of being, while I was among them. My being Vezo was undoubtedly contextual; however, I shall argue that Vezo identity is always contextual for *everyone* who acquires it and performs it.

Inevitably, the modes through which the Vezo constitute and define their identity in the present profoundly shaped my fieldwork and determined the kind of questions I asked; the experience of inclusion – through the process of becoming Vezo, which at times I felt was almost being forced upon me – brought into focus the issues and problems around which the first part of this book is organized. Experiencing the *limits* to my inclusion, on the other hand, made me aware of a second identity, one which stands in opposition with Vezo-ness as I describe it.

Towards the end of my stay I happened to be in a very dangerous situation at sea. I was sailing back home at night, when the young man who was in charge of the canoe lost the paddle that was being used as a rudder, and realized that he had forgotten to take the spare paddle which is normally kept on board. We were thus left with no control over the canoe. We quickly took down the sail, and made out that the current was pushing us into a shallow inlet where the sea was very rough. Although the canoe began to take on a lot of water, and the hull was in danger of splitting under the strain, we managed nonetheless to push ourselves slowly to shore with the aid of the two sail poles. Although I kept myself busy trying to reassure a small boy who was travelling with us, I realized on reaching shore that we could easily have drowned. A few days later, someone told us they had found one of the watermelons we had thrown overboard that night many miles to the south, lightly remarking that they could well have found our bodies instead if the canoe had been wrecked or capsized. This episode prompted a question that had been hovering in the back of my mind for a long time: would my Vezo family have buried me in its tomb if I had died? The answer was that they would *not*, because my parents 'on the other side of the ocean' would want my body and bones to bury in *their* tomb.

Like all other people in Madagascar, the Vezo attach great significance to the 'placing of the dead', that is, to the choice of the burial tomb (cf. Bloch 1971). Among them, burial into different tombs divides people into 'kinds', which are called *raza*; by excluding me from their tomb, my Vezo relatives effectively barred me from being incorporated into their *raza*. The reason for this is that, contrary to Vezo-ness, *raza* identity is a state of being and not a way of doing; it is an identity based upon descent, upon a person's ancestry which cannot be changed contextually in either time or space.

The existence of 'kinds' of people, the *raza*, among the Vezo who claim that they are *not* a 'kind of people' poses a theoretical puzzle. How can two opposed identities co-exist among the same people, one that evolves through practice and the other that is fixed by descent? One that is inclusive and the other that is exclusive? How can the Vezo be at the same time 'un-kinded' and 'kinded' people? These are the questions addressed in the second half of the book.

Kinship will be used as the backdrop against which one can perceive the 'kindedness' of the Vezo. Two different domains can be distinguished, one which establishes relatedness in the present, and the other which divides people into 'kinds' (*raza*) and operates only in the future, after a person's death. This distinction, based upon the experience of time, is vital for understanding the co-existence and interplay of what have traditionally been referred to as cognatic and unilineal descent; it also sets the context for the analysis of the identity ('kindedness') experienced by the dead. The latter can be reconstructed by analysing funerals and mortuary rituals, during which the living Vezo separate themselves from the dead, and yet at the same time create distinctions of kind among them.

Finally, we shall be in a position to understand how the Vezo both deny and recognize the continuity between their identity and the identity of the dead, between 'un-kindedness' and 'kindedness', between the past, the present and the future.

I spent my fieldwork among the Vezo (from November 1987 until June

1989) living in two villages: Betania and Belo-sur-Mer (Belo for short).[11] Morondava, the main town in the area, which includes governmental offices, a market, a hospital, a post office and an airport, lies about 3 km north of Betania. For most of the year Belo, 60 km south of Morondava, can be reached from the town only by sea. While living in Betania and Belo I spent short spells of time in other nearby Vezo villages: Lovobe, Bemangily, Ankevo, Begamela, Antanimanimbo, Manahy an-driaky; at the market in Morondava I met women from many Vezo villages north and south of Betania. I also visited some Masikoro villages in the interior: Ambohibary, Manometinay, Beleo, Marofihitsy, Manahy an-tety (see Fig. 1).

Betania lies on a long and narrow tongue of land, surrounded by water on three sides: to the north, an inlet which grows and shrinks according to the tide; to the west the ocean, a mere 200 m away; to the east, a mangrove swamp. The village in its entirety can be seen only from the sea. The sun and moon both rise from and set in the water.

Like all other Vezo villages, Betania is built not on 'hard land' (*tany mahery*) but on 'soft sand' (*fasy malemy*). The beach merges with the village; the only boundary demarcating them is a range of coconut palms scattered between the houses. Looked at from the ocean, Betania can be recognized by the disposition and height of its palms, and by one large umbrella-shaped tamarind tree at its northern tip.

The houses are built on a band of sand along a north/south axis running parallel to the sea, and canoes are beached in a similar manner. Most houses consist of a wooden frame. The walls are stuffed with dried *vondro* (a long grass which grows in the interior), the roof is made of layered coconut leaves, and the floor is covered with woven mats spread out over the sand. Besides these there are a few brick houses, with corrugated iron roof and cement floor. The openings in both kinds of dwelling are in the eastern and western walls.

Most people have a separate hut for cooking; otherwise food is cooked outdoors. Nothing is ever cooked in the dwelling used for sleeping. Small enclosures near the houses are used as 'showers' (*ladouche*), where one can undress and wash with the help of a bucket. Cooking, drinking and washing water comes from a number of wells dug between the houses. Chickens and pigs roam freely around the village; but if they get too close to a house, and especially if they belong to 'enemies', they risk being clubbed, stoned or scalded with boiling water. Casualties have been known to occur.

If one were to ask the people of Betania what the most important feature

Fig. 1 Area of fieldwork

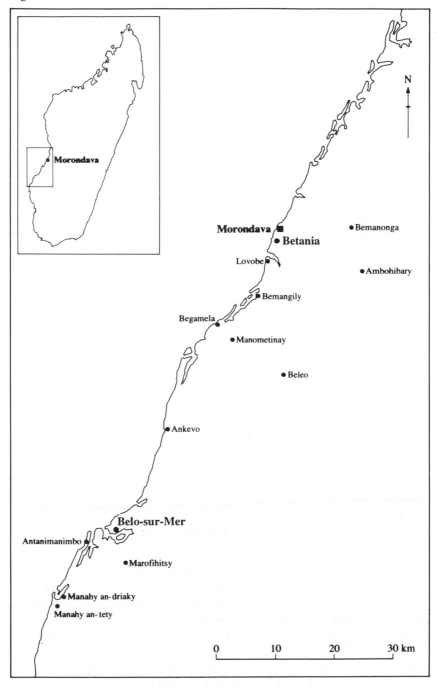

of their village is, beside being a Vezo (i.e. a coastal) settlement, they would probably answer that its 'character' (*toetsin-tana*) derives from its proximity to the Morondava market. This market is an integral part of the villagers' social space. To the question, where they were going, people heading north would most often answer that they were walking to the market (Q. *Ho aia nareo?* A. *Handeha a bazary añy zahay*). Although I soon learned that this answer can be a polite equivalent to 'mind your own business', most of the time the reply was truthful. Villagers go to the market every day to sell their fish and to buy provisions for the day's meals; they buy rice and, if they earn enough money, they buy ingredients to make 'rich side-dishes' (*laoke matavy*) such as pork with potatoes, or beef with manioc leaves. In fact, they will often point out that proximity to the market enables them to avoid the monotony of eating fish every day (*oma fia isanandro isanandro*); as a result, people will seldom be bored with their food (*tsy morimoritsy*).

On mentioning that I wanted to move to Belo, a village with no market (*tana tsy misy bazary*), friends in Betania insisted that I would be miserable: I would eat fish day in day out, and life would be so quiet (*bangy bangy*) that I would soon get homesick (*jangobo*). When a relative from Betania subsequently came to visit me in Belo, he asked teasingly whether we could make a quick visit to the market before supper, and made a great show of surprise at hearing that there was no market nearby.

One of the first things I noticed on arriving in Belo were the deep ruts in the sand left by carts with which inland Masikoro periodically carry maize, manioc or rice to Belo to sell or barter for fish. Villagers in Belo say that these carts are their market, but they will readily admit that they do not provide the same excitement as the market in Morondava. They also recognize that their diet is more monotonous than in Betania because they eat fish every day; however, they pride themselves both for the greater variety of fish and crayfish and for its being both fattier and tastier.

The atmosphere in Belo is quite different from that in Betania. The village lies on one side of a vast lagoon and is further away from the open sea, and it is therefore hotter than Betania. The sand, which is much darker, also heats up more and makes it painful for small children to walk on; one will see more frequently than in Betania older children carrying their younger siblings piggy-back from one shaded area to another across a stretch of scalding sand. Also in Belo most houses are built with solid wood planks, making them much more durable than in Betania; on the whole, the settlement has a more solid and permanent appearance. This impression is reinforced by the many *botsy* under construction, massive schooners made with very hard, long-lasting timber. It is these schooners, and people's involvement in their construction, that is regarded by the inhabitants as making the 'character' of their village.

When I moved from Betania to Belo and whenever I travelled to another Vezo village I was encouraged to notice the differences in ways of doing (*fomba*), mostly with respect to people's livelihood (*fiveloma*), but also to their manner of speech, their diet, the location of the villages, and the build of houses. As one of my closest adoptive relatives once explained to a visitor who had never met me before, I had come to Madagascar to learn about the Vezo, and I had been travelling to different places in order to see the many different ways in which the Vezo do things.

Despite widespread awareness of these differences, my interlocutors used the term 'Vezo' in conversations with me or among themselves to refer to all the people who 'struggle with the sea and live on the coast' (*olo mitolo rano, olo mipetsaky andriaky*). The fact that in one place people dive for lobsters while in another they line-fish for Spanish mackerel is irrelevant, in so far as in both places – in *all* places along the west coast – people base their livelihood on the sea and are therefore Vezo.

In this book I employ the term 'Vezo' in two complementary ways. First, I refer to the small fraction of Vezo people I got to know in the two villages where I lived for long stretches of time; I write about what they taught me of themselves and about those things they did which made them Vezo. Second, I write about 'the Vezo' in the same way as my informants talked about them(selves), with the awareness that despite differences in practice, the people of Betania, of Belo and of any other village on the west coast are all Vezo because they are all 'people who struggle with the sea and live on the coast'. Following my informants' usage, I assume that this criterion of identity transcending local differences (as well as the notion that 'the Vezo are not a kind of people') is shared by all Vezo people, even though I lack empirical confirmation that this is the case outside the region where I worked.

I chose to live in Betania initially for reasons of convenience, for it was the closest village to the administrative centre of Morondava, and thus the easiest place I could arrange to move to at short notice. At that point I was anxious above all to learn the language, and life in Betania seemed an easy solution to acquiring linguistic competence before moving to a more distant location, which I identified as Belo.

In the end, despite these plans and a first visit to Belo four months after settling on the coast, I spent most of my time in Betania, where I was able to establish an ideal human and working environment which I felt I could not leave lightheartedly. In Betania, I was adopted within the kinship network of the man whose house I rented. Within these bounds, which included eight households, I could join in any conversation, meeting, argument, gossip, fight, joke, whispering, laughing or crying I wished to be part of. I could ask questions and require explanations. Although some people were remarkably better than others in providing answers I could understand, most were at ease with the idea that I was interested in learning about them and were highly committed to teaching me what to learn and how.

Outside this close kinship network, I soon got on familiar terms with a number of other households, where I could ask questions freely and provoke discussions on topics I was interested in. Although I sometimes made formal interviews, I found it more useful to participate in conversations and activities I had not initiated myself. Nonetheless, even though I could visit these households informally whenever I wanted to, I lacked the intimacy of my adoptive family. At times this greater formality was compensated by the fact that for more distant people I was a special kind of outsider to be treated with special attention, so I was allowed or even encouraged to watch certain rituals from a privileged viewpoint. Within my adoptive family, by contrast, I lost these sorts of privileges as soon as my daily presence began to be taken for granted. Other villagers instead remained distant throughout my stay. Some I felt did not like me; some I found it hard to like. Others were indifferent towards me, or uninteresting to talk with. Yet even with these people I had some degree of familiarity, since we lived in the same village and shared many important activities like attending funerals and the market in Morondava. Finally, there were those I could neither talk nor exchange greetings with, for by becoming part of one kinship network I was forced to adopt all my kin's hatreds and enmities.

When I finally arrived in Belo after more than a year in Betania, I was regarded as a 'visitor' (*vahiny*) from Betania. I was accompanied by a woman who had married into my family in Betania and whose old father lived in Belo. I was considered her daughter and her father's granddaughter, and I was integrated accordingly into their vast local kinship network. Except for my adoptive grandfather and a few others, however, relations in Belo were more formal than in Betania, partly because I spent far less time there, and partly because I had reached a point in my research where I wanted to ask questions on very specific points. I made a large number of structured interviews and I visited people on the basis of the information I hoped to get from them, rather than according to the strategy of non-selective involvement in any conversation or activity I had followed in Betania.

This book is based on an extensive use of my fieldnotes. Since I often quote informants' statements as I recorded them in my notes, it is necessary to say something about how I wrote them down. I took notes from the first day I arrived in Betania when I hardly knew a word of Vezo. At first I wrote down simple descriptions of what people did, how they dressed, sat, moved or laughed. As my linguistic abilities improved, I was able to incorporate more and more of what people said; I wrote down bits of sentences or expressions that seemed to recur and were easy to remember; sometimes I could ask people to repeat what they or others had said and I wrote it down in full. But mostly I paraphrased conversations, choosing specific points I found more interesting or reporting explanations I asked for or that were volunteered. Because of the informal way I met, talked or listened to people, I made very little use of a tape-recorder. Nonetheless, the few transcriptions I have and which I use extensively in the book include particularly effective statements that express crucial aspects of Vezo-ness.

Both in Betania and in Belo I was able to participate in almost all the activities I wished. The most significant exception was that I was not allowed to go into the forest to observe the first stage in the construction of canoes. Although women rarely join in this undertaking, the reason I was not taken was not my gender but the inconvenience of having me around while working in a hostile and unfamiliar environment. More generally, I never felt that my gender or age significantly affected the information or activities I had access to. A far more determining factor was the intimacy that grew between me and my foster kin, an intimacy that required as much commitment and loyalty on my part as on theirs.

2

Acting Vezo in the present

You, when you arrived here, people said: 'Ha! this lady [*madame*] often goes out fishing', and now I say: 'Haven't you become Vezo?'; and yet you are a *vazaha* [a white] from far away. But if you go fishing every day here: 'Ha! that lady is Vezo!', because you struggle with the sea, because you paddle the canoe, and [therefore] you are Vezo.[1]

The first intelligible conversation I had in Betania was about swimming. I wanted to find out whether I could swim in the ocean, and I was told that I could; when people saw me swimming, they told me that I was Vezo (*fa Vezo iha*). Later on, when I began to imitate my hosts in the way they ate fish – stuffing my mouth with a piece of fish, flesh, skin and bones all together, swallowing the flesh and skin and spitting out the bones – I was told that I was really Vezo (*fa Vezo tokoa iha*). The first time I was taken out fishing, I found a large crowd of people waiting for my return on the beach; they asked whether I had been sick, if I had been hungry or thirsty, whether the sun had burnt my skin. I told them that I had been fine, that I had liked it, and that I had actually caught a fish. They then wanted to see my hands: did my fingers have 'the signs that one is Vezo' (*famantaram-Bezo*)? Yes indeed, my hands were burnt with red lines, the scars that the fishing line leaves when one retrieves a particularly large and heavy fish; that afternoon, other villagers came to see my hands and to tell me that I was becoming Vezo (*fa mihavezo iha*).

But the first time I was told that I was '*very* Vezo' (*Vezo mare*) was on my return from my first visit to Belo. We had been stuck in Belo for much longer than we had expected because of a spell of bad weather; finally, after checking that I was not afraid, my adoptive father decided to 'steal' our journey back (*mangalatsy lala*) even if the weather was still 'difficult', that is, dangerous (*sarotsy*). We sailed back in a strong wind and a rough sea, and as we tried to land at Betania the canoe almost capsized, and the sail

14

collapsed into the water. After retrieving the sail, my father paddled back to shore, skilfully guiding the canoe through the breakers so as to avoid the waves directly hitting the hull and capsizing us. Although I had done nothing except to sit quietly crouching in the bottom of the canoe, marvelling at the hull's pliability as it responded to the pressure of the waves, my father and the people who had watched us from the beach praised me that I had been 'very Vezo' because I had not been afraid (*tsy mahataotsy*). If ever I was on a canoe that capsized, they also explained, I should not attempt to swim ashore but should climb onto the hull and wait for the tide to draw me back to the beach.

As this episode suggests, my Vezo friends gave themselves the task of teaching me many of their activities related to the sea. They would often comment that I was a fast learner (*malaky mianatsy*), mainly because I was not shy (*tsy menatse*), I asked a lot of questions (*mañontany raha isanandro isanandro ie*, lit. she asks questions all the time), and I was not afraid of the water (*tsy mahataotsy rano*). Their efforts also taught me that the various tasks I learned to perform – swimming, eating fish, fishing, sailing, paddling a canoe – were what rendered me Vezo (*mahavezo*). I soon realized that this experience was not at all peculiar to myself; it was shared by some of the Vezo's neighbours who are cultivators and cattle keepers.

Take for example a Masikoro who comes from the interior to live here in Betania, and then marries here. He observes people's livelihood: there are no rice fields, people only go fishing, they only have fishing nets and only go out to sea. After all this, his brothers- or father-in-law might take him out fishing. There he is, his mind works hard: this is how one does this, this is how this other thing works! Yet his forefathers did not know about these things. He goes out again with his friends, and so on and so on, until in the end *he knows*: he becomes Vezo.[2]

Anybody can become Vezo, even people whose forefathers knew nothing of the sea; this is because anybody can learn to perform Vezo activities like sailing and fishing. On arriving in Betania, a Masikoro from the interior is not Vezo because he knows only that which he has learnt from his forefathers: how to cultivate maize, rice and manioc, and how to raise cattle. But when he settles with the Vezo on the coast, he learns and begins to do other things. When he knows what the Vezo know, and does what the Vezo do, he becomes Vezo. The process through which an outsider becomes Vezo was referred to with the expression *mianatsy havezoa*, which means literally 'to learn and to study Vezo-ness'; it is when one learns (*mianatsy*) and therefore one knows (*fa mahay*), that one becomes Vezo (*manjary Vezo*).

However, this process of becoming Vizo through learning is not a rerogative of outsiders; children of Vezo parents must also learn and study Vezo-ness:

one can't yet say that small children are Vezo, one can say that they are a little Vezo . . . These children you see, their school is there in the water. They learn how to swim; when they have worked on learning how to swim, when they have learnt and know how to swim, when they are not afraid of the water, then one can say that they are Vezo.[3]

Children are not born into the world already knowing how to swim, sail and eat bony fish; when they are born, they are as yet unable to do the things that render people Vezo. For this reason, they cannot yet be said to be Vezo; like any Masikoro or any distant outsider, they become Vezo through the activities they learn to perform.

The fact that a white anthropologist, a Masikoro and little children *become* Vezo when they learn how to fish, to paddle a canoe or to swim in the ocean suggests that Vezo-ness is not a *state of being* which people are born into; rather, it is a *way of doing* which people perform, and which renders them Vezo (*mahavezo*). Below, I argue this point in two stages.

First, in sections on swimming, making canoes, sailing, fishing, eating and selling fish, I discuss a number of examples in which women, men and children are rendered Vezo by their activities; I also show that when someone fails to act Vezo effectively, s/he is rendered Masikoro. Although the activities I discuss by no means exhaust the many things that render people Vezo, this incompleteness does not affect my argument, for in order to be rendered Vezo a person need not perform *all* Vezo activities. As many of the following examples suggest, Vezo-ness is not defined formalistically as a given set of activities, all of which must be performed in order for a person to attain full Vezo identity. On the other hand, the detailed descriptions of how the Vezo choose a tree to carve a canoe, how they fish shrimps, how they market the fish, and so on, are meant to convey an image of who the Vezo *are* through what they *do*; this is how the Vezo I have known presented themselves to me and, as far as I could understand, how they perceived themselves.

I then turn to a discussion of the general implications raised by this material. I argue that in order to understand how people can be Vezo at one moment and Masikoro at the next, we need to appreciate that 'being' Vezo is *acting* Vezo. Vezo identity, in other words, is an activity which 'happens' intermittently through time; it is only by acting Vezo *in the present* that a person 'is' Vezo. I expand this point further by arguing not only that Vezo-ness is bound to the present, but that the Vezo deny that a person's identity in the present is ever determined by her past. By looking at how the Vezo describe the process by which a person learns to 'be' Vezo, as well as the nature of the relationship between people and the place where they live, I suggest that a person's identity – what one 'is' through what one does – remains at all times *contingent* on one's actions in the present.

Swimming

We saw earlier that little children have their schooling in the shallows close to the shore; this is where boys and girls learn how to swim (*mianatsy mandaño*) as they play at fishing or sail their toy canoes. They are never taught how to swim; they just learn as they become increasingly confident with water. These water games give rise to considerable apprehension in adults, especially women, who fear that the smaller children might drown, and children are often scolded for playing in the sea because the sea-salt ruins their clothes. Nonetheless, children are expected to learn how to swim, for this is a necessary prerequisite for safe sailing and fishing, and they will not be taken out to sea for fishing or other exciting expeditions until they know how to do so.

The fact that the Vezo know how to swim is rather taken for granted. When I asked two young men if they could swim, they smiled at having to state the obvious: they know how to swim, because all the people who live on the coast know how to do so (*fa mahay mandaño zahay, ka laha olo mipetsaky andriaky mahay mandaño iaby*). Conversely, the fact that a Masikoro cannot swim is also taken for granted; if a Masikoro can swim, she is *ipso facto* Vezo (*fa Vezo ie laha mahay mandaño*).

Yet even if it is assumed that the people who live on the coast know how to swim, the fact that some of these people are unable to do so does not prevent them from becoming Vezo. During the dangerous journey in canoe from Belo to Betania I recalled above, I discovered to my horror that one of the other women in the canoe could not swim. This had never been mentioned before, and indeed I had seen this woman demonstrate great ability on previous sailing expeditions in leaning over one of the booms, way out over the water, to keep the canoe on an even keel. She later explained that the reason she is unable to swim is that she was raised by her mother in a Masikoro village in the interior. When she subsequently went to live with her father in a Vezo village she was already too old to play with smaller children, and she therefore missed her chance of learning how to swim. This did not stop her from learning many other Vezo tasks, which she performed *as if* she could also swim. She explained that she is rendered Vezi (*mahavezo anakahy*) by what she is able to do – she can fish, she can sell fish, she can paddle and sail, and so on; her inability to swim has not interfered with her becoming Vezo, despite the potential danger, and at times the actual fear, caused by being a Vezo who does not know how to swim.

Marofasy's story is somewhat different. A young man who moved to Betania a few years ago, he was born in the south, near Tsiombé. He is Antandroy. He came to Morondava to look for wage employment, and he has been on and off a variety of jobs in the area. He was welcomed on his arrival in Betania by his relatives (*longo*), the descendants of three brothers who came from Antandroy country, settled in Betania and became Vezo. When Fañolana first arrived, he was very impressed by the huge fish that his relatives caught and sold daily at the market, and by the large sums of money they earned. He is convinced that he would be better off fishing, rather than being a night-guard in Morondava for a small albeit regular wage; but he 'does not know the sea' (*tsy mahay rano*), and he thinks that learning its skills is very hard (*mahery mianatsy rano*, lit. to learn about the sea is hard). Fañolana's main problem, I was told by one of his Vezo relatives, is that he cannot swim (*i mahavoa azy tsy mahay mandaño*). For the rest, he has managed well: he has learnt the names of the different parts of the canoe and the names for the positions of sail and rope, and he would probably know how to tie the sail in correctly if ordered to do so. Every morning Fañolana goes to the beach to help his Vezo relatives set out to fish, and he helps them tidy up the canoe when they come back. When I asked Fañolana whether he would like to learn more, he replied: 'I would like to learn, but I am too afraid' (*ta hianatsy, nefa mavoso*). Yet his relatives expect that he will eventually overcome his fear and will go out fishing – 'if he knows the sea, that's it, he is Vezo' (*ka laha mahay rano, fa tsy mañahy, fa Vezo ie*).

Canoes

The canoes used by the Vezo are dug out of the trunk of a tree called *farafatse* (*Givotia madagascariensis*). Once the tree has been felled and left to dry for a few weeks, the wood becomes soft, light and extremely supple. Two types of canoes are made with the same wood: the outrigger canoe, *laka fihara*,[4] and the canoe without the outrigger, *laka molanga*.[5] The first type is commonly referred to as *laka*, the second type as *molanga*.

The first task in building a canoe is to fell a tree and carve out the trunk (*mivan-daka*); the hull that emerges is called *roka*. Once the wood has fully dried out, the *roka* is transported to the village. If the *roka* is for a *molanga*, there is little further to be done on it; if it is needed for a *laka*, a second major operation takes place (*miasa laka*). The tree that is chosen will depend on the type of canoe that must be built, whether a *laka* or a *molanga*, and on its size. First of all the height and the circumference of the tree must be estimated, not an easy task in what is normally a very densely grown forest;[6] the trunk is also checked to see that there are no knots in the wood. Once the tree has been chosen, the area around it is cleared so that the trunk finds no obstacles as it falls to the ground; but if in falling the trunk breaks it is abandoned, and the search starts afresh. If the trunk falls safely, it is dug out immediately. The branches are chopped off, and slowly the bow, the stern and the hull begin to take shape.

The *roka* will be made into a *molanga* or a *laka* only after it reaches the village. In the first case, it is only a matter of planing down and shaping the hull. But if it is a *laka* that is being built, there is still a lot of work to be done. First, the sides of the hull must be extended in height by fitting onto the *roka* planks of *farafatse* taken from an old canoe.[7] To avoid leakage at the joints, the planks and the *roka* must achieve a perfect fit; long wooden nails are used to join the parts together. Once the sides of the canoe are the required height, they are evened out all around and the edge is flattened. The hull's inner surface is smoothed out, and any unevenness at the point of juncture between the *roka* and the planks is removed.

The supports for the booms and the seats are then fitted into the hull. A wooden rail, divided into six long pieces, is forced into shape and nailed onto the edge of the hull; this frame helps keep the seats and boom-holders in place, and partly counteracts the extreme flexibility of the hull. The next step is to plane down and give shape to the outer surface of the hull; the shape of the bow line is of particular concern, because it affects the canoe's speed and stability at sea. Once the hull is ready, its bottom part is waterproofed with tar. If the makers have any extra cash available, they may paint the canoe's upper half with commercial paint, which also helps protect the wood. Once the tar and paint have dried, the hull is ready to be assembled with the booms and the outrigger, and the canoe can be rigged and set sail.[8]

The operations undertaken in the forest are considered very difficult (*sarosty mare*). Although the *roka* is not a proper canoe yet (*mbo tsy azo atao laka*), it is the first carving out of the trunk that will make it into a canoe (*mahalaka azy*), for it gives the canoe-to-be its structure and shape. The transformation of a trunk into a *roka* is therefore regarded as the most difficult step in the making of a canoe.[9]

Things are not made any easier by the conditions in which the Vezo

Plate 1 Making a new canoe (*miasa laka*)

undertake this work. When my adoptive father set off to build a *roka* in the forest, I asked to be taken along; for the first and only time, I was told very firmly that I could not join in. The reason, I was told, was that the forest was too difficult and dangerous for me; it was also obvious that the two men in the team were worried that I should be the only woman travelling with them. Although making canoes is not considered a woman's job (*tsy asan'ampela*), women are not banned (*tsy falin'ampela*) from this activity; if they accompany the men, they will cook and fetch water for the working team. In this particular instance female help was considered unnecessary, and none of my women-friends showed any eagerness to accompany me. When the team returned from the forest, my father and his friend made a lot of effort to put into words what they had done, so as to teach me how the Vezo build their canoes. But they also described the huge wasps which came in swarms and attacked them; they talked about their fear at night at hearing wild dogs rummaging about; they showed me mosquito bites all over their bodies; they told me how they longed to have a good night's sleep, after sleeping on the hard and cold earth of the interior. They were clearly trying to prove that, had I accompanied them, I would have been miserable and that my presence would have made their work even harder than it had been. But they were also formulating a view of the forest as an alien environment, in which the Vezo find it difficult to move, to work or even to sleep.

The remoteness of the forest makes learning how to carve the *roka* less accessible than learning how to transform a *roka* into a proper canoe.[10] When a canoe is being built at the village, people come by, sit around, watch and make comments on technical aspects of the work. Most notably, young boys are encouraged to attempt a few of the easier tasks, and will join a few small decorative parts to the bow and the stern of the canoe, using the same techniques used for building the hull. These children also seem to enjoy most of all the aesthetic aspects of canoe building, as they circle around the hull to admire its shape, and touch its surface to feel its smoothness.

The chunks of *farafatse* that are discarded after joining the side planks to the *roka* are used by little boys to make toy canoes, which are often precise replicas of the real one under construction. I once asked an expert canoe builder how he had learnt to make canoes, and he pointed to his grandson's toy canoe: little boys begin to learn by messing about with small bits of *farafatse*, giving shape to the hull and joining it with the outrigger, the masts and the sail.

Building canoes is one of the activities that renders people Vezo; the following example is meant to show what they may actually mean. Once, when I was in Belo, I asked my foster father to accompany me to Marofihitsy, a nearby Masikoro village. I had heard that his blood-brother (*fatidra*) was very skilled at carving the *roka*, and I wanted to commission him for a canoe I planned to give to my adoptive mother in Betania. The two men did most of the talking. First came the usual light conversation about people's health, the weather and the oddity of my presence for people who had never met me before. Soon, however, they moved on to real business. The tone of the conversation changed abruptly; the two men started to talk shop. My father asked whether there were still *farafatse* in the area, and if there was one large enough for a canoe of such and such a size. Of the two, the man from Marofihitsy struck me as being the expert. He gave a detailed description of the quality of various trees he had seen, and carefully described the shape of a *roka* he had recently built, which he heard had turned into one of the fastest canoes in the area. He was boasting, but he was doing so very knowledgeably. Finally, he agreed to build the *roka* I wanted.

This man lives in the interior, where he cultivates maize and manioc. He seemed rather apologetic as he explained to me that he is 'rendered Masikoro' (*maha-Masikoro anakahy*) by the fact that his mother married a Masikoro and moved to the interior and that he therefore ended up living there also. He also confessed that he was becoming more and more Masikoro, proof of this being that he cannot sail a canoe from Belo to Morondava (*mihamasikoro mare aho, ka tsy mahay milay laka ho avy a Morondava añy*). But when I asked him whether the Masikoro know how to fell a *farafatse* and build a canoe, he replied that the Masikoro are only good for hunting tenrecs, and that if they try to build a canoe they produce a 'cattle's canoe' (*lakan'aomby*) – in other words, a cattle trough.[11]

In so far as this man knows how to build canoes, he is *not* Masikoro. On the contrary, since his *roka* produce canoes that go faster than any others, he was described by my father as 'very Vezo' (*Vezo mare ie*). On the other hand, he *is* Masikoro because he lives in the interior and because he does not know how to sail. As such, this man seems to be a living contradiction: how can he be a skilful canoe builder, and at the same time claim that the Masikoro, of which he claims to be one, cannot build canoes? How can he be Masikoro and 'very Vezo' at the same time? Once again, the contradiction can be solved if we, like my father and the man himself, define what he is through what he *does*, and *when* he does it. When he says that he is becoming more and more Masikoro, he refers to the fact that he does not and cannot act Vezo (he does not fish, he cannot sail); he is drifting out of

Vezo identity by lack of doing Vezo things, and when he does not act Vezo, he is Masikoro. He is Vezo, by contrast, when he builds canoes which are fast and beautiful.

Sailing

Except for the smallest canoes that can be sailed by a single person, sailing normally requires a team of two people; others can travel on the canoe as passengers. One person sits at the rear with the steering paddle, while the other sits behind the masts and follows his companion's orders by changing the masts' and sail's position, by adjusting the sail ropes and by perching out on the outrigger or on the booms to keep the canoe balanced against a sudden change of wind.

A first requirement for sailing is to know the terminology used to give and carry out orders; one must know the names of all the parts of the canoe, of the various sail positions, of the arrangements of ropes and knots. This technical lore is the first thing that Marofasy, the Antandroy who would like to know more about the sea, was taught by his Vezo relatives. Adults say that children learn the basic sailing techniques by playing with their small toy canoes; they learn the correct terminology by carefully trying out various positions of the sail, with older children often leading the game.[12] Solo (aged six) often impressed me, though he was probably trying harder to impress his father, by demonstrating in which position he would put the masts and arrange the sail if he were sailing in a certain direction, given that the wind was blowing from such and such a quarter. He would put up his hand proudly and indicate with his fingers the exact position of the masts.

It is often said that children and young adolescent boys are not strong enough to sail. Although strong arms and hands are required to steer the paddle against the current, the steering is not particularly tiring if one knows how to do it correctly. But the operations involved in changing the position of the masts following shifts in the direction of the wind or, more seriously, the rigging of a canoe at sea, when one has to stand on the narrow edges of the canoe, plunge the 5 m masts vertically into the water, pull them up high enough to lift them over the sides of the hull and gently slide them into their place, are tasks which no young boy is able to perform. Solo is an unusually small and frail child who will have to wait a long while before he can hope to take an active role in a canoe; yet when he puts up his fingers and positions them like the long and heavy masts, he is obviously pleased to be praised that he 'knows the canoe' (*fa mahay laka iha!*) and that he is Vezo (*fa Vezo aja io*).

Knowing how to sail implies being able to predict the directions of the wind, the conditions of currents, waves and tides, changes in the weather, the configuration of the sea-bed and the reference points along the coast. Before setting out to fish, one has to wait for the right wind: coconut tree branches are carefully observed to decide when the wind becomes strong enough for sailing, and to predict how the wind will change during the day; the latter will affect the decision about where to go fishing. Knowing the weather (*mahay toetrandro*) is a prerequisite for safe sailing; if predictions are for bad weather, a rough sea or a strong wind, all sailing will be deferred. It is recognized that sailing is always potentially dangerous and difficult (*sarotsy*), but danger is also inversely related to expertise: the more one knows, the less difficult and dangerous sailing becomes. Thus, after the episode at sea recalled above, my adoptive father was scolded by his sister for having taken the risk of sailing back from Belo in bad weather; but the woman also accepted that she should have been less scared when she watched the canoe approaching: knowing how knowledgeable and 'very Vezo' her brother was, she should have trusted that we were not in serious danger.

Courageous or dangerous feats at sea are recounted again and again in the evenings, or at gatherings for funerals or village meetings; conditions of sea and wind, dangers braved and actions taken are dwelt on at great length and with a wealth of detail. Women are part of the audience but are seldom protagonists of these tales, for they are not usually in control of sailing. Indeed, the presence of women on a sailing expedition can produce a reduction of the level of risk one is prepared to take. A journey may be put off because 'the waves are not women's waves' (*tsy lozokin'ampela*). I myself witnessed how, when two canoes that had set out on the same journey began to come against exceptionally strong winds, the sail of the canoe which transported four women was doubled up so as to reduce speed and to minimize the impact of the waves on the hull, whereas the second canoe with only men was allowed to run spectacularly at great speed. During this particular journey, however, another significant incident occurred. At the critical moment when the two canoes left the mouth of the mangrove swamp and entered the open sea, the canoe with the women on board found itself in serious trouble. One of the women took a leading part in getting it out of danger. She jumped into the sea and, standing in shallow water, held the canoe against the wind, changed the position of the masts and rearranged the sail to prevent the canoe from capsizing. Months later, a man recounted a difficult journey he had had on the same route. His tale was followed by that of the woman who told of her own past performance; she recalled that her brother, the only man with her on the canoe, had been far more scared than she had and that, if it had been for him, they would never have made it back to the village. Amidst jokes and cheers, the crowd drew the inevitable conclusion: the woman's brother had behaved like a Masikoro, while she had been very Vezo.

I referred earlier in this chapter to the case of a Masikoro who is taken out fishing and learns how things work at sea. In another instance, the definitive confirmation that a Korao[13] had become fully Vezo came after his canoe happened to capsize; after spending three days drifting at sea, he eventually made it back to shore. Faced with my surprise that an event that was meant to prove that a Korao had successfully become a Vezo should involve an accident at sea, I was told that 'when capsizing happens, whether you are Vezo or not, it just happens' (*fa ny arendrea, na Vezo na tsy Vezo lafa tonga, lafa avy ny arendrea, fa avy avao*). The point was, that had the man not been Vezo, he would have tried to swim ashore and would have drowned; but having learnt the ways of the sea, he knew that his only chance of survival was to hold on to the canoe and wait for the currents to push him back to land. In so doing not only did he save his life, he also made himself truly Vezo (*fa Vezo tokoa ie*).

Fishing

The types of fishing practised by the Vezo, the instruments they employ and the techniques they use are many and vary considerably from place to place.[14] In this section I describe some fishing activities I witnessed and took part in Betania, which form part of the many practical pursuits that render people Vezo.

The first fishing activity I undertook soon after arriving in Betania consisted in catching a kind of very small shrimp called *patsa*. At certain times of the year these shrimp swim in huge shoals towards the shore. To catch them, people use small push-up nets made with a rectangular piece of mosquito-netting, hemmed with thick cotton cloth which is looped at the four corners. Two people stand in the water and hold the net, one corner in one hand and the other loop tied around a big toe; they move slowly, parallel to the shore, holding the net well stretched out and almost entirely immersed. As they walk, they sweep up the shrimp; after a certain number of steps, depending on the weight of the catch, they take hold of the immersed loop with their free hand and slowly raise it, folding the net like a sack. A third person carries a basket where the shrimp slowly pile up. The full basket is carried to the sand flats between the shore and the village, where the shrimp are scattered to dry under the scorching sun. At mid-afternoon of the same day, the desiccated shrimp are gathered

Plate 2 Children look on as Somaly prepares his catch of *pepy* for smoking

together in little heaps mixed with sand, which are then carefully sieved with large tin sieves. Finally the dried shrimp are put in large jute bags and are ready for sale.

When the shrimp are close to the shore, it is easy to catch them; but their comings and goings are quite sudden, and a successful catch depends to a great extent on the ability to predict or guess the exact moment when the shrimp will swim towards the shore. Changes in the weather, in the intensity and direction of the current, in the colour of the ocean, in the behaviour of certain kinds of fish, in the food that can be found, half digested, in the entrails of freshly caught fish – all of these provide useful clues to the *patsa*'s movements. As the shrimp's expected arrival gets closer, the village hums with bustle and excitement. The women impatiently check the conditions of the sea and send off the children to check if other people have sighted anything. As soon as the shrimp appear, everyone rushes to the shore carrying their nets and baskets. The colour of the water and the ripples on its surface are scrutinized for tell-tale signs of shrimp shoals; as in other fishing pursuits, the most successful in this art are said to be very Vezo.

Children are very active in shrimp fishing. Although I soon found out how exhausting pulling a shrimp net against the tide can be, it is generally claimed to be simply a matter of having strong toes. Children develop them by using a shrimp net to catch small fish, close to the shore or near the mangrove swamp, at times when there are no shrimp. This half play, half serious activity keeps children busy for hours. It is usually little more than a game, which grown-ups dismiss as 'nonsense fishing' (*maminta fahatany*), and which ends with the children cooking their miniature catch in miniature pots on miniature fires. But the game can also turn into something more productive; in some instances, the catch can contribute significantly to the family meal or it can even be taken and sold at the market; thus a twelve-year-old girl got into the habit of catching a bucketful of little fish, which she then took for sale at the market. Just as the water where children act their 'nonsense fishing' is considered a kind of school for learning to be Vezo, as the earlier quotation suggests, this girl's activities in the water and at the market prove that she had learnt her lesson – 'she knows, she is very Vezo' (*fa mahay, fa Vezo mare ie*).

Despite the use of nets for shrimping, most fishing in Betania is done by line. Dozens of canoes sail out in the morning to reach one of the fishing beds (*riva*). The actual location will be chosen on the basis of the day's sailing conditions and with reference to the previous day's catch at different fishing sites; generally, however, the majority of the canoes converge on the same *riva*. On arrival, the canoes scatter out across the fishing bed, weigh anchor and begin to fish. The most sought after fish is called *lamatsa* (*Scomberomorus leopardus*, a kind of Spanish mackerel). Since *lamatsa* move in shoals, the fishing day is made up of long periods of boredom and inactivity, during which people sit or lie awkwardly snoozing in the bottom of the canoe, followed by hectic activity as a shoal swims by and the fish begin suddenly to nibble at the bait.

Pulling a fish that has been hooked close to the canoe and hauling it on board requires strong arms and tough hands to keep a hold on the line, for the fish has to be played, often for a long time, giving it length when it pulls harder and hauling it in when it shows signs of tiring. The first time I was taken out fishing, I noticed that one of my companions had a badly infected cut on his middle finger. As we headed slowly for the fishing bed he had chosen for the day, he complained of the pain in his hand; but as soon as the first *lamatsa* bit on one of our lines, he was carried away by excitement and seemed to forget all about the injury. Later in the evening, as he sat giving a blow by blow account of the day's main event, my first fishing expedition, he told us how he had begun the day in a bad mood because of his cut, but that the pain had ceased as soon as we caught the first (of nine) *lamatsa*; and it was suggested that he was Vezo because catching nine *lamatsa* had made him forget entirely about his hand (*fa Vezo ie, ka laha mahazo lamatsa sivy isanandro, de tsy mañahy tanany!*).

The most difficult part of fishing is being able to fool the *lamatsa*, which is believed to be a very clever fish (*mahihitsy*). Whereas other fish can be caught simply by baiting a hook and having some patience, the *lamatsa* is very particular about the quality of its bait, which in addition has to be prepared with great care in the shape of a fish. The hook must be made invisible, and the bait has to be put on the hook at an angle so it appears to be swimming like a real fish.

Although people use 'fish medicines' (*aolim-binta*, lit. medicine of the hook), no-one admits to doing so personally. I only discovered that a member of my adoptive family used the 'medicine' by chance, when he came to tell his sister in a frenzy that it had been eaten by a mouse. From what I was able to understand, the 'medicine' works on a highly individual basis. It attracts fish only to the person who owns it, and what is more, apparently, only to one particular line among those the owner employs (a team of two on a large canoe will use up to five or six lines simultaneously). In the case of this relative of mine, I could hear him whispering some kind of formula as he launched one of his lines; this, of course, was the line he caught most fish with, whereas his other lines and his companion's seldom caught anything. Yet despite this, the catch was always divided equally among the two.

Although I attempted many times to get my friend to talk about his *aolim-binta*, I failed to evince any information on the matter from him, or, indeed, from anyone else. I got the impression that people are loath to admit that they use 'fishing medicines', because to do so would diminish their personal skills; they prefer to attribute their success to the fact that they are 'very Vezo'. By contrast, if someone is consistently unsuccessful, s/he will claim to be a victim of sorcery through *fanabaka*, a special kind of *fanafody gasy* (lit. Malagasy medicine). Such claims usually remain a matter of suspicion and a source of simple conversation and are seldom taken any further. If the matter is pursued further, on the other hand, the victim will approach a diviner (*ombiasa*). The *ombiasa* will confirm that the victim's canoe (rather than the person itself) has been attacked and has been polluted (*mampaloto*, lit. made dirty), and he will recommend a counteractive medicine to cleanse the canoe. The fact that the canoe, rather than its owner, is identified as the victim is significant; although the attack is thereby made to be potentially more disruptive, for anyone employing the dirty canoe will be affected,the responsibility of failure is deflected from a person's individual ability, and the person's Vezo-ness is unaffected.

In addition to the technical aspects of line fishing, there are serious practical difficulties in spending long stretches of time on the canoe. Children have to learn to cope with the hardship involved in sitting for hours under the high tropical sun, slowly rocking on the waves. They are not yet Vezo, and thus it is understood, and even expected, that they will suffer somewhat to begin with. Children will be sea-sick or they will feel hungry, and they are troublesome and fussy about relieving themselves in the sea. A child I witnessed being sick half an hour into his first fishing expedition was lifted by his father and plunged into the sea; the man, smiling all the while, then proceeded to clean the canoe and to build a small shelter for the boy by draping his shirt over a paddle. The boy managed to recover after a long nap, and by the time we had returned to the village he was cheerful again and hungry. The father later described the incident, and the boy was made fun of and told that he had been Masikoro (*ka manao akory, fa Masikoro aja ty?*); only a few minutes before, as he walked up to the village carrying the canoe's steering paddle over his shoulder, the boy had been told that he was being 'very Vezo' (*fa Vezo mare iha!*).

Fish

'The Vezo know fish' (*Vezo mahay fia*). They know where to find fish and when fish is at its best and fattest. The behaviour and location of different kinds of fish varies with the seasons; some 'close their mouths' at certain times of the year. Knowing fish also means knowing their names.[15]

The Vezo eat fish. Adopting the technique I previously described, they hardly ever choke on the bones. It is easier of course to eat the larger fish; those with small bones that are hard to detect can be dangerous for younger children or for non-Vezo guests. An Antandroy woman who had come to visit her relatives in Betania was difficult (*miola*) about eating fish. As she sat struggling with her meal, my adoptive mother told her baldly that she really was Antandroy (*Antandroy tokoa iha*); somewhat to my embarrassment, I was quoted as an example to be followed: after all, if a *vazaha* (a white person) had succeeded in becoming Vezo, couldn't she also learn to do so? A few weeks later, however, the Antandroy woman (who had since returned to her village) was somehow avenged. We were eating crabs, and my adoptive mother mistakenly ate the crab's 'heart', which the Vezo avoid because it is known to cause an allergic reaction; immediately after the meal she had what looked like an asthma attack and almost fainted. After she had recovered, her closest sister-in-law suggested that she had made the mistake of an Antandroy, and had become one like her relative who had just visited us!

Children not only learn how to eat smaller fish; they must also acquire a taste for certain fish that 'smell' (*misy fofony*, have a strong taste). Sea turtle is particularly 'smelly', and it is cooked according to customs (*fomba*) and prescriptions (*faly*) that make its meat and broth a peculiarity of Vezo cuisine. Since it is forbidden to cook sea turtle with salt, sea water is used instead: not only does the cooked meat 'smell' very strong, it also tastes sharp and tangy (*mahatsiro*). When I first ate sea turtle and remarked matter of factly on its saltiness, I was assured that that was the way the Vezo liked it; conversely, if one likes salty sea turtle (as I claimed I did) one is Vezo.

Knowing one's fish also implies that one knows how to cure it and preserve it, and how to sell and barter it. The marketing of fish caught in Betania is centred on the nearby town of Morondava, and is almost exclusively in women's hands (see below, ch. 3); trading follows different patterns in the village of Belo, which lacks a nearby urban outlet.

The ability to trade fish in Betania rests in the first place on the ability to keep fish fresh until it is taken to the market to be sold. One has to be able to evaluate how long it will be before the fish goes bad on the basis of its kind and the general weather conditions, and how long it will take on average to sell it, which will depend on factors of supply and demand. An able tradeswoman will obtain and evaluate the most information about the (highly variable) conditions of the Morondava market so as to pursue the most effective sales strategy. Daily fish prices are known to be affected both by the quantity and quality of fish on offer and by the price of meat, which is the main available alternative to fish. If meat become scarce, for example because local supplies have been bought up for a funeral in a neighbouring village, fish sells more easily and at a higher price. Curiously, rice supplies have the opposite effect on the fish market. The Vezo explain that they have difficulty in selling fish when rice is scarce and expensive because people do not eat fish if they have no rice to accompany it with.[16]

When the canoes return with their day's catch, the women have to decide how they will go about selling the fish. They can choose either to go straight to the market themselves or to sell the fish to another saleswoman; they can take the catch to a nearby cooperative, which buys wholesale for freezing and sale in the capital Antananarivo; they can smoke the fish or clean it and leave it to hang during the colder winter weather. Direct sale at the market is the usual and most profitable choice, but if it is known or expected that the market will be overstocked, a woman may decide to smoke the fish and sell it the next morning (hung or smoked fish only lasts one day), even if the price of smoked fish at any one time is always lower than that of fresh.[17] Clearly this second strategy will work only if few women choose it; otherwise, as sometimes happens, the excess supply is simply carried over to the following day, when everyone brings smoked rather than fresh fish to the market. Finally, selling at the cooperative is normally the least profitable choice, but it has the advantage of being faster; when, as is not uncommon, money from the day's catch is needed to buy the rice for the evening meal, a woman will accept the loss of income for the convenience of having immediate cash from the cooperative.

Trade is not restricted to the family catch. Some women specialize as intermediaries, buying and reselling fish for a small profit (*manao tongotsy*). Every day a steady flow of fish moves north along the coast to reach the wooden trestles of the Morondava market. Baskets of fish, both fresh and smoked, are carried by a female trading chain involving a great number of transactions. When the fish reaches Morondava, it will either be sold for consumption or enter a new chain of intermediation, which now takes the direction of the Masikoro villages in the interior. Since the profit margins in this system are very small (*vola kelikely*), it is very easy to make a mistake and lose money (*maty vola*, lit. dead money). When my adoptive mother waited on the beach for the women carrying fish-baskets from villages further south, she carefully noted the contents of the baskets that went by so as to assess the risk involved in buying her own supply; if she came late to the beach, she would look at the sand for tell-tale signs of the traders' footprints, searching for clues to how much fish had already gone by. At the marketplace, my mother and the other tradeswomen were tense and intent, ready to pounce on the least opportunity for a profit however small. These women know the trade better than anyone else because they are 'used to selling at the market' (*fa zatsy mamarotsy a bazary*).

It is undoubtedly true that not only Vezo women are involved in these forms of trade. But what makes these tradeswomen Vezo – what makes those who are particularly good at it 'very Vezo' – is the fish they handle and the smell on their hands and their clothes when they come home from the market. What makes them Vezo is also the tricks and deceit they deploy. Compared with some of their non-Vezo clients, these women 'know fish' (*mahay fia*), and they are more than happy to sell bad-quality merchandise to unwitting clients. In Vezo terms, someone who buys fish without realizing that it is going bad must be Masikoro, and when a Vezo manages to sell some bad fish, her friends will congratulate her that she is 'very Vezo' because she has fooled a Masikoro client who doesn't know the difference.[18]

Identity as doing

The preceding sections have all reiterated the same point: that people are Vezo if and when they learn and know how to swim, make canoes, sail, fish, and eat and sell fish. This reiteration of ethnographic accounts has been deliberate; it is meant to convey the constant stream of commentary on the making and undoing of Vezo-ness which I experienced (neither always nor most frequently in response to my presence) throughout my stay with the Vezo.

That this was so may seem rather odd. The reader may wonder whether the fact that people reiterate so incessantly that they are Vezo is an indication of existential insecurity; or whether the running commentary on skilful hence Vezo sailing, and on blundering hence Masikoro shopping, demonstrates merely that to be Vezo or Masikoro is a rather trivial matter. In fact, the Vezo are singularly lacking in identity crises, and they consider their identity to be a quite central feature of their lives. The reason why being or not being Vezo is such a meaningful point of everyday conversation is that 'being' Vezo is an *activity*, rather than a state of existence.

Malagasy is a language that lacks the verb 'to be'. To say that a woman is beautiful in Vezo, one says '*soa* (beautiful) *ampela io* (that woman)'; to say that she 'is' Vezo, on the other hand, one says '*fa Vezo ampela io*'. The particle *fa* in the second statement conveys the notion of an accomplished act: as in *fa vita*, it's finished; *fa matanjaky iha*, you have gained weight; *fa*

Plate 3 Trading fish on the beach of Betania (*manao tongotsy*)

maty, it's dead, broken, done in. Thus, whereas being beautiful is a quality and a state of being, 'being' Vezo is the outcome of an activity.

Once we begin to think of 'being' Vezo as an activity, we are able also to appreciate that Vezo-ness – the activity that renders people Vezo – either happens or fails to happen through time; thus, to say that a child 'is' very Vezo when he carries the canoe's paddle on his shoulder is meaningful, because his action *at that point in time* renders him Vezo – but *at a previous moment*, when he was sick on the canoe, he 'was' Masikoro. The reason why the same person can 'be' Vezo at one moment and 'be' Masikoro at the next, is that a person 'is' what she does.

As an activity, Vezo-ness is intermittent rather than continuous. It 'happens' in a succession of minute incidents – eating fish, tricking Spanish mackerel in biting the line, sailing in a strong wind. According to the context, a white anthropologist 'is' Vezo merely by taking a swim in the ocean; an old man, who can no longer sail or fish, 'is' Vezo when he eats fish and spits the bones, or when he recounts old stories about sailing and fishing as if they had occurred that very same day; a child 'is' Vezo when he uses his fingers to show how he would place the canoe's masts. In other words, Vezo-ness is experienced contextually as people act Vezo in the *present*. As a way of doing, as opposed to a state of being, Vezo-ness is bound to the present because it is only in the present that it can be performed – and performed it must be in order for people to 'be' Vezo.

Learning to 'be' Vezo

I mentioned at the beginning of this chapter that the argument that people 'are' Vezo through their performance in the present ties in with the denial that 'to be' Vezo in the present is something determined by a person's past, and that it determines her future. This denial rests on the fact that a person's identity – what she 'is' through what she does – remains at all times contingent on her actions in the present. To argue this point, I begin by analysing how people say that they 'learn' Vezo-ness.

At first sight, the fact that people learn to 'be' Vezo appears to contradict the claim that Vezo-ness is bound to the present. This is not only because learning as we conceive of it is a process which extends over time, but also because we assume that what a person learned yesterday will (to a certain extent) determine what she does today, and what she learns today will (partially) determine what she will do tomorrow. Although the Vezo appear to recognize these assumptions, they also expound a very different view of what learning entails and how it is brought about.

Keeping in mind that I am not describing how a person (a child, a foreigner, or an anthropologist) actually learns to become Vezo,[19] but the way the Vezo themselves describe this process, we can usefully turn to Rolpha, an old man who was born and lives in the coastal village of Lovobe. Rolpha's forefathers came from Bekoropoka, a village in the interior. When they moved to Lovobe, Rolpha explained, they were Masikoro because they had previously lived in a Masikoro village.[20] But following their move to Lovobe, they learnt to go out to sea and became Vezo.[21] I asked Rolpha who taught his forefathers to be Vezo, and he answered as follows:

When they first came here, of course, this place was already Vezo. So when they came here, they just took up learning; this is not difficult to do. Even little children, when they learn, learn quickly. This is because there are no papers involved, one gets no diploma; there are no diplomas for these things. When one learns how to paddle, however, one knows how to move on a canoe. This is how one learns about the canoe. Thus our ancestors knew; and we learnt in their steps. For one does what one's parents did; as whites say: 'tel fils tel père' [sic]. And so, what one's father did is what one does also. This is how things go. We learnt about the canoe and we know about the canoe; our grandchildren learn about it also. This is how things go.[22]

Rolpha was addressing what seem at surface to be two distinct issues, how the children of Vezo parents become Vezo themselves and how non-Vezo become Vezo. On the one hand, children and grandchildren follow their parents' steps and *become*, rather than being already, what their parents and grandparents were before them. Vezo-ness, in other words, is not inherited; it has to be learnt in order to be transmitted over the generations. On the other hand, Rolpha's description of his ancestors' transformation into Vezo seems to underestimate the difficulty for a former Masikoro of learning to be Vezo; it is a fair guess that to learn from scratch how to dig a canoe, sail or fish is rather more challenging than Rolpha suggested. The reason for this is that Rolpha's story completely ignored the learning process, or rather he ignored its *duration over time*.

Rolpha's attitude was in fact quite typical. All my Vezo friends portrayed learning as a sharp transition (a 'jump' rather than a process) from a state of not-yet-knowing to a state of full knowledge. Rolpha himself suggested what causes this 'jump', when he stated that his ancestors were Masikoro because they lived in the interior, and explained that they began to learn and master Vezo practices as soon as they settled in a Vezo village. In other words, the learning process was triggered by the transition from one place of residence to another; and since a movement through space tends to be fast and abrupt, the learning process is similarly portrayed as an abrupt and easy 'jump'.

This is not to say that people did not also readily recognize the time involved in learning and becoming Vezo (' . . . *and at the end*, when he knows, he becomes Vezo'). They would agree wholeheartedly with Marofasy, the Antandroy boy who would have liked to become Vezo but was too afraid to do so, that learning about the sea can be very difficult; in the case of swimming, moreover, people accept that if a person brought up in the interior came to the coast as an adult, she might easily never learn the skill. In this second representation of the learning process, a person's past does impinge on her actions in the present; yet Rolpha's view is quite different. Although we can assume that he was aware that his forefathers learnt to be Vezo over a lengthy period of time and with some effort, in the context of our conversation he was trying to make a different point, a point not of fact but of principle: the principle that his forefathers, like any other person, could *shed the past* and become Vezo *by acting in the present*.

The place where people live

Rolpha suggested that what people learn is determined by where they live – in the interior his forefathers had learned to be Masikoro, on the coast they learned to be Vezo. However, this is rather more than the common-sense observation that people who live off the land learn about rice, maize and manioc, while people who live off the sea learn about fish and canoes. Because it determines what people learn, the place where people live is *actually* what 'renders the Vezo Vezo' (*mahavezo ny Vezo*): 'all the people who live near the sea are Vezo', because 'being Vezo is a consequence of where one is, of the place where one lives'.[23]

My Vezo friends would sometimes joke about the possibility that people in the interior might act Vezo, and those who live on the coast might act Masikoro. Once, the rumour spread that the government was planning to donate Japanese fishing nets to the Vezo and that a number of Masikoro had given their names to a local official in Morondava in the hope of obtaining one. People in Betania wondered whether, since they couldn't fish in their fields, these Masikoro would use the nets to catch birds in the forest; someone also suggested that if the government decided to donate ploughs to the Masikoro, the Vezo would try and obtain some to use as anchors for their canoes.

As this joke suggests, there is no doubt in people's minds that the place where one lives determines what one does and hence also what one 'is': people who live on the coast and fish 'are' Vezo, people who live in the interior and cultivate 'are' Masikoro. If one moves from the interior to the coast (or vice versa), one must change one's activities and identity accordingly. This may seem a rather trivial and self-evident proposition; it appears to be less so if we investigate more closely the notion that 'ways of doing things' (*fomba*)[24] are associated with certain places. I shall do so by considering 'ways of doing things' that are associated with specific localities along the coast, and by investigating how the changes that accompany the movement of people through space are explained.

Take the example of a group of siblings who moved years ago from Belo to Betania. Certain changes in their activities are easily accounted for; given the different ecological conditions in the two villages, fishing techniques they used in Belo ceased to be feasible in Betania, and there is thus nothing surprising in the fact that they started line fishing like everyone else after they moved north to Betania. But they did more than this. They also changed the way they position the masts of the canoe.

I discovered that people in Belo sail differently only when I moved to this village and went out on a canoe. I noticed that whereas in Betania both masts were placed in the mast-step at the bottom of the canoe's hull, in Belo only the shorter mast was placed in the mast-step; the other mast was tied to the first one with a kind of slip-knot (*dinikily*).[25] When asked, people in both villages gladly expounded on the advantages and inconveniences of each system; however, my suggestion that the use of different techniques was the result of different sailing conditions in the two areas was rejected out of hand. It was just a matter of villagers in Betania and Belo being used to different systems, they insisted.

Here 'to be used' to something (*fa zatsy*) means, in effect, to have *become* used to it. Thus, the siblings who had moved from Belo to Betania claimed, somewhat tautologically, that people become used to sailing in a certain way because they live where that way of sailing is what people are used to. Interestingly, they invoked the same kind of argument to explain why they had stopped collecting sea-cucumbers, an activity widely practised in Belo. Although the most obvious reason is that there are too few sea-cucumbers in Betania to make it worthwhile to collect them, the explanation they gave me was 'we do not do it, because here people are not used to it'.

The actual process through which newcomers conform (or are made to conform) to the 'ways of doing things' peculiar to the place where they settle is not under debate. The issue we are concerned with is the Vezo's description of the process, which suggests that they attribute to the place of residence the power to force its character upon them. As a result, whereas the association between place and 'ways of doing' is thought to be *enduring*, the association between people and the 'ways of doing' peculiar to a place is considered entirely *contingent*: 'ways of doing things' do not stick to people and they are dropped as individuals move from one place to another. Although the terms 'stick' and 'drop' are not Vezo I use them advisedly, for I wish to emphasize that the link between the place of residence and the way one becomes by living there is not, and does not become, of *essence*.

If we now return to what had earlier appeared to be a matter of fact consideration, that moving from the coast to the interior or vice versa will change one's activities accordingly, we recognize the same association between people, the place where they live, and 'ways of doing things' that I have just described. For although people are made what they 'are' by the place where they live ('being Vezo is a consequence of where one is'), when they move they drop their old 'ways of doing things' and adopt (learn and/or become used to) new ones. Here too, the association between a place and the 'ways of doing' peculiar to it is enduring, whereas the association between people and 'ways of doing' is contingent upon movements through space. Thus, while points in space can be imagined as being determined by the past (by the 'ways of doing' that 'stick' permanently to various localities), people are not so determined, for upon moving they 'drop' what they did and 'were' in the past in order to acquire a new identity in the present.[26]

So far, I have chosen to emphasize the contingency of the relationship between people and what they 'are' in the place where they live, a point to which I shall indeed return again. However, one should also note that the Vezo's geo-determinism of identity (i.e. the claim that what people 'are' is determined by where they live) does in fact extend the duration of a person's identity beyond the intermittent performance of the various acts described above.

If we compare the transformation undergone by Rolpha's forefathers when they moved from the interior to the coast with that of a Betania villager who makes a blunder while sailing, we find similarities as well as differences. The similarity lies in the fact that Rolpha's forefathers, like the incompetent sailor, share the experience of 'being' (or failing to 'be') Vezo through performance. With a single 'jump', their identity is altered. There is however no doubt that the Vezo also recognize that there is a difference between what the sailor does and is able to do and the transformation undergone by Rolpha's forefathers; the first may last a moment, the second can last as long as a person's lifetime and beyond, even across many generations. The reason why one 'jump' into a different way of doing is short-lived, while the other is drawn out over time, is that only in the second instance did the actors move through space and change their place of residence. I do not wish with this to argue that when people shout at a sailor who has nearly made a canoe capsize: 'What's up? have you turned Masikoro?' (*ka manao akory? fa Masikoro iha?*), they do not mean what they say. For at that point in time, the sailor 'is' indeed a Masikoro; and yet, he 'is' also Vezo in so far as, and *as long as*, he lives on the coast. Similarly, the man in Marofihitsy we encountered earlier 'is' Vezo when he builds canoes, but he 'is' also Masikoro in so far as, and *as long as*, he lives in the interior.

Nonetheless, the longer duration of what people 'are' by virtue of where they live does not contradict my previous claim about the contingency of Vezo identity. This is because no matter *how* long a person remains in the same place, she never becomes fixed in what she 'is' by virtue of living there.

Let me make this point more clearly with a story about the Kainantu of Papua New Guinea (Watson 1990). During his fieldwork, Watson discovered a taro field in a most inconvenient and unlikely place: on the top of a rocky cliff (pp. 29–32). When he asked why the field's owner, who was unknown to his informants, had gone to the trouble of making a field on top of a rock, he was told that the person must have done so because his ancestors taught him to do so. When Watson asked the same question of someone who belonged to the same phratry as the field's owner, he discovered that the latter belonged to a group of immigrant refugees. Together with the curious practice of growing taro on top of rocky cliffs, the new informant suggested, the members of this group 'had doubtless brought some of their old ways with them' (p. 31).

The reason why people who move from place to place 'bring their old ways with them' can be found in the nature of the link between land and people. As Watson points out, the Kainantu have a Lamarckian theory of identity;[27] they accordingly stress the role of the environment in creating identity. Like the Vezo, they also distinguish between kinds of technical knowledge required for different environments; for example, such distinctions account for the difference between grassland people and forest people. But although the Kainantu maintain that people are different because they do different things, they also stress that other people do certain things differently because 'their fathers/ancestors taught them so' (p. 29). As Watson explains,

the ancestors' legacy is transmitted through growing up in a particular community where, thanks to the peculiar [magical] powers of its members, a unique competence is *instilled* in the young, *infusing* them and forming them after the community's own local character. Indigenous identity is partly a question of belonging to the country itself, *imbibing* the local waters and *ingesting* the foods that spring from the local soil. (pp. 34–5, added emphasis)

By absorbing these substances, people 'come to have the land in them'. At the same time, 'the land . . . comes to have people in it', for the landscape bears the heritage of the ancestors – in their gardens, their animals, their food and their water, their knowledge, skill, immunities, competence, power (p. 35). The terms used by Watson to describe how the Kainantu come to acquire their identity – to instill, to infuse, to imbibe, to ingest – suggest that in this case locality comes to be fused with, or becomes akin to descent (see A. Strathern 1973).[28] By living in a certain place, the Kainantu gradually acquire or absorb an identity that 'sticks' to them permanently, as it becomes the constitutive substance of the person.[29]

Terms such as those used by Watson are, however, totally foreign to the Vezo. Vezo people never 'come to have the land in themselves': they adopt the 'ways of doing' of the place where they live, but when they move, they do not take their old ways with them. Thus, whereas locality determines what one does, what one 'is' does not become a permanent feature of the person – identity remains at all times contingent on the present, and is never determined by the past.

By contrast with Kainantu identity which is gradually absorbed as an ancestral substance, Vezo-ness is better thought of as a shape that people take while they live in a place and when they act in the present: it is a temporary shape, a shape that never hardens. This is more than a play of words, however, for Vezo-ness does in fact shape people's bodies, and leaves deep, albeit impermanent, traces on them.

The signs that one is Vezo

The hands of men are scarred by Vezo-ness. When a particularly large, heavy and strong fish bites on the hook, the nylon line cuts the men's fingers. This rarely causes an injury, for their hands are very thick-skinned, but the fishing line will burn a white scar in the tissue and a sort of streaked callus will gradually develop. Fishing lines leave other, more noticeable scars on the men's waists. When a fishing team decides to search for a better location, both men paddle the canoe and let their fishing lines trawl in the water behind. In order to avoid missing a bite while they paddle, the men tie the lines loosely around their waists; if a fish does bite, the line will tighten around the men's waist and burn a red line in the skin. As the skin heals, the sharp red lines slowly turn into whitish scars. These scars were often displayed for my benefit. When Vezo men told me that one is made Vezo by one's activities at sea, they would show me their hands and, twisting their bodies slightly, point to the scars on their waists. The scars on their bodies were the 'signs that one is Vezo' (*famantaram-Bezo*).

When I asked women whether they had 'signs of Vezo-ness' on their hands, they suggested I look at the hands of Masikoro women, which have a callus at the base of the thumb which comes from the daily pounding of maize and rice. It was thus the *lack* of a callus on the Vezo women's hands that demonstrated their Vezo-ness.

Another way of recognizing Vezo men and women is by the way they walk and move their bodies. Because they live on the coast, they are used to walking on the sand. However, to do so effectively requires a special technique: to avoid getting stuck in the sand one must grasp it with one's toes, while making at the same time a slight rotating movement with one's heels. When people who are not accustomed to walking on the sand come to the coast, they look clumsy and quickly lose their breath. On the other hand, when the Vezo visit the interior and walk on hard ground, they tend to grasp the ground as if it were soft sand and get blisters as a result. Thus, while my friends were quite impressed that I learnt to walk properly on the sand, they became enthusiastic when after my first visit to the interior my toes got covered with blisters!

The practice of Vezo activities shapes people's bodies profoundly; it could therefore be argued that just as Vezo-ness becomes inscribed in the flesh, it is indeed 'absorbed', 'instilled' and 'infused' in the person. But although the traces which 'being' Vezo leaves on the body mark people profoundly, they are also impermanent. Thus, my friends remarked that when they resume fishing after the long period of inactivity of the wet season, their fingers are soft and more easily hurt. Once, during a rice shortage, the women in my village were forced to buy maize which they had to pound every day. They showed me their hands, remarking that they were becoming Masikoro: at the base of the thumb, a blister was starting to develop into a callus. If a Vezo spends some time in the interior, the blisters on her toes will gradually harden into a sign of Masikoro-ness. To bear the 'signs that one is Vezo', in other words, people must act Vezo *in the present*; if not, the signs accumulated through past activities are simply shed away. To return to the example of the Kainantu, one could say that when people move away from the place or practice that makes them Vezo, they leave behind not only their 'old ways of doing things', not only their Vezo identity, but also the old shape inscribed in their body. Like everything else, a person's body is created in the present and is not determined by the past.

Difference by analogy

Although this chapter has been concerned with the identity of the Vezo, the Masikoro have been a constant background presence as those who 'are' what the Vezo 'are' not. The reason for this subterranean dialogue, I shall argue, is that although the Masikoro are irreducibly different from the Vezo, they are at the same time also identical to them.

I quoted above a number of examples in which a child, a sailor or a woman were said to be Vezo, very Vezo or Masikoro, according to what they performed at a specific moment in time. When I first arrived among the Vezo, I was struck by the range of behavioural traits that were recognized as being either Vezo or Masikoro: the way a man wears his blanket, a person talks, a child answers when ordered to fetch water, women's hair is braided, distance at sea and inland is perceived, funerals are conducted and so on. In all these instances, a person 'is' Vezo if she behaves Vezo-like, she 'is' Masikoro if she behaves Masikoro-like. This minute differentiation of Vezo- and Masikoro-like behaviour, which is often a source of crowd amusement and of mild harassment of a Vezo-turned-Masikoro, derives from a basic contrast between two distinct types of livelihood and place of residence: living off the sea and on the coast as opposed to cultivating and living in the interior. This contrast, in turn, is at times expressed in terms of what the Vezo and Masikoro have *not*: the Masikoro do not have canoes (*tsy manan-daka*), and the Vezo do not have fields (*tsy mana tanim-bary, tsy mana baiboho*).

We have already seen that if a Masikoro were to dig a canoe, he would end up with a cattle trough; and if a Masikoro were to try to sail a canoe in the ocean, he would capsize and drown. On the other hand, if the Vezo had fields, they would just be wasting their time (*tsy misy dikany*). The reason for this, I was told, is that when a rice or maize crop is almost ripe and the fields need to be constantly supervised to scare off the birds (who can destroy an entire harvest in a few hours), the Vezo will only stand guard to the fields for a few days; for as soon as they hear that the fish are biting well, they will take off to the sea for the day. On that one day, their harvest will be totally destroyed and all their efforts will have been in vain.

This story portrays the difference between the livelihood of the Masikoro and that of the Vezo in terms of occupational *incompatibility*.[30] The same person cannot be simultaneously engaged in cultivation *and* in fishing; people cannot simultaneously be living in the interior *and* on the coast; and, as we shall see in the next chapter, they cannot be simultaneously 'wise' (as the Masikoro are when they plan their economic strategies) and 'unwise' (as the Vezo claim to be in the management of theirs).[31] Yet the incompatibility of Vezo and Masikoro livelihoods implies nothing about the *people* who practise such different activities, with such different strategies and in such different places. That is to say that the source of the absolute difference between Vezo and Masikoro lies *in the things they do*, and not in the people themselves.[32] Although it was stressed that Vezo and Masikoro activities – including apparently trivial ones like the braiding of women's hair or blanket-wearing by men – are done by different people, this does not mean that such people differ *before* they act as Vezo or Masikoro.

Borrowing from Comaroff, we could suggest that the Vezo adopt a totemic mode of dividing people into 'units within a common humanity'; while collective identities are defined 'in contrast to one another', the various units portray themselves as 'similar yet different' (Comaroff 1987: 304). Although I have no evidence to suggest that the Vezo conceive of an abstract humanity, existing prior to the specific place it occupies and to the specific activity that keeps it alive, the Vezo do indeed appear to regard the Masikoro as 'similar yet different'. We have seen why the Masikoro are absolutely different; the reason why they are also *similar*, or even identical to the Vezo, is that the identity of the Masikoro is produced by a process *analogous* to that which produces the identity of the Vezo. For the Vezo, the Masikoro are different because, like themselves, they 'are' what they do – they are rendered different by their different livelihood, by the different place where they live, by the different skills they learn as a consequence of where they reside, and by the different 'signs' marked on their bodies.

If difference is constituted through analogy, we may argue with Wagner (1977) that what is differentiated must be assumed to have been the same. In the context of his analysis of Daribi kinship, Wagner argues that *if* we assume, for analytical purposes, that kin relationships and the kin identified through these relationships are basically alike, and that the difference between them must therefore be actively created, the only way to create *difference* is by *analogy*, since what is differentiated is originally assumed to be the same. In the case of the Vezo, I would argue that the reason why difference *cannot* be analytically assumed is that difference, like identity, can only be *created* through people's practice in the present. Other people are contingently other, just as the Vezo are contingently Vezo.

3

People without wisdom

I realized very soon after settling in Betania that there was little point in attempting to plan my days ahead, as I had initially tried to do to keep anxieties under control. I found it difficult at first to grasp how villagers managed their time, for they seemed to move erratically from days of hectic activity at sea and at the market, to long spells of time spent playing bingo in small groups dotted around the village. A few weeks after I arrived, I wrote in my diary that the only sensible thing to do was to take each day as it came, and forsake any desire for long-term planning.

As I later discovered, by learning how to cope with the short-termism of my daily life in Betania, I was actually learning about a fundamental trait of Vezo identity, about a type of 'doing' that renders people Vezo. Wholly unawares, I was making myself Vezo. I argued in the previous chapter that what people do, hence what they 'are', is not determined by the past, and remains at all times contingent on people's activities in the present. We have seen how a person's past is shed when he moves from place to place and learns new 'ways of doing things'; and how a person who 'is' Vezo at one moment can become temporarily Masikoro by making a blunder in sailing – he replaces his past Vezo-ness with a new identity created in the present.

This chapter discusses a further context in which the Vezo deny, both implicitly and explicitly, that the past impinges upon the present. This context is the livelihood of the Vezo (fivelomam-Bezo), which is portrayed as an activity that is bound to the present and does not extend into the past or stretch into the future. As a result, 'being' Vezo consists in starting one's activities from scratch every day, as if what happened yesterday had no bearing on what happens today and, consequently, what happens today has no bearing on what happens tomorrow. This short-termism, which eschews all forms of planning, is what renders people Vezo: people without wisdom (*tsy mahihitsy*), who are constantly surprised (*tseriky*).

The livelihood of the Vezo

Although the Vezo employ specific terms to describe the various kinds of fishing they practise – line fishing (*maminta*), drift-net fishing (*mihaza*), barrier-net fishing (*mitandrano*), diving (*maniriky*) and so on – they possess no *generic* term for fishing as such. To denote what they do 'to keep themselves alive' (*velomampo*), the Vezo use the generic term *mitindroke*, which means 'to look for food' (*mila hany*).[1] This term does not specify what kind of technology is employed, or the kind of food that is sought. *Mitindroke* can refer equally to people fishing in their canoes, to a person hunting tenrecs or searching for honey in the forest, to the pigs endlessly rooting for food in the village sand,[2] or to the inhabitants of Belo who collect sea-cucumbers, which they consider inedible but sell to Indo-Pakistani traders for export to China. *Mitindroke* denotes the gathering of any kind of object that provides a source of livelihood. For example, *mitindroke* does not apply to children who look for wild plums in the forest. The reason is not, as I originally thought, because they are children, but because the plums do not contribute to anyone's livelihood; if anything, as the children are repeatedly admonished, the plums will make them sick. Usually, therefore, what is collected through *mitindroke* is edible and will be either consumed personally or traded; but *mitindroke* can also apply to inedible objects like sea-cucumbers whose sole purpose is to be sold.

The term *mitindroke* is of particular analytical interest because it describes the livelihood of the Vezo without referring to their productive technology and activity, fishing; *mitindroke*, in other words, describes generic (rather than technologically defined) features of what the Vezo do to keep themselves alive. To illustrate these generic features, my informants contrasted *mitindroke* with what is *not mitindroke*, namely agriculture (*fambolea*). Thus, while a person who 'looks for food' goes out today (*androany*), sees things (*mahita raha*) and collects a little something (*mahazo raha kely*) every day (*isanandro*), an agriculturalist must wait (*miamby*) for her products to grow (*raha mitiry*); at the end of the productive cycle she will reap a large crop (*mahazo vokatsy bevata*). People who 'look for food' do not have land (*tsy mana tanim-bary, tsy mana baiboho*); cultivators, by contrast, possess land which comes to them from the past (*avy bakañy*).

From this contrast we can identify two important features of the livelihood of the Vezo. First, 'looking for food' occurs on a clearly specified time-scale: it is a day-by-day affair, which does not require waiting and does not involve the transmission of property over time. Second, 'looking for food' is characterized by the unmediated acquisition of objects that exist independently of the person who seeks and acquires them. I shall discuss each of these two features in turn.

By contrast with agriculture, the livelihood of the Vezo does not stretch into the *past* because the Vezo do not own land; it does not project into the *future* because the Vezo do not need to wait for their large crops to grow and mature. *Mitindroke* is repeated over time, day after day, but each new search for food is a self-contained enterprise. Interestingly, the same contrast, according to the same criteria, was drawn by my informants between Vezo livelihood and wage labour. The Vezo commonly object to wage labour because 'it does not make sense' (*tsy misy dikany*), since one good catch at sea can earn the Vezo as much as an average month's wage in Morondava (or even as much as functionaries, *foncionera*, earn in the capital Antananarivo), and wage-earners have to work according to a rigid schedule, day in day out, and under a boss. However, my friends in Betania also recognized a significant advantage of working for a wage, namely the security of income it provides when the sea is rough or when the rainy season sets in (see below). They would go on to suggest that wage labour lies somewhere between agriculture and 'looking for food'. At one extreme, people who cultivate must wait a whole year to earn their income; at the other, people who 'look for food' earn their income every day; in between are those who engage in wage labour and are paid an income once a month. The interesting point here is that, at one end of the continuum, 'looking for food' stands for a mode of livelihood that is short term and bound to the present. With no land that attaches people to the past, and no need to work and wait for a crop or a wage to be delivered in the future, the Vezo's search for food starts afresh every day.

This statement might seem in contradiction with the fact that the Vezo employ canoes which, as technological artifacts, do in some sense attach people to the past. Although canoes do not last very long (a maximum of two years), this is far longer than any individual search for food; and although, by contrast with agriculturalists who inherit land, the Vezo do not inherit canoes from the past, they do inherit the technical knowledge they need to build canoes in the present. In the Vezo representation, however, the canoe remains bound to the present. This is because its origins are represented in a form that could in theory be re-enacted at any point in time, including the present.

When asked about the origins of the canoe, who first thought of building one, and how the techniques for building it had been devised, most people would acknowledge that their predecessors already knew how to make canoes (*olo be taloha fa nahay niasa laka*), but they would leave it at that. But on one occasion an old man recounted the following story. The people who lived on the coast in the past knew how to make canoes. The first time they tried to make one, they used a tree called *mafay*. They cut down the tree, they carved the trunk out and gave it the shape of a canoe; they carried it to the sea and the canoe sank. They returned to the forest, and there they saw a *farafatse* (which is what present-day Vezo use for their canoes); because of its lightness, they thought that this might be a suitable tree for making canoes. They carved out a *farafatse* in the shape of a canoe, they dried it and carried it to the seaside; and it floated. And this, the old man concluded, was the origin of canoe-making.[3] Wanting to know more about these original inventors, I was told that there was nothing more to be said. The old man himself had never thought of asking further, and people older than himself had not volunteered to tell him more. He made it quite plain that I also had no need to know any more.

At first sight, the story seems to be saying that the Vezo canoe originated in the past, for we are told that the canoe was *invented* by past inhabitants of the coast. In fact, the narrative is rather more ambiguous. The invention appears to occur in a timeless void, undetermined by historical or mythological events. The actual site of the invention is not recorded; the names of the inventors are not remembered; the time of occurrence is a generic 'for the first time'. In other words, the story fails to transform the accidental and contingent invention of a dug-out tree trunk that fortuitously did not sink, into a distinct and unique, historically or ancestrally grounded event. The narrative thus achieves two conflicting ends. On the one hand, it acknowledges that past Vezo people knew how to build canoes; on the other hand, it abolishes the distinction between the past and the present, by depicting the invention of the canoe as an event that happened, and may still happen, *at any point* in time. The story thus establishes *both* that the Vezo do not need to re-invent the canoe each time they need a new one, because they have inherited the knowledge from the past, *and* that if necessary they *could* re-invent it at any time. If, for some unknown reason, the Vezo lost the knowledge of canoe-making, they would simply rediscover it through another contingent act of invention.[4]

We can now turn to the second feature that defines the livelihood of the Vezo. The contrast that my informants drew between 'looking for food' and agriculture draws on the basic assumption that the food they look for to keep themselves alive is readily available 'out there'; the Vezo need only find it and gather it. In this respect, the Vezo are resource biased, rather than activity biased (Bird-David 1992: 39); instead of assuming that 'products exist *by definition* only after they have been produced', the Vezo assume that resources 'exist *a priori*, and activities follow to suit' (p. 39). In the case of the Vezo, the resources people need to keep themselves alive exist *a priori* in an ever present and ever abundant container – the sea.

When the Vezo refer to something that is in the sea, they use the adverb *amboho*, literally 'behind one's back'. A Masikoro, on the other hand, will use the term *añatiny*, which means 'inside'. A Vezo will say 'take this fishing net *back there*' (*atery amboho eñy harata iñy*); a Masikoro will say 'take this fishing net *inside* the sea' (*atery añaty riaky eñy harata iñy*). Someone explained this difference to me by referring to the Vezo's position with respect to the sea: 'When one goes out looking for food, when it's over, one returns home; but one does not return home in a westward direction [towards the open sea], but heading eastward, so that one climbs up to the village from the sea.'[5] The Vezo thus perceive the sea as lying behind their back because they position themselves in the act of returning home from a day spent fishing.[6]

From where they stand, the Vezo view the sea as the container of what they need 'to keep themselves alive' (*velomampo*). The presence of fish in the sea appears to be taken for granted. When questioned about the origin of fish, my informants would look puzzled and would tentatively suggest that *Ndrañahary* (the creator, commonly translated as God in the western literature) must have thought of putting it there; as far as the Vezo can tell, fish *has always been* in the sea.

People also assume that fish *will always be* in the sea, essentially because they do not see that their fishing activities affect the fertility and abundance of the sea. The only times I saw people worry about fish stocks was when they discussed the recent massive influx of Japanese industrial fishing-boats, which were trawling the sea off the coast of Morondava. The scale of the Japanese catches – which people estimated when they went with their canoes to collect the smaller fish that the Japanese had thrown overboard – was so out of proportion compared to the Vezo's, that people could not but wonder whether the fish might actually run out (*holany fia*). It is significant in this context that the Japanese fishing enterprise, with its big boats and high-tech fishing equipment, was seen as something very different from *mitindroke*; consequently, it also became admissible to think that it might have different consequences on the sea. Barring the Japanese, however, people never seemed to worry about the sea's fertility. They did not propitiate the sea, nor did they think themselves otherwise capable of interfering either positively or negatively with the size of the fish stock.

There are, in fact, very few prescriptions (*fomba*) or prohibitions (*faly*) concerning people's behaviour at sea that are believed to affect the quality of the catch. The only *faly* I was told of was that one should never show surprise, scream or point one's finger at the sight of big creatures like whales, sharks or giant octopuses out of respect (*fanaja*) for them. If one acts disrespectfully towards these powerful creatures, a gale and high waves will rise all of a sudden to endanger the canoe.[7] On the other hand, it sometimes happens that a 'woman with gills' (*ampela mañanisa*) will seduce a fisherman by posing alluringly on the canoe's outrigger; if he accepts her marriage offer, he will from then on fill his canoe to the brim with huge, fat fish. Unfortunately, such marriages are destined to break up, for the husband will inevitably do what he is forbidden on all counts to do: he will look under his wife's armpit, see her gills, and thus cause the woman to depart in a rage for the sea.[8]

Another rather special but different creature of the sea is the turtle (*fano*). Although the Vezo hunt *fano*, they consider them to be very different from fish: 'Sea-turtles are not animals to be killed very frequently, for they have power; fish instead is killed every day. Sea-turtles are not killed by people every day, but once a month or once a year.'[9] *Fano* are 'difficult' (*sarotsy*). This is both because they are hard to catch and because a number of restrictions (*faly*) must be observed in order to harpoon them or even merely to see them; most of these rules define how to treat and eat the turtle after it is caught. In particular, it is *faly* to kill a sea-turtle by cutting its throat (hence, the carapace is ripped open and the meat is cut up while the animal is still alive), to cut through the chest muscles, to let any blood drip on the sand, to roast the meat, and to add salt to the cooking water (hence, sea-water is used as a substitute); the meat must be cooked by men and must be distributed to relatives and friends, whereas it is *faly* to sell it; certain parts of the meat and entrails are also taboo for women and children. These *faly* are meant to be signs of respect for the turtle (*manaja azy*). If the rules are broken, the people on the canoe which caught the particular turtle involved will never see another one again until the canoe's owner makes appropriate acts of compensation (see also below, pp. 63–4).

By contrast, fish is 'easy' (*tsy miola*) in terms of *faly*; some fish may be particularly 'clever' (*mahihitsy*), like Spanish mackerel, but we saw that the Vezo know how to fool it with their well-prepared bait. The only problem with fish is that one must know where to catch it; if *lamatsa* (Spanish mackerel) are not biting, the Vezo will assume that they are somewhere else, rather than that they are actually unavailable. Fish is assumed to be invariably in the sea, even if no-one is there to catch it.[10]

The sea that the Vezo leave behind their backs on returning to their village contains large quantities of fish which have always been and always will be available. Thus, whereas agriculturalists have to wait a long time for their produce to mature, the Vezo feed on demand: when they need food, they go out to sea and look for it. I witnessed how easy this supply system can be in Manahy, a small settlement south of Belo. As I sat chatting with a woman and her husband, we suddenly realized that the sun was very low on the horizon; it was late, and they had no *laoke* (side-dish) for their evening meal. The man excused himself for having to leave us to 'provide for some *laoke*' (*mikarakara laoke*). He went to the back of the house to fetch a small fishing net, which looked very old and full of holes; he walked to the shore, which was just a few metres away from where we were sitting, strode into the water up to his shoulders and unfolded the net. He then waded back to shore, wrapped himself up in a blanket and sat down on the beach, with his eyes fixed on the net; his cat came rushing up to sit next to him. The net's small floaters moved four or five times; after a quarter of an hour, the man walked back into the water, retrieved the net, and brought back four medium-sized *bica* (mullet) to the house. He dried himself and sat down to clean the fish; in the meantime his wife had started a fire. The whole episode had taken less than half an hour. He resumed our conversation after assuring me that people in Manahy need not worry about their *laoke* (*tsy manahira laoke zahay ato*).

But life is not always so simple. The sea is not just a plentiful container of the things the Vezo need to keep themselves alive; it is also *masiake*, quick tempered and violent, unpredictable and unreliable. As people will tirelessly repeat, one day the sea may be 'angry' (*meloke*) and force the Vezo to stay home; another day, the sea is calm and smooth, and people will go fishing; the day after, however, the sea could well be 'wild' (*masiake*) and the Vezo will be back to inactivity and boredom (*morimoritse*). Because of this dual character of the sea – a generous source of food but with a nasty temperament – the Vezo cannot always feed on demand: they cannot always 'look for food' when they need it.[11] Instead, they are confronted with the one feature that all fishing communities are said to share and which has become the main subject of the 'anthropology of fishing' (Acheson 1981): they are faced with uncertainty.

The Vezo know that in order to cope with the uncertainty of fishing, they would have to be wise (*mahihitsy*). Wisdom, in this context, is the ability to learn from past experience, and to know how to plan for the future by saving in the present; to be wise, in other words, means to extend one's perspective beyond the present, to include both the past and the future. The Masikoro agriculturalists and cattle-raisers are wise, because they work according to a long time-scale, and act on past experience for future benefits. Conversely, one of the main and constantly reiterated features of Vezo people is that they are *not* wise (*tsy mahihitsy*), because in their practice of *mitindroke* they start their search for food from scratch every day, and they do *not* learn to cope with uncertainty from past experience. Despite the whimsical temperament of the sea on which they depend, the form of livelihood that renders people Vezo remains bound to the present. And it is for this reason, as we shall see, that the Vezo are constantly open to surprise (*tseriky*). The remaining part of this chapter discusses the Vezo's lack of wisdom in two very different contexts, the villages of Betania and Belo.

Betania

When people sit around and chat after their meal in the evenings, someone may be asked if he is planning to go out fishing the next day. Unless there is a known reason for *not* going – for example, a funeral that must be attended, an illness, or an appointment with a diviner to choose the favourable day for a ritual – in other words, if one *is* planning to go fishing, the answer is likely to be: 'I don't know yet, it depends on the sea' (*mbo tsy hainteña riaky io*). In such exchanges, the sea is sometimes referred to as a *vazaha*, white man; this is because the sea is not only the Vezo's boss (*patron*),[12] but is also, as whites are, quick tempered and violent, unpredictable and unreliable (*masiake*). The next day, early in the morning, those who plan to go fishing go down to the shore to look at the sea (*mañenty riaky*); they check the dew on the canoe and the movements of the coconut trees (see above, p. 24) to know whether they can go out to sea. If, owing to a rough sea or a bad wind, they decide to postpone their trip, they will return home saying how *surprising* the sea or the wind are (*mahatseriky riaky ty; mahatseriky tsioky ty*).

The return of the canoes in the evening is quite spectacular. Slowly, tiny specks of white begin to dot a long and narrow strip of sea just below the horizon; gradually the number and size of the specks increases. Women and children wait on the beach for the canoes to approach; soon, they begin to recognize individual canoes by the size of the sail and by distinctive features like a coloured patch or a torn corner. Soon after, the guessing game on the day's catches begins. A first indication that the catch has been successful comes from a canoe's position in the fleet, for often a team that has had a good day's fishing will stay behind to have a further, last go while the others hoist their sails to return home. On the other hand, if a canoe is unusually fast, or its sailors are especially skilful, it can leave last with a heavy catch and still beat everyone else to the shore. As the canoes come slowly closer, the day's catch will be estimated more accurately by looking at the hull's water-line; evening tales will later describe the canoe as overflowing with fish, practically shipping water because of its exceptionally large load. Yet even the canoe's water-line need not be an accurate clue to its contents, for the boat is sometimes weighed down by water taken in on the way back.

The catch is not immediately visible when the canoe is beached, and no-one waiting on the beach asks how large the catch is; no-one even *looks* at the catch as it lies inside the canoe, protected from the sun by a large piece of wood. Little is said as the fishermen jump out of the canoe and are helped by their womenfolk to furl the sail, to take the masts down, and to lift and carry the canoe inshore. Only then, rather off-handedly, as if this were merely part of the task of tidying up, the fish are caught one by one by the tail and swung up elegantly from under the cover for everyone to see.

Although no-one is caught looking openly inside the canoe when it lands and is being beached, the women will admit that they 'peep through the back of the canoe' (*mitsikiroke am-porin-daka*) to have a look at the day's catch. If it is good, they will be very happy; if the catch is poor, on the other hand, they will put no strength in their arms when they help to haul the canoe up the beach. As they return home, empty handed or nearly so, they say how *surprised* they are that today they will not earn money from selling fish at the market (*tseriky teña tsy misy vola androany*).

The market of Morondava is indispensable for Betania's livelihood. The market, as I would be told on admiring a freshly caught catch just in from the sea, transforms fish into goods that people need but do not find in the sea. The fish has to be sold on the market because the Vezo need to 'buy money' (*mivily vola*) in order to buy food (*mivily hany*). This makes them full (*vintsy*) and happy (*falifaly*), since 'it is not proper to eat only fish day after day' (*tsy mety laha oma fia avao isanandro*).

So after beaching the canoes, the women take off for the market carrying on the head several huge mackerel, tied together by their heads and tails, the skin wet and shiny, the spine bending slightly over the carrier's shoulders. They will later return to the village with big, heavy baskets, half filled with rice and topped with a few tomatoes, a couple of onions, some meat or even fish for the evening meal, five or ten cigarettes, a small paper bag with some sugar, another with a handful of coffee beans or a tiny envelope with a few tea leaves inside. Crowning all this, bought at the last minute with whatever money is left over from the day, is some sugar cane stuck up straight along the side of the basket, a *baguette*, some bananas, perhaps a slice of *godrogodro* (a rich cake make with rice flour and coconut milk), a couple of *mokary* (rice cakes) and a few *bonbom-boanio* (coconut sweets).

When I walked back from the market with my women-friends, I would often be urged to take note what they carried back home in their baskets (*tsy hitanao raha andesin' ampelan' Betania lafa mimpoly baka bazary?*). Was I aware how, as soon as they earned some money from selling fish, Vezo women (including those I was speaking with) would tour around the marketplace buying good, rich food like pork, beef and manioc leaves? And how they would top up their baskets with bread, sweets and snacks? Surely I would agree that the Vezo are unwise (*tsy mahihitsy*): they binge on good food when they have cash, without thinking that if the following day's sea is rough there will be nothing to sell, nothing to buy, nothing to eat, and they will go dead hungry (*maty mosare*)!

The Vezo are fully aware that the rational alternative to this high-quality but short-sighted consumption would be to build up food stocks, which could be used to buffer against dearth when fishing becomes impossible. But like regular wage labour compared with irregular fishing, stockbuilding 'does not make sense' (*tsy misy dikany*). The reasons are both economic and cultural: saving and stocking would oblige one to give one's rice or beans away to hungry (and 'free-riding') relatives; and 'Vezo women like to go to the market every day' (*tian'ampela Vezo mamonjy bazary isanandro*) to buy provisions, for they are unused to (*tsy zatsy*) and dislike (*tsy tia*) storing food at home (*hany an-trano*).

Women's tastes and customary preferences (*fomba*) with reference to food stocks illustrate what the inhabitants of Betania regard as a more general and fundamental trait of Vezo economic behaviour. This is that 'the Vezo make a lot of money, but they don't know how to "manage" it [lit. make it work]' (*zahay Vezo mahazo vola maro ka tsy mahay mampiasa vola zahay*).[13] The Vezo, I was told with some pride, find money in the sea (*mahita vola añaty rano*),[14] but are incapable of managing it because they do not know how to save: they spend immediately what they earn.

We have already seen how this feature applies to the management of food expenditure. It makes the eating habits of the Vezo similar to those of certain invisible forest creatures known as *kalanoro*. To 'eat like a *kalanoro*' (*atao sakafon' kalanoro*) means that one eats up all the food one has prepared for lunch without giving any thought to the evening meal: 'in the evening there is no food and one just sits around' (*lafa hariva, laoke tsy misy, de mipetsaky avao teña*). The same kind of attitude prevails in the consumption of liquor, specifically rum. Women see spending on alcohol as a male prerogative,[15] and consider that money squandered on rum could be better spent on good food, or even more on clothes (see below). But when the drinking is only occasional and does not compromise the family welfare (as sometimes happens), women can be remarkably tolerant of, and often amused by, male drunkenness, which they will take as evidence that, just like Vezo women, Vezo men are incapable of saving and planning ahead.[16]

Another prominent item of Vezo consumption is clothing (*siky*). However, buying clothes is contrasted sharply with spending money on food, and all the more on rum. The habitual complaint that 'the Vezo just eat and stuff' (*oma, oma avao ny Vezo*) would often be followed by the firm resolve to spend one's next earnings on a blanket or a sarong. If there is money available, spending it on food somehow seems inescapable;[17] the only way to get round the compulsion is to spend the cash quickly on something else. Clothes are an especially valued alternative because they last longer than food.[18] But this has its drawbacks as well, as people in Betania would often point out; after New Year, the Vezo can be seen at the Morondava market wearing smart new jeans and shiny, synthetic dresses – but they lack the money to buy food.

Their inability to manage money often causes people in Betania to be surprised (*tseriky*), or even very surprised (*tseriky mare*). They are surprised when, after indulging in some luxury good, they are 'dead hungry' or are forced to eat a meal with a dull side-dish or with none at all; they are surprised at having no firewood to cook with, or when they have to sit in the dark because they have no money to buy even a few drops of paraffin; and they are surprised when they 'do not see money' (*tsy mahita vola*) to buy a new blanket, or a few medicines, or a bar of soap, or some coconut oil for braiding the women's hair.

Writing about Malay fishermen, Rosemary Firth noted that 'life is an alternation between plenty and scarcity. A Malay who could not plan would starve in the months when he cannot go to sea.' 'A typical complaint of poor fishing results [is that] "there is just enough for food only. One cannot save"' (1966: 141–2).[19] The contrast with the Vezo is noticeable. Where Malays complain that a poor catch allows them to buy food but not to save, the Vezo boast that the earnings from a large catch will all be spent on rich food. Where Malay fishing people survive because they plan and save, the Vezo claim that they are often forced to go 'dead hungry' because they are incapable of either saving or planning.

While the Vezo of Betania do indeed buy fancy clothes and eat pork every time they can afford to, even at the risk of compromising future basic needs, it is also clear that they do not 'die of hunger' when fishing fails them because of a rough sea or a bad wind. They survive thanks to a variety of small income-generating activities;[20] thanks to assets like chickens and pigs which can be sold during a subsistence crisis; thanks to short-term emergency support by their relatives; and, finally, because they do not in fact entirely avoid some forms of saving and planning. For the purposes of our discussion, however, what is significant is the choice by the inhabitants of Betania to *ignore* this evidence of strategic ability to reduce insecurity, and by contrast to emphasize what they consider to be peculiarly Vezo characteristics, namely the contingency and short-termism of decision making, and the lack of foresight and wisdom, all of which generates 'surprise'. Yet the inhabitants of Betania will also happily acknowledge that their neighbours to the south, in the boat-making village of Belo, are much wiser than they are.

Belo

The most striking and prominent feature of the village landscape on arrival in Belo is the large number of schooners (*botsy*). Some, fully rigged with masts and sails, float in deep water in the lagoon; others are in need of repair and squat in the mud, slowly tilting to one side and losing shape over the years. The most noticeable, however, are those that are still under construction, which look like huge bare skeletons rising up out of the sand, their innards visible, made of huge pieces of the hardest, most resistant timber known as *nato*.[21] These schooners were the most visible reason for believing, as I'd been told in Betania, that people in Belo were very wise (*mahihitsy mare olo reo*).

Belo villagers often told me that building schooners had become 'the character of the village' (*toetsin-tana*), thus indicating that building and sailing schooners was already 'done in the past' (*natao bakañy*) and that the villagers are now 'used to it' (*fa zatsy*). In fact, nowadays the entire population of the village (*olo iaby an tana eto*) is said either to have a schooner at sea, to be building one or to be planning to do so. The people of Belo were first taught how to build schooners by a white man, a *vazaha*, from Réunion called 'Beibe'.[22] Initially only a few villagers learnt the boat-building skills; subsequently, other people, wishing to build a schooner themselves, learnt the techniques by imitation. Their children followed in their footsteps, and so the activity slowly spread to the entire village.

The inhabitants of Belo live surrounded by many half-finished skeletons of schooners. Villagers are aware that it often takes longer to finish building a *botsy* than a person's lifetime, but I was assured that this 'doesn't matter' (*tsy mañahy*), because the timber is so hard that it will last for decades without rotting so long as it is kept out of contact with sea-water. The reason why *botsy* take so long to build (twenty to thirty years is not uncommon), I was told, is that they are built entirely with money from the sea (*vola bakan-drano ro mahavita azy*). The capital for the building materials (up to 300 kg of nails and 400 planks for a 30 ton schooner) is collected 'little by little' (*mivory vola tsikelitsikely*) by saving over daily consumption. Building is therefore done piecemeal, a pound of nails or a few planks at a time.

Once building is completed, the schooner is ready to be employed for cargo transport along the coast. In most cases, the owner of the *botsy* (*tompom-botsy*) is also its captain and is responsible for arranging the journeys, which mainly involves obtaining freight from the Karany (Indo-Pakistani traders) in Morondava and in other commercial towns along the coast. A captain who can arrange for freight on a regular basis will earn a lot of money (*vola bevata*). When he returns to Belo after a journey, a boat owner will bring back stocks of food (rice, maize, manioc, sugar, oil) for his family; it is precisely this abundance of 'food at home' (*hany an-trano*), I was told, that makes the inhabitants of Belo desire a schooner.

The reasons why people in Belo *want* a schooner was often discussed in conjunction with the reasons why they *need* to have one. In the first place, they have schooners because Belo has no markets close by (*tsy misy bazary ato*). The difference between Betania and Belo, I was told, is that in Betania people go to the market, whereas in Belo 'it is the market that comes to us' (*ka zahay atoy mandalo ami'hay ny tsena*) – the 'market', in this context, being the carts of the Masikoro who periodically visit Belo to sell maize, manioc and rice. Thus, whereas food is always available at the Morondava market, the inhabitants of Belo know that carts only come every one or two months; they therefore must have 'food at home', for otherwise they would be 'dead hungry' (*maty mosare*). An alternative way of securing 'food at home' would be to engage in cultivation; but since in Belo 'there are no rice fields' (*tsy misy tanim-bary*), it is the schooners that 'are the kind of agriculture that people do here' (*fa io no sahala fambolea atao'hay eto*). By further analogy, the large income produced by the schooners is compared to the 'big crops' (*vokatsy bevata*) that the Masikoro cultivators harvest at the end of the agricultural season.

My friends in Betania had warned me that in Belo I would meet very wise people (*olo mahihitsy mare*), who know how to manage money (*mahay mampiasa vola rozy*) and how to make it grow (*mitombo*). According to their own criteria, then, the inhabitants of Belo were not very Vezo. But a villager in Betania also told me that 'they are still Vezo, these people who build schooners, yet the root of the Vezo is the canoe' (*mbo Vezo olo ro miasa botsy, fa laka ro fototsim-Bezo*). In another instance, I was told that 'the schooners do not make people Vezo, but it is the Vezo who get involved with the schooners' (*botsy tsy mahavezo, fa Vezo ny olo ro mamonjy botsy*). Echoing these statements, I found that people in Belo would emphasize how 'the work of the schooners is white's work, not Vezo's work' (*asa botsy asam-bazaha, tsy asam-Bezo*); they were also keen to state that despite the widespread use of schooners, everyone in the village still owned canoes and went out fishing with them. Thus, after a journey along the coast, the captain of a schooner will up and go fishing with his canoe (*de roso ie, mandeha mihaza, mandeha maminta*). As portrayed in Belo, *mitindroke* is compulsive: 'whatever happens, looking for food is never given up' (*na ino na ino, tindroke tsy afaky*).

Everyone in Betania and Belo agreed that building schooners is *not* a Vezo activity; but they also agreed that Belo villagers 'are' Vezo nonetheless, in so far as they act Vezo by going out to fish with their canoes. Yet if to 'be' Vezo is to act wholly Vezo, the occasional ride on the canoe seems more like a sentimental allegiance than a strong claim to identity; and, to a certain extent, Belo villagers would agree with this view. Although they consider themselves 'very Vezo' because they hunt sea-turtle successfully (*mahay mitoraky fano*), they seem to have little doubt that they practise Vezo livelihood less consistently than those of Betania. Of them they say with admiration that they are 'very Vezo' (*Vezo mare*) or 'really Vezo' (*Vezo tokoa*), because they are strong (*matanjaky*) and only fish at sea, day after day (*maminta an-drano avao rozy, isanandro*), and their women go off daily to the market (*de roso ny ampela, mamonjy bazary isanandro*).

As far as their livelihood is concerned, there is no doubt that the people in Betania are 'more Vezo' than those in Belo. Yet in a curious reversal of meaning, the inhabitants of Belo also claim to be acting, and therefore to 'being', Vezo because of the way they *deploy* that most un-Vezo-like object, the schooner. Although they ostensibly build schooners in order to achieve economic security through 'big crops', the actual management of the schooners at sea is an uncertain affair, the proof being, as I was often told, the many boats in the village lagoon which were slowly disintegrating because their owners were unable to face the cost of repairing them.

A schooner reaps a 'crop' when its captain finds a cargo. For this he is paid a fixed rate by ton, out of which each member of the crew (*matelot*) receives the value of one ton's freight. When the schooner is inactive, the captain is still responsible for feeding the crew, although the *matelots* receive no further payment. This makes it very hard to retain a crew at times of inactivity, for *matelots* will waste no time in finding better employment elsewhere. But I was also told that finding cargoes in Belo was becoming increasingly difficult, for in recent years a couple of ship owners in Morondava had come to control the freight business through their political and trade connections, and they therefore monopolized the transport of sugar, cement and other bulk commodities.

Nonetheless, these recent developments simply exacerbated a condition of insecurity that had existed already before. The main source of uncertainty were the Karany, the Indo-Pakistani traders who are also the main cargo suppliers. The Karany are *masiake* like the sea – violent, unpredictable and unreliable. As a result, Belo's ship owners are often forced to ply the coast in search of opportunities for trade they have no certainty of finding. At times, for want of a better alternative and if they have some available capital, they will be reduced to buying a load of coconuts at one end of Madagascar in order to sell it at the other end for an insignificant profit.

Someone pointed out to me that to employ the schooners in this way is analogous to what the women in Betania do when they buy and resell fish on the beach (*manahaky mpanao tongotsy reñy*): instead of a 'big crop' one earns only a 'very little profit' (*manao profity kelikely*).[23] Thus, external constraints transform the long-term, large-scale enterprise represented by the schooners into a short-term and largely unpredictable affair. Needless to say, the Vezo in Belo find this transformation very surprising. Ship owners in Belo were *tseriky* to find no cargoes for their *botsy*; they were *tseriky* that the unemployed boats lay disintegrating in the village lagoon; they were *tseriky* by the behaviour of the Karany.

People in Belo were aware that the only way to ensure a continuous and reliable source of cargoes was to stipulate long-term agreements with the Karany. The problem is, they are not wise (*tsy mahihitsy zahay*), and therefore they refuse to enter such long-term commitments. *As Vezo*, they declared, they are unwilling to relinquish their independence: 'the Vezo do not like to have bosses' (*tsy tiam-Bezo laha misy patron*) (see below, ch. 4). Whether the people of Belo actually refuse long-term agreements with the Karany, or are simply unable to ensure them because of their lack of market power, is not of particular relevence in this context. What is of significance here is their choice to emphasize – among a broad array of equally significant practices and constraints – the typically Vezo features of 'unwisdom' and surprise. Although Belo villagers 'are not' Vezo when, by dint of wise long-term planning and saving, they manage to complete a large, expensive and long-lasting schooner, they 'are' Vezo during the long periods of enforced idleness, when their schooners lie in the docks or are grounded in the village lagoon; they are so more generally in their 'unwise' inability to engage in long-term, binding contracts with the Karany that would enable them to avoid the insecurity and unpredictability of *mitindroke* with schooners.

Unwisdom and surprise

In both Betania and Belo I met with repeated and widespread expressions of 'surprise'. This was such a common feature of daily life that I soon learnt to express surprise myself in order to prompt people to talk about things I did not understand. Unfortunately, I never thought of expressing surprise at the fact that my friends were so often 'surprised'; so I was unable to test how 'real' those expressions were.

Can the Vezo be 'truly' surprised by the fact that they cannot go out fishing because of a rough sea, when they spend long evening hours discussing the sea's unpredictability? Can they 'really' be surprised that the day's catch is small, if they know that the fish is not always where they think it is? Could the people of Belo be 'actually' surprised that they could not find a cargo, when they spent much of the time complaining that the Karany and their powerful clients were monopolizing the carriage industry?

I noticed that my friends never admitted to being surprised when something unusually *good* happened to them. They were surprised when the rain prevented them from fishing, but a protracted drought would be accepted in good spirit (*falifaly*); they found a poor catch surprising, but an exceptionally large one would be reason for boasting their abilities; lack of cash was an endless source of surprise, but finding a lost wallet stuffed with banknotes would be a sign of a fulfilled blessing: 'that you may find a lost wallet' (*hohita kitapo raraky*). I concluded that my friends were surprised not because they were faced by the unknown and the unpredictable; they were surprised – rhetorically rather than emotionally – *because they were unwise*, because they ignored what they should have 'known' from past experience.

Both the Vezo's surprise and their lack of wisdom have a significant temporal dimension. Surprised and unwise people are those who act (or are subjected to the acts of others, like those of the sea or of the Karany) in the present, with no knowledge of the past and no expectations of, or plans for, the future. The Vezo of Betania show surprise when they are faced with a rough sea, because they ignore past experience that tells them that the sea is *masiake*; they are surprised if they have no food to eat after spending everything on fancy clothes, because they are unwise and ignore that past actions affect the present. The schooner owners of Belo are similarly surprised by the lack of cargoes, because they 'unwisely' ignore the need for long-term relationships with the Karany that extend beyond the present, back into the past, in order to ensure a predictable future.

This rhetoric of unwisdom and oratory of surprise defines a world in which there is no past and no future, only acts in the present. This world revolves around *mitindroke*. As we saw in the first part of this chapter, 'looking for food' is an activity that starts anew every day and, although it is repeated day after day, remains self-contained in the present. *Mitindroke* neither requires nor engenders wisdom, because it consists of activities that do not extend back into the past and do not stretch forward into the future. By contrast, people who do not 'look for food' are very wise (*mahihitsy mare*). Agriculturalists like the Masikoro are wise because they know how to wait and plan, save, and make their money grow; similarly, the people of Belo reveal wisdom by building schooners, an activity that – significantly – is considered analogous to agriculture.

Lack of wisdom and a disposition to be perpetually surprised are two fundamental traits of Vezo people. As the comparison between Betania and Belo has shown, the more people are unwise and surprised, the more they 'are' Vezo. What is more, any activity people engage in – be it fishing, trading in the market or running a schooner – will be perceived as a Vezo activity, as an act of *mitindroke*, if and when it can be construed as a short-term, present-orientated activity which people perform unwisely and which engenders surprise. In the same way in which the Vezo deny that what a person was in the past determines who she is in the present, so the Vezo's lack of wisdom and perpetual surprise constitute them as a people whose livelihood has no links with the past or with the future, and thereby binds them at all times to the present.

4

Avoiding ties and bonds

We saw in the preceding chapter that when the Vezo say that they are 'unwise' they are making a statement about economic strategies that are short term and present bound. When they say that 'the Vezo do not like ties and bonds' (*tsy tiam-Bezo fifeheza*), on the other hand, they are making a statement about their political strategies whereby the power of the past over the present is denied or neutralized. This chapter discusses three different contexts in which the Vezo experience forms of power and authority that stake claims over people's actions and identity through time: the claims of custom and tradition, the claims of affines in marriage, and the claims of the Sakalava kings of the past. In all three instances, the Vezo acknowledge the constraining force of the 'ties and bonds' of power and of the past; in all three instances, as we shall see, these 'ties and bonds' are manipulated, contextualized or fled.

Customs and taboos

Anthropologists are used to being told by their informants that the reason they perform a ritual in a certain manner or adopt a certain behaviour is that it is customary to do so. Anthropologists seldom find this kind of answer satisfactory, however, for they suspect that an invocation of 'tradition' is a way of hiding the 'true' meaning behind a ritual or a certain pattern of behaviour; and they feel frustrated that their capacity to understand is so abruptly brought to a halt by an appeal to seemingly arbitrary 'custom'.

My Vezo friends often invoked custom to account for certain traits of their behaviour. The reason why they do certain things in the present is that they were done in the past: *fa fomban' olo taloha* (they are customs of the people of the past); *fa fomba bakañy bakañy* (they are customs that

61

come from the past).[1] *Fomba* are considered to be 'difficult' and 'serious' things (*raha sarotsy*), that constrain people and which they must obey, willy-nilly, because if they do not they risk falling 'dead on the spot' (*maty sur place*). I was often told that I was fortunate to be a *vazaha*, a white person, because, as far as my friends could judge, I had far fewer 'customs' (*fombanao tsy maro*, 'your customs are not many'), hence a much easier life. Was I not surprised at the many prescriptions and prohibitions that the Vezo must follow? If one eats honey, one cannot laugh; one cannot carry cooked food outdoors at night, unless one places a small fire-brand next to it; if one eats crabs, one cannot throw away the shells until the following morning and one cannot wash one's hands outdoors; if one is a woman, one cannot pull out facial hair; and so on and so on. All these rules must be obeyed because they are upheld by 'custom' (*fa fomba*) – and the arbitrariness of these kinds of 'ties and bonds' seemed as striking to my friends as it did to me.

Yet, I was also assured that I had been very wise to choose to do research on the coast rather than in the interior, not only because the coast is a far healthier and cooler place to live in, but also because the Vezo have much 'easier' customs than most other people in Madagascar (*fombam-Bezo mora, tsy sarotsy loatsy*, 'the customs of the Vezo are easy, they are not too difficult'). The reason this is so is that it is part of the Vezo nature and disposition to be 'soft' and 'easy' (*malemy fanahy, mora fanahy*), and to have a 'soft heart' (*Vezo malemy fo*). This is proven, I was told, by the fact that they always travel unarmed (*tsy manday kobay*, 'they don't carry sticks'), which shows that they have no penchant for fights; or by the fact that they get drunk only to be happy (*falifaly*) and act silly (*adaladala*), and they never become violent. Vezo 'softness' is demonstrated by their manner of speaking; the intonation and the speed of their speech are said to be slow, easy or quiet (*moramora*).[2] Their 'softness' also transpires in the way they treat children. Parents will say that they spoil their offspring: 'we people of the coast do not scold and punish our children' (*tsika olo andriaky tsy mandily anaky, tsy mamohotse anaky*)[3] because they are 'gentle' and 'soft'. For example, if a child is rebuked and starts to cry, her parent will immediately comfort her and tell her to stop, because crying will make her ill (*mamparary*); the child will be reassured in a special sing-song voice that everything is now all right (*fa soa io, fa soa*). Thus the 'softness' of Vezo parents gently reproduces further 'softness' in their children.[4]

It is due to their soft character that the Vezo must have 'easy customs' (*fomba mora*), for they would be unable to cope (*tsy saky*) with more 'difficult' ones (*fomba sarotsy*). A good example of what is meant by this concerns the behaviour expected of women who give birth. During a visit to some Antandroy relatives of my adoptive family, one of our hostesses told us how she had behaved during her labour, describing how she had to keep her head and arms completely still and stay quiet throughout her pains, for such were her people's customs (*fomba'hay*). The Vezo women present showed surprise at the 'difficulty' and strangeness of these customs (*fombanareo sarotsy sady sambihafa mare*), for Vezo women can scream in pain, clench their fists and twist their bodies; doing this is both 'good' (*fa soa io*) and not to be ashamed of (*tsy mahamenatse*). One of the Vezo women present was of Antandroy parents who had come from the south to settle in Betania, where they had become Vezo. Consequently, this woman knew little about Antandroy customs, and 'followed the customs of the people of the coast' (*manaraky fomban'olo andriaky*); as a result, she had become 'soft' and easy-going and would no longer be strong and tough enough to have a baby among her people of origin, the Antandroy.

A further example of the 'easiness' of Vezo customs that was quoted to me is the short duration of their funerals. Vezo people are too 'soft' to endure the sight and smell of a decomposing body: it makes them unhappy (*malahelo*) and sick (*mamparary*), and it frightens them (*mampatahotsy*) (see below, pp. 113–15). The contrast with other peoples of Madagascar, most notably with the Masikoro, among whom funerals were said to last for weeks or even months, was frequently stressed. No-one ever suggested that other people are less afraid, unhappy or sick through close contact with human putrefaction; but whereas other people have the courage to endure their 'difficult' customs, the Vezo 'dare not, because they are too scared' (*tsy mahasaky, ka mahatahotsy mare zahay*).

Besides having 'easy customs', the Vezo also do not have many taboos (*faly*).[5] On one occasion I worried that I had sat on a doorstep (*mipetsaky an-varavana*), which I knew was taboo in southern Madagascar, but I was reassured that for the Vezo it is not *faly* to do so and that I could go on sitting there and enjoy the breeze. My friends explained that the Vezo do not like to have 'too many' *faly* (*tsy tiam-Bezo laha misy faly maro*), because their soft and easy-going nature makes it hard for them to respect very many prohibitions. Since *faly*, like customs, are 'difficult' things, which kill people if they are violated (*raha sarotsy mahafaty olo*), the Vezo would be 'dead all the time' (*maty isanandro isanandro*) if they had to bother about too many.

Whether Vezo customs and taboos are in actual fact any less 'difficult' or numerous than those of other people is clearly a matter of judgement. What interests me here is that the Vezo consider themselves able to *decide* which

customs and how many taboos their 'soft' nature and easy-going character
can cope with, and able to *manipulate* both customs and taboos in order to
accommodate their desires and inclinations in the present. A striking
example of this concerns the *fomba* and *faly* connected with hunting
sea-turtle. I mentioned in the previous chapter that sea-turtles (*fano*) are
considered 'difficult' creatures, both because they are hard to catch and
because of the many restrictions (*falim-pano*) that must be observed by
hunters. When I enquired about these restrictions, I was assured that
people in the past used to follow them far more strictly. The origin of all
rules and restrictions on hunting the sea-turtle, I was told, resided with the
ranja, a kind of altar where sea-turtles were killed, cooked and eaten, and
where their carapaces and heads were kept on display. In an attempt to
make things easier, however, some people decided to eliminate the altar
and see whether they could still catch sea-turtles. The experiment turned
out to be a success, and hence (my informants told me) the altars gradually
disappeared and the *falim-pano* were eased.

Nevertheless, people still follow most of the prescriptions, whether they
have a *ranja* or not: they rip open the carapace and cut up the meat while the
animal is still alive, they ensure that no blood falls on the ground, they
refrain from using salt, they set aside those portions that are prohibited to
women, they refrain from selling the meat at the market, and they continue
to display the head of the turtle on a fence near the house or on the latter's
roof. All this they do, I was told, because they are a sign that they are Vezo
(*famantaram-Bezo*). On the other hand, having rendered their customs
'easier' means that they no longer risk being 'dead on the spot' if and when
they fail to obey a *faly* – which explains why an old woman, who had been
given a portion of sea-turtle meat by her son, could safely go to the market
the following day with a small dish hidden in her basket to sell her highly
prized delicacy.

As my friends pointed out, the very 'easiness' of the Vezo with their
customs and taboos – their willingness to find a way around a *faly* which
proves too difficult, or to soften a custom that they find too hard – is also a
source of uncertainty about what such customs and taboos are meant to be.
I witnessed endless debates – not always and not even most often generated
by my own curiosity – about the correct way of performing a certain ritual,
about its appropriate timing, or about the people that should be invited to
attend. On one occasion, after a long and fruitless discussion, someone
suggested that *I* might know the correct answer since I had been studying
Vezo customs intensively for some time.

A participant in the discussion later remarked to me that one reason why people die so often (*maty isanandro isanandro*) is that they do not know how to act properly. Interestingly, it is the *hazomanga*, elderly people who mediate between the living and the ancestors (see below, pp. 99–103), who are especially vulnerable and in constant danger of dying. They are in a particularly difficult and dangerous (*sarotsy*) position, because if the ancestors are unhappy or upset by the wrongdoings (*hadisoa*) of the living, they will most probably vent their anger on the *hazomanga*. Thus, if a mistake is made in the timing of a ritual, or the wrong sequence of events is followed, the *hazomanga* may easily 'die on the spot'. In one instance, an offering of food to the ancestors was postponed for more than a week, as people debated whether the ritual should be done at dawn or at sunset. What is significant about this episode is that everyone understood that a mistake would have been fatal for the *hazomanga*, but no-one expected him to know the correct answer to the problem. The *hazomanga* was thus caught in an impossible situation: he was recognized to be the repository of a traditional knowledge which could not in effect be known. His authority and power, which should have been based on the 'difficulty' of his knowledge, were thus being perpetually undermined by his inevitable and life-threatening mistakes.

Ties and bonds in marriage

The 'easiness' of Vezo customs results in a reduced danger of 'being dead all the time'; but it also implies far greater individual freedom. This is particularly evident in the case of marriage, which is recognized as being one of the easy customs of the Vezo (*fanambalia amin'ny Vezo mora mare*, 'getting married among the Vezo is very easy'). Its 'easiness' is due to the fact that only a few litres of rum are needed for a wedding (*filako raiky avao, de vita amin'zay*, 'just one bottle and it is over'), and for establishing a union for which 'the customs have been completed' (*fa vita fomba*).

In the marriage ritual the groom and his elders offer drinks to the bride's relatives who have gathered for the occasion. The groom's party will bring a can of locally made rum (*nañosena*), a couple of bottles of legally distilled rum (*toakem-bazaha*) and four or five bottles of soft drinks.[6] Because marriage is so cheap[7] (when one of my relatives performed this ritual, for example, he spent only 25.000 FMG, the earnings of a good day's catch, and was praised by his in-laws for having provided so much drink), one marries 'just for pleasure' (*plesira avao*), like 'going for a stroll' (*mitsangat-sanga amin'zay*).[8]

The very 'easiness' of marriage means that Vezo men and women will have up to 'twenty spouses' (*roapolo valy*) in succession. My friends in

Betania liked to impress me with the numbers of wives or husbands, lovers and children they had had. When I asked Moty, a man of thirty, to tell me about his love affairs and marriages, he admitted some difficulty in remembering all the lovers he had had 'here and there' (*mañatoy mañaroy*). We therefore agreed that he need only count the women for whom he had performed the marriage ritual, and the lovers who had 'dropped children' (*latsaky anaky*) of his. Moty's first memory concerned a woman he had met during a wake when he was about fifteen; although she became neither a lover or a wife, he remembered her because she was the first woman he had sex with. Next, he mentioned the first woman who bore him a child. She delivered the baby at her father's house; a month later Moty performed the marriage ritual and the woman came to live with him in Betania. After a while, Moty decided that he wanted to register the baby with the government to get the equivalent of an identity card for him, but the woman forbade him because, she said, 'this child is not your child' (*anaky io, tsy anakinao*).[9] Moty thought that these were 'difficult words' (*safa sarotsy*); a fight ensued and he sent the woman away, who took her child with her. Soon after, he found a new lover in Lovobe, just south of Betania. The woman had a baby by him, but Moty did not perform the marriage ritual and the woman never came to live with him. When the baby fell seriously ill, however, the mother came to Betania looking for Moty. Moty accompanied her to the hospital, where the baby died. Two years later, a lover Moty had had for a short while gave birth to another child; again he did not perform the marriage ritual for her. Three years after that, a woman who had come to visit some relatives in Betania became Moty's lover and had another child by him. Moty would have liked to keep the child with him but the woman refused. A few months after, Tesa, who had been Moty's lover for over a year, moved in with him. Moty only performed the marriage ritual three years later; soon after, Moty's last wife finally became pregnant; when I left Betania, Tesa was still living with him.

Although I have chosen to recount the biography of a man, I could have just as easily reported the experiences of a woman who married and divorced five different men, and left and returned to her present, sixth husband three times; or that of Tesa, who at the age of 24 had already been married once before she moved in with Moty, and had had two children by two other lovers. Thus, although Vezo men may have an easy time paying for the cheap marriage ritual, Vezo women also benefit from the 'easiness' of marriage. When I explained the marriage arrangements I had observed during previous fieldwork in Swaziland, where the husband gives ten or more cattle to the family of his wife-to-be, my women-friends declared that the Swazi 'have customs that are very hard on women' (*fombandrozy sarotsy mare amin'ampela*); in such conditions, they thought, the women's relatives would force their daughters and sisters to stay married so as not to have to surrender the cattle. Vezo women, by contrast, see themselves as being very unaccommodating with men, because if they want to leave them, nothing and no-one can stop them from doing so.

From both the woman's and the man's point of view, the most significant feature of Vezo marriage is that it does not bind (*mifehy*) people permanently to one another: it is an easy custom because it is easy to contract and easy to dissolve.[10] By contrast, if a marriage is registered with local government officials (if it is 'written down', *vita soratsy*), it becomes difficult to divorce (*sarotsy saraky*). It is for this reason, I was told, that 'the Vezo do not like to contract marriages through the government' (*tsy tiam-Bezo mahavita fanambalia an-fanjakana*). A friend in Belo, who knew a little French and liked to practise it on me, said that the Vezo prefer their own 'easy' customs because they like to be *libre*. Other people made a similar point, stating that the reason the Vezo avoid 'writing' their marriages with the government is that 'they dislike ties and bonds' (*tsy tiam-Bezo fifeheza*). In this context, the easiness of Vezo marriage is seen as part of a more general approach to giving structure to non-binding personal relationships.

As long as it lasts, marriage creates a relationship between two sets of people who were previously un-related (*olo hafa*, lit. different people, see below, pp. 84–5). Through marriage, these people acquire new (affinal) roles, as they position themselves with respect to each other. The Vezo stress that this positioning engenders equality because marriage is a 'barter of a woman for a man' (*ampela takalo johary*), in which the side which loses a daughter acquires a son and vice versa; as a result, 'no-one is below, no-one is above' (*tsy misy ambany, tsy misy ambony*). This principle of equality was clearly stated in answer to a question about the terms of kinship used by parents-in-law when they address one another. I was told that although they would use tekno-names rather than kinship terms for address, the two pairs of parents-in-law should be regarded as siblings because they are linked by their children's marriage. Like siblings, the two groups are equal because they enter into an equal exchange, whereby both sides say to each other: 'here is my child, it is not mine but it is yours' (*anako ty tsy anako, fa anakinao*). Each side honours the other because each has a child who has married among the other (*zaho manaja an-drozy satsia anako manambaly amindrozy, de rozy manaja anakahy satsia anakindrozy manam-*

baly amiko, 'I honour them because my child has married among them, they honour me because their child has married among my people').

Yet, despite all this emphasis on equality, marriage is also recognized to put one side 'up' and the other 'down'. On one occasion, an old man began to expound on the equality of marriage, using many of the expressions that I have just quoted. A younger man who was repairing his fishing net nearby interrupted him, pointing out that it was also the case that 'their [the old man's daughter's in-laws] begging places you [the old man] higher up' (*fangatandrozy ro mañambony anao*). In this case the old man would be in a superior position, he argued, because his prospective in-laws would have to come to him and ask to marry his daughter (*hoavy ato mangataky valy*), and they would have to come to him again to ask to perform the ritual through which they obtain her children (*hoavy ato indraiky mangataky anaky*) (see below, pp. 92–8). The old man agreed with his younger interlocutor (*eka, marina io*, 'yes, that is true'), but then reiterated that in marriage 'no-one is below and no-one is above'.

At first sight, the exchange seems fruitless: whereas the younger man's comments appear to call into question any equality between the two sides contracting marriage, the old man remains adamant in stating that equality exists. In fact, the two statements complement each other. Far from contradicting the statement that in marriage 'no-one is below, no-one is above', the higher position in which the wife-givers are put by the begging of the wife-takers and by their movement towards them is actually what *makes* the two sides equal (cf. Bloch 1978).

For the Vezo, a proper marriage should either be neolocal or virilocal, with the groom taking the woman to live in his home (I discuss uxorilocal marriage below). From the point of view of the woman's side, such a marriage entails the movement of a daughter or sister away from home; and although marriage is described as an exchange in which the side that surrenders a daughter gains a son in turn, the outward movement of the woman is not offset by the inward movement of the man; the woman's movement actually causes her side to suffer a net loss. Just before she moves out, however, the groom and his people move towards the woman's side in order to 'beg' for her.

As the young man suggested, this movement renders the wife-givers (momentarily) superior. This movement will be repeated many times, whenever the son-in-law visits his in-laws (*mamangy any rafoza*), either together with his wife or alone; each time he will re-enact his first visit, when he had to move towards his in-laws-to-be to beg for his wife. During these visits, which are meant to honour (*manaja*) his in-laws, the son-in-law is once again 'put down' (*mañambany*). His inferiority will not be stated through an explicit display of authority by his in-laws, but will be expressed by subtle changes in body language and tone of voice and by the motives and timing of the visit.

The superiority as such of his in-laws on these occasions derives from the fact that they remain in their place, thus forcing their son-in-law to move towards them. But when the visit is over, the son-in-law once more moves out, as he had on the first 'wife-begging' occasion. He, now, is the one 'above'; his superiority over his in-laws derives from the original outward movement with which he took his wife away. It is these regular, pendulum-like movements of the son-in-law towards and away from his in-laws that over time achieve an overall equality between the two sides ('no-one is below, no-one is above').

If equality between the parties is achieved through this alternation of inward and outward movements by the son-in-law, it is easily appreciated why the reverse so seldom occurs, why in-laws so rarely visit a son-in-law. Needless to say, when for some reason such a visit is called for – when in-laws, for example, are invited to attend the 'work for the dead' described in chapter 8 below – the outward-moving party will find a means of neutralizing its potential inferiority and of reaffirming its (temporarily) superior status. Thus, whereas the majority of those invited to the 'work' will present the organizers with small donations in cash, the in-laws will offer a live head of cattle or a whole case of beer; such offerings in kind set off a series of events which draw attention to the unusual character and importance of the contribution (see below, pp. 142–4). What is more, the boastful and somewhat aggressive manner with which the offer is made is meant to demonstrate that the incoming party's contribution is essential to the completion of the 'work' and thereby to humiliate the receivers, so offsetting what would otherwise be the in-laws' weakness as incomers. On his part, the son-in-law will be particularly careful to look after them and honour them by providing plenty of drink. In this context of time and space, he has to play down his superiority as the host so as to maintain the delicate balance of equality effected by the offerings of his in-laws.

A counter example of this exercise in achieving equality by cancelling out opposite positions of hierarchy is the case of a son-in-law who was asked to attend a similar 'work for the dead' by his in-laws. Normally a son-in-law would be expected to contribute to the 'work' of his in-laws in order to show them respect; but he would also be expected to be careful not to overshadow them with too large a contribution. In this particular instance, the son-in-law attempted to do precisely that when he announced during a visit that he would contribute one head of cattle that would be larger than what anyone else could afford. His father-in-law's reactions to this were immediate: no-one had sought the son-in law's help, he shouted, nor was the in-law needed to complete the work successfully; the son-in-law was then brusquely enjoined to leave.[11] Afterwards, the two sides agreed that both the son-in-law and the father-in-law had been too drunk really to mean the difficult words (*safa sarotsy*) they had said to each other, and the incident was hushed up. It was nonetheless clear to everyone that the son-in-law had acted improperly (*tsy mety*) and was therefore in the wrong (*diso ie*). He had failed to act respectfully and submissively in a context in which he should have been 'put down' by his in-laws; the point was made repeatedly that if one takes a wife from someone, one must always talk softly (*moramora*) to them on visits.

These examples suggest that when the Vezo say that marriage is an equal relationship in which 'no-one is below, no-one is above', they are not thereby denying that marriage engenders relations of hierarchy between someone who *is* below and someone who *is* above. However, they emphasize that hierarchical relations are defined by *context*. Who is below and who is above is defined by context, in a certain place and at a certain point in time. The reason why saying that wife-givers are superior is not in contradiction with saying that marriage engenders an equal relationship is that the two statements originate from two different perspectives which complement each other. On the one hand, marriage is construed as a hierarchical relationship because it is envisaged at one specific point in time and space; on the other hand, marriage is construed as an equal relationship because it is envisaged as a process, in which opposite hierarchical contexts offset each other to provide a neutral equilibrium. As we shall now see, it is precisely its lack of equilibrium (its lack of contextualization produced by movement) that renders uxorilocal marriages so problematic for the Vezo.

Uxorilocal marriages are considered to be 'bad marriages' (*fanambalia raty, tsy soa*), which go against custom (*tsy fomba*) and are shameful (*mahamenatse*). They are characterized spatially by the formula 'the man follows the woman' (*johary manaraky ampela*). Vezo dislike for such marriages was explained as follows. People must assume that *all* marriages will break up after a while. When a couple have a fight and separate, either momentarily (*tezitsy*) or for good (*saraky*), the partner who has 'followed' the other must leave the couple's home. It is customary and proper (*fa fomba, de mety io*) that it be the woman who 'carries her stuff on her head' (*miloloha enta*) back to her kin, for it is 'shameful for a man to carry his things on his shoulder when he leaves' (*mahamenatse laha johary milanja enta lafa roso mandeha*). This of course occurs if 'the man has followed the woman' after marriage. Because he first follows the woman and then is forced to leave home, 'the man is like a woman' (*mitovy amin'ampela johary iñy*).

Both the definition of uxorilocal marriage and the explanation of its shameful character emphasize the movement engendered by this kind of union. Because he *follows* the woman, the son-in-law remains where he was when he begged his in-laws for a wife. He is thus *permanently* (except when he leaves his wife or is sent away by her) in the same position in which a son-in-law who marries neolocally or virilocally puts himself *temporarily* when he visits his in-laws. Whereas the visiting son-in-law oscillates between inward visits and outward residence, the man residing uxorilocally is stuck in the same place. Therefore, instead of experiencing submission only in definite and temporally restricted contexts, the in-marrying son-in-law experiences it as a permanent feature of his life.

Although uxorilocal marriage is stigmatized as 'shameful', a closer look reveals some interesting nuances in attitudes. Uxorilocal marriage is said to be liked by the *receiving* in-laws, because they acquire a new hand, someone who can help them (*mañampy azy*). By contrast, it is supposed to be disliked by the *incoming* man for a variety of reasons: the man is constantly in fear of being sent away (*mahatahotsy horoasiny*), he lacks power (*tsy mana povoara*) because his in-laws, rather than himself, are the 'masters of the house' (*tompon-trano*), and he is forced to work too hard because his in-laws can boss him around (*miasa mare teña ka rafozanteña maniriky an-teña*).

If a man who 'follows' a woman expects to be exploited to such a point, one is bound to wonder why he enters an uxorilocal marriage in the first place. The answer is that he is an idler (*ebo*), otherwise described as 'someone who follows the shade: if the shade is in the west, he goes west; if the shade is in the east, he goes east' (*manaraky aloke ie: andrefa aloke, andrefa; antiñana aloke, antiñana*). The only reason for a man to 'follow the woman' is that he is too lazy to build a house where he can move with his wife and her possessions, either at his kin's place or on a vacant lot elsewhere in the village. Since it is both easy and cheap (*mora mare*) to build a new house (Marofasy, I was told, had collected the timber for a house in less than a week), a wise (!) young man (*kidabo mahihitsy*) will build a house well before he marries, so that when he begins 'to look for a wife' (*mila valy*) he already has somewhere to take her to.

This explanation I discovered to be somewhat misleading. When I asked for real-life examples of uxorilocal marriages, people admitted that most men who 'follow the woman' come from far away; quite understandably, it is newcomers with no local kin to rely on who prefer moving in with their partners rather than being isolated in a house of their own. (This is especially true, of course, if the man is not a Vezo and has also to learn to become one).[12] Yet despite these counterexamples, people still insisted on the 'idleness' of 'the man who follows the woman'.

Looked at more closely, the claim that a man will only enter an uxorilocal marriage because of idleness rests on a curious paradox. While the in-laws' advantage is supposed to derive from the fact that they acquire additional labour force, someone they can command and who is available to help them, any gain they might have can only be curtailed (if it is not entirely nullified) by the fact that an in-living son-in-law is, by definition, lazy: instead of an ideal *super son*,[13] he turns out to be a useless *super idler*. Indeed, the uselessness of such an acquisition was actually often acknowledged.

Nonetheless, the presumed idleness of the in-marrying son-in-law subverts the otherwise straightforward relations of dependence, fear and exploitation in which he would normally expect to find himself; and it similarly subverts the position of superiority of his in-laws. Thus, although his marriage does not engender overall equality, his idleness does nonetheless undermine hierarchy. And of course, by stressing the fact that the *only* reason for a man to put himself in a subordinate relationship with his in-laws is his laziness, this theory suggests an easy way out of dependence and of a shameful power relation: stop being lazy and move out! By doing so, the son-in-law would free himself of the 'ties and bonds' that fix him in his inferior position; he would recontextualize hierarchy, and join the oscillatory movements that transform positions of inequality at certain points in space and time into overall and long-term equality.

Stories about kings

'Ties and bonds', however, cannot always be manipulated and contextualized. This section looks at how the Vezo respond to *inflexible* constraints by examining their recollections of the domination by Sakalava kings (*mpanjaka*), who formerly reigned over the western regions of Madagascar. Like all holders of power and authority, for present-day Vezo the *mpanjaka* were violent, unreasonable and uncontrollable (*masiake*);[14] confronted with their intransigence and their demands for subjection, the Vezo fled. It is in particular this flight that they choose to remember in the present.

When I asked whether the Vezo had formerly been subjects of the Sakalava kings (*nanompo mpanjaka ny Vezo?*), the stock answer I received was that after the white man arrived in Madagascar there had been no more kings (*mpanjaka tsy misy*), the implication being that there was little point or interest in talking about something that no longer exists. Although, through sheer persistence, I did succeed on a few occasions in drawing my friends' attention back to the past, no consistent picture of Vezo relations with the Sakalava monarchy ever emerged. Thus, the statement that 'the Vezo had no kings' (*Vezo tsy mana mpanjaka*) might be followed by an admission that if a king demanded a tribute of sea-turtles or of *fiantsiva* (*Naso unicornis*) the Vezo could not refuse, because kings were wild and aggressive (*masiake*) and killed (*mamono*) anyone who did not obey them. On the other hand, it was once suggested that in actual fact the Sakalava kings took little interest in the Vezo because 'the Vezo have no wealth, they have no rice-fields and cattle' (*ka Vezo tsy manan-kanana, tsy mana tanim-bary, tsy mana aomby*). On yet another occasion, I was told the following story as evidence of the *mpanjaka*'s stupidity. One day a king came to a Vezo village to collect tribute. The villagers presented him with baskets full of high-quality dried fish (*fia venja, maiky soa*); but because the *mpanjaka* was afraid of being poisoned by his subjects, he asked for the fish to be soaked in water which one of the villagers then drank. The person survived the ordeal, and the king took the fish away; but by then, of course, the dried fish had been ruined: what a stupid waste! (*mosera*).

Most of my informants, however, responded to questions about kings and kingdoms of the past with a stereotypical tale of an act of defiance: 'if the king came to the coast the Vezo would just take to sea, because they couldn't be bothered to wait at the village to meet him' (*de lafa niavy andriaky ny mpanjaka, de roso an-driva ny Vezo, ka tsy nahefa mipetsaky an-tana mandramby azy*). But although the Vezo have indeed often been portrayed in the literature in the act of fleeing with their canoes from kings and enemies,[15] I am not concerned with the historical accuracy of this claim. Rather, I am interested in understanding what the Vezo claim to have fled *from*. For this, I turn to the (failed) encounter between the *mpanjaka* and their Vezo subjects in order to ask: what did the *mpanjaka* do when he came to the coast?

As my interlocutors recounted it, the *mpanjaka* came for two reasons. First of all, they came to collect tribute, in the form of typical Vezo goods like sea-turtle and certain especially prized fish;[16] but they also came to 'survey people's ancestors' (*mitety raza*), that is, to ask people who their ancestors were and where they came from. This explains why, when I first attempted to write down the genealogy of an old man, I was asked somewhat aggressively whether I thought I was a *mpanjaka*.

Giving tribute to a *mpanjaka* was a way of showing allegiance and of proving to be a subject (*manompo azy*); hence, when the Vezo took to sea instead of meeting the *mpanjaka*'s demands, they were effectively refusing to recognize subjection. But why did the *mpanjaka* want to 'survey people's ancestors'? And why were the Vezo anxious to avoid being questioned? Whereas the first question went unanswered, the reply I was given to the second one was, once again, that 'the Vezo do not like ties and bonds' (*tsy tiam-Bezo fifeheza*).

In order to pursue these issues further and to clarify what is implicit in these statements, we must briefly turn to the literature on the Sakalava kingdoms, in particular to the analysis of relations between the monarchy and its subjects. Although there are significant differences in approach between scholars like Lombard (1986, 1988), Feeley-Harnik (1978, 1982, 1991), Baré (1977), Schlemmer (1983) and Fauroux (1980), and although the political and ritual organization of the southern and northern king-doms differs,[17] a theme that is shared by all these studies is that which we might gloss as the 'politics of identity'. Very schematically, this consisted in the creation through conquest of a new social and ritual order in which formerly independent and now subject people were defined through criteria that referred to, and were centred around, the monarchy. The area in which this redefinition of identity occurred was history (*tantara*).[18]

Like other people in Madagascar, the Sakalava distinguish between two types of narration about the past. *Angano*[19] are tales about plants, animals and people that are stated emphatically to be untrue (i.e. to be lies, *mavandy*) by both the narrator and the listeners; their main attribute is their timelessness (Feeley-Harnik 1978: 410). By contrast, *tantara* are true stories about the past, typically about the ancestors, which are tied through time to the present: they relate 'a succession of events that actually happened, and rank them in time from past to present' (p. 411). As Feeley-Harnik notes, 'history [as *tantara*] is not evenly distributed because to have it is a sign of politico-religious power and authority' (p. 402). Thus, while 'the only *tantara* of significance to Sakalava as a whole is the history of the Sakalava monarchy, from its origin to its present-day location' (p. 411), the only *tantara* of significance to individual Sakalava is that which recounts how they and their ancestors came to be associated with the monarchy as nobles or workers (pp. 404, 411). It is only through this association that people are placed within 'history' (that is, within *royal* history) and are defined as subjects and members of the kingdom.

We can now return to the Vezo who fled with their canoes when the *mpanjaka* came to the coast to 'survey their ancestors'. In view of the unequal distribution of 'history' between royals and subjects and among different subjects, we are now better able to appreciate the deep *political* significance of the *mpanjaka*'s questioning. To ask people who their ancestors were and where they came from was tantamount to asking them about their *tantara*; the *mpanjaka*'s survey of the 'history' people claimed for themselves through their genealogies was a means of redefining those 'histories' as a fragment of their own, royal, history. Because 'history' was carried in one's genealogy, 'surveying people's ancestors' was a means to transform previously autonomous people into subjects of the monarchy by subsuming them into the general history of the kingdom. By taking to the sea with their canoes, by refusing to pay tribute and to disclose to the *mpanjaka* who their ancestors were and where they came from, the Vezo were avoiding being so subsumed. Because under the Sakalava the only 'history' available became royal history (which attached people to a sequence of royal events unfolding from the past to the present), the Vezo's refusal of 'Sakalava history' was also a refusal of 'history' as such.

As the Vezo remember it, the flight from the *mpanjaka* constitutes a clear assertion about their past and present dislike for 'ties and bonds'. This in turn can be read as a powerful statement about their identity in the present. We just saw that a consequence of the Vezo's real or imaginary flight was to deprive them of 'history'. Feeley-Harnik notes that to have no history, or to have 'lost history' (*very tantara*) (1978: 411), has disastrous consequences, because 'severed from his past, a person has no identity in the present' (p. 411). This of course is true only if a people's identity is constructed by reference to the *past*; it applies only if people are what their 'history' makes them, by virtue of what their ancestors were and were recognized to be through the *mpanjaka*'s questioning. Once we admit that identity need not be defined by the past, the Vezo's flight from the *mpanjaka*'s questions achieves not a loss of identity, but rather a defiant assertion of an *alternative* mode of defining identity, a mode in which people 'are' what they do in the present rather than being determined by their own or someone else's 'history'.

Resisting fixity

The unifying theme of this chapter has been the Vezo's dislike for the 'ties and bonds' (*fifeheza*) they encounter in different contexts and domains of experience, and the specific strategies of resistance, negotiation and avoidance of these constraints that they develop.

The Vezo recognize the constraining power of tradition, of rules and prohibitions that come to them from the past; they call this power 'difficulty', on whose account people may even die. However, the Vezo claim that because of their soft nature they are unable to cope with too many 'difficult' things. If they were to follow every *fomba* and *faly* according to the rules, they would be 'dead all the time'; they therefore consciously *choose* how much of the 'difficulty' of tradition they can actually take on. This conscious deliberation has the effect of reversing the holistic assumption that rules and constraints are imposed by 'society' on its members. Rather than being inherited, unchangeable constraints that shape and define, *fomba* and *faly* can be manipulated – softened and eased – to suit the Vezo's character and inclinations. Once tradition has become negotiable, it is no longer felt to be a heavy burden. Although the Vezo recognize that customs are 'difficult', people's 'softness', and the limits this dictates on what they are able effectively to endure, provides them with a significant degree of autonomy to decide pragmatically which customs of the past they shall follow in the present. By deploying their 'softness', the Vezo effectively loosen up the 'ties and bonds' imposed on them by the past.

A similar strategy is followed in the context of marriage. Although marriage among the Vezo is an 'easy' custom that does not bind people permanently to one another, it nonetheless engenders inequality between those who are 'down' and those who are 'up', between those who lose a daughter and those who gain a wife. Marriage fixes people into positions that last through time; it defines roles and constrains action. The Vezo's solution to this dilemma is to render contextual and time-bound those situations in which a role of superiority and/or inferiority is engendered and acted out. Structural positions of inequality are constantly redefined in the present. As in a complex Baroque dance, wife-takers and wife-givers move towards and away from each other, bringing 'up' those who are 'down', and putting 'down' those who are 'up'. By contextualizing what is 'difficult' and fixed in marriage, the Vezo once more neutralize the 'ties and bonds' that last through time.

Analogously, the Vezo's flight from the *mpanjaka* remembered today, when their formidable power is no more, is a flight from a source of authority that claimed to establish and control people's identity. The Sakalava kings not only forced people to pay tribute, which they then wasted through their diffidence and stupidity; they also exercised the power of telling people who they were or, more precisely, of telling them that they were only to be fragments of a more general 'history' controlled and articulated by the kings themselves. But as they recollect it today, the Vezo could not be bothered to attend on the *mpanjaka*, and they took up and left. Exploiting their mobility and lack of physical ties to the land, they once again refused to let the present be determined by the past.

5

Intermezzo

The Vezo are soft people. Their customs are easy and their taboos are few. They dislike ties and bonds, which they avoid through complex strategies of manipulation. When the binding power of kings becomes too strong to be manipulated or contextualized, they choose to flee in order not to be told who they are. The Vezo are people who keep themselves alive by searching for food in the sea. But they are unwise, and so they fail to learn from past experience and to plan ahead for the future; this makes them unusually prone to surprise. They are people who live on the coast, who know how to swim, how to make canoes, how to sail, fish, eat and sell fish, and how to walk on soft sand without losing their breath. They are people who bear on their body 'the signs that one is Vezo'.

The Vezo are people who 'are' what they do. Their identity (Vezo-ness) is an activity, not a state of being; it must be performed for a person to 'be' Vezo. When people learn Vezo-ness, they learn to 'be' Vezo; when they perform it skilfully, they 'are' *very* Vezo; if they perform it only intermittently, they 'are' Vezo at one moment and Masikoro at the next; if they stop performing it, they stop 'being' Vezo. Whether people 'are' Vezo or not depends on their actions in the present, for it is only in the present that they can act Vezo.

The Vezo are people undetermined by the past; only their activities in the present are relevant to what they 'are'. What they were before can be shed in an instant: by making a mistake in sailing, or by being sick on a fishing expedition; by moving their home from the interior to the coast, or by changing their livelihood from agriculture to fishing. As people shed their past identity by acting a new one in the present, their body also sheds the signs of what they used to be; as the old signs fade away, their body becomes inscribed with their new identity.

The Vezo can be described as *transparent* people, because they lack the residues deposited by the passage of time. The Vezo have a shape, but this shape never hardens; they acquire experience and knowledge, but these can be shed in an instant; they require wisdom in order to learn from the past, but they claim to have none; they find the constraining power of the past so 'difficult' that they either adapt it to their taste and inclinations or they flee it altogether. The Vezo are transparent because what they 'are' in the present is not the outcome of events in the past; the past does not become history for the Vezo person, because what the person 'is' is made anew and from scratch every day.

Recall the statement which first introduced me to the Vezo theory of identity: 'the Vezo are not a kind of people' (*Vezo tsy karazan'olo*). As I explained in the opening chapter, the meaning of this statement is that Vezo people are not *inherently* such. Hence, if one were to search for Vezo identity 'inside' the Vezo person, one would be unable to *see* it; one could only see *through* it, as one sees through transparent matter, because there is no lasting Vezo core 'inside' the Vezo person. Vezo-ness can only be perceived if one looks at what the person *does* in the present.

Yet the Vezo are not *entirely* transparent. There is inside them a zone of opaqueness, a residue of history: a scar left on people by the past which cannot be shed and which does not fade away; an inherent quality, a state of being, which a person acquires by virtue of ancestry and which lasts unchanged through time. It does not need to be performed because it *is*, outside and beyond the present. It is a fragment of 'kindedness' inside people who are otherwise 'un-kinded'.

It is to this zone of opacity in the Vezo person that we now turn. In the following three chapters, we will be looking at the 'kindedness' of the Vezo, at how, where and at what time it is experienced by them. We shall start, however, by analysing, with the aid of an old man, the backdrop against which 'kindedness' is made visible.

6

Kinship in the present and in the future

Kinship in the present

Dadilahy (grandfather) is a very old man (*fantitra be*). He does not know when he was born, but he thinks maybe in 1905. *Dadilahy* is very tired (*rerake mare*); he spends his days sitting in front of his house, which his grandchildren (*zafy*) built for him a few years ago. He occupies himself with making knives out of small scraps of iron that his grandchildren find for him. He hammers the iron on a flat stone; now and then he stops to recover his strength, and at times he falls asleep over his work. His grandchildren tease him that he spends more time sleeping than hammering, so it takes him many days before he finishes a blade and can start carving the handle. Although *dadilahy* is barely able to walk from his house to the kitchen, which is just 10 m away, he says he would go fishing if he could find a companion; at this, his daughter reminds him how weak his legs are and how bent his back is. A few hours later, in the evening, a small audience gathers around *dadilahy* to listen to him telling one of his many adventures at sea as a young man. He gives marvellously accurate details on the wind, the current, the waves and the position of the sail. His audience strains to hear his feeble voice, for his stories are always very engaging. His grandchildren say that he is a good story-teller (*mahay mitantara ie*).

Dadilahy knows other stories as well. He knows how people come to be related to one another, 'what makes them kin' (*mahalongo an-drozy*). *Dadilahy* knows a lot about *filongoa* (kinship), because his great age has meant that he has been able to follow the setting up and expansion of *filongoa* over many generations. I spent many hours in Belo talking with *dadilahy*, often interrupting his work since he was unable to talk and hammer knives at the same time; mostly we discussed kinship. *Dadilahy* was very patient with me. If I asked meaningless questions, he would take time to explain why they were meaningless. If he felt that I assumed to know what I did not know, he would gently lead me to raise the relevant questions. On his part, he seemed always to understand fully what my questions implied and answer accordingly.

Things had started out rather dispiritingly, however. Seated in front of him with a large notebook firmly in hand, I had begun by asking him to list all his kin, everyone he was related to; could he please give me their names and how they were related to him? *Dadilahy* looked at me in disbelief mixed with exasperation. How could I possibly imagine that my paltry little notebook would be even distantly capable of containing his list of kin?

I should indeed have known better. The most frequent remark I had heard about Vezo kinship was that 'the Vezo have very many kin' (*Vezo manan-dongo maro mare*). As *dadilahy* pointed out, this is because the Vezo have kin on both their father's and their mother's side (*amin' ilan' babanteña, amin' ilan' neninteña*); in other words, because they do not draw distinctions between the two sides, thereby including as their *longo* (kin) all the people with whom they can trace a shared link of generation – with whom they, or one of their ascendants, 'share a mother [and/or] share a father' (*miharo neny, miharo baba*).

Having set my importunate notebook to one side, *dadilahy* proceeded to teach me about *filongoa* his own way. He began by explaining how the audience that gathered in the evening around his house and the people who brought him scraps of iron for his knives had all come to be grandchildren of his. This led on to an explanation of how these grandchildren relate to each other as *longo* because they share him or an ascendant of his as a source of generation. In the first instance, *dadilahy* made me look *down* at his descendants; in the second instance, he indicated how his descendants first look *up* towards him, and then *sideways* at each other. *Dadilahy* was showing me a system of ungendered relations[1] in which sameness between persons is stressed over difference between genders.

To put it somewhat differently, this is a system of kinship in which gender is a difference that makes no difference. As I learnt to look at *filongoa* through *dadilahy*'s and his grandchildren's eyes, I discovered that in this domain people are gender-blind. The Vezo do indeed recognize, even emphasize, that men and women differ in procreation (men place children inside the women's body with their semen, but women are responsible for the hard work of housing and feeding the baby inside them), and that women ought therefore to be considered 'the real source – origin – hence the owners of the children' (*ampela ro tena tompony*).[2] Nonetheless, they also actively transform this difference into sameness. They achieve this transformation through a complex ritual which elaborates and defines both genderedness and ungenderedness in relation to each other, as two attributes that mutually constitute rather than contradict one another (see Astuti 1993). The end result, which is what concerns us here, is the ungenderedness of *filongoa* and people's blindness in this context to gender difference.

When *dadilahy* looks down at his descendants, he has a vision of growth and expansion. This he finds very pleasing.[3] *Dadilahy* looks down at his children (*anaky*), at the children of his children (*zafy*), at the children of the children of the children (*kitro*), and so on. As his eye moves downwards, he draws no distinctions between his descendants: his brother's children are the same as his sisters' children, his sons are the same as his daughters, his sons' children are the same as his daughters' children, and so on further and further down the generations. *Dadilahy* considers all his descendants as his grandchildren (which he consequently can claim to have very many of, *maro mare*); in so doing, he construes the link between himself and his descendants as ungendered. Under his gaze, filiation is non-gender specific.

The converse of *dadilahy*'s view is that of his grandchildren, who look upwards and recognize him as their ascendant. For the young boy who comes with a scrap of iron, *dadilahy* is the man who generated the woman who generated his own mother; the woman from Betania who visits him when she goes to a funeral in Belo recognizes *dadilahy* as the man who generated her father; for a small baby, he is the father of the father of the mother of his own father. When *dadilahy*'s descendants look upwards, they trace back to him along the same ungendered paths that *dadilahy* follows to embrace them all as his descendants; if *dadilahy*'s sight reaches Dany by 'descending' through his sister and his sister's son, Dany's sight reaches *dadilahy* by 'ascending' through his father and his father's mother – in this case, by moving once through father's side (*amin' ilan' babanteña*) and once through mother's side (*amin' ilan' neninteña*). In the descendants' view, parenthood is non-gender specific: to have been born by a woman and to have been born by a man makes no difference.

While the people who gather around *dadilahy* in the evening look upwards in order to recognize him as their grandfather, they also look sideways at one another to recognize themselves as *longo*. They are *ampilongo* (reciprocal kin) because they share the old man as a source of generation, or because they share one of these sources with *dadilahy*. Lefo and Dany, for example, are *ampilongo* because they are the grandchildren of a sibling pair which was generated by two brothers, one of whom was

Fig. 2 Lefo and Dany

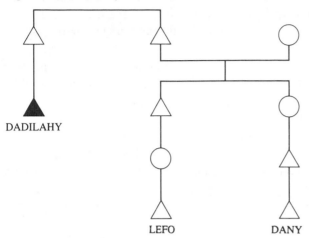

Fig. 3 Sary and Lefo

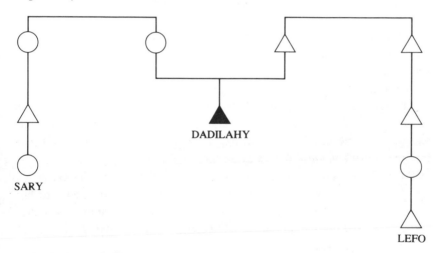

also a brother of *dadilahy*'s father (see Fig. 2); *dadilahy* is therefore their grandfather, while Lefo and Dany are brothers of each other. Sary and Lefo, on the other hand, know that they are *ampilongo* because *dadilahy* is both Sary's father and Lefo's grandfather; *dadilahy*'s mother was the sister of Sary's father, and *dadilahy*'s father was the brother of Lefo's grandfather (see Fig. 3). The fact that Lefo and Dany, and Sary and Lefo are *ampilongo* by reference to sibling pairs rather than by reference to a common apical ancestor is of significance, because siblingship is a non-sexual, ungendered relation. Thus, like the old man who looks downwards, and like his descendants who look upwards, people who look sideways at each other retrace the source of their relatedness through ungendered links of generation.

As it was often pointed out by *dadilahy* and his descendants, the number of a person's relations in the present depends upon the memory of older men and women who know how people were related to each other in the past. That is why *dadilahy*'s grandchildren will often come to him to ask if and in what way a certain person is their *longo*; it is also why, every time an old person dies, some knowledge of *filongoa* is lost, and some of their descendants who are related will become forever unaware that they are so. In some ways, this periodic loss of knowledge is regarded as a good thing (*raha soa*). Marriage among the Vezo should only occur among people who are unrelated, called *olo hafa*: 'different people'. But as Sary once explained, having so many *longo* makes it impossible to find 'different people' to marry (*maro mare longonteña, tsy misy olo hafa*); inevitably, one has to marry a *longo* (as she did Lefo).[4] The loss of genealogical knowledge makes it easier to avoid having to do so.

Although she often fights with him over the money he spends on rum, Sary seems very fond of Lefo; but she also acknowledges that her marriage is not good (*fanambalia ty raty, tsy soa*) because she has no in-laws: 'I don't have a father-in-law, because my father-in-law is already my father, my sister-in-law is already my sister' (*tsy mana rafoza zaho, ka rafozako mbo babako, velahiko mbo rahavaviko*). Yet when I told Sary's father that his daughter had no in-laws through her marriage with Lefo, he replied that this was mistaken (*diso io*), because Lefo's father *is* now Sary's father-in-law and Lefo's sister *is* now her sister-in-law. Thanks to the marriage, Lefo's father, who was previously Sary's father, is transformed into her father-in-law (*babany manjary rafozany*). It is thus the act of marrying that makes Sary and Lefo and their respective kin – *who are related* – *unrelated*, 'different' from each other.

On one occasion *dadilahy* expressed the same idea in broader terms. During a lecture on the vast numbers of kin that the Vezo have, he paused briefly to tell me: 'people are really just one people, but it is marriage that separates them' (*olo raiky avao, fa fanambalia ro mampisaraky*). Although *dadilahy* felt he could not explain this statement any further,[5] I am inclined to interpret it in the sense that the old man's view of *filongoa* is so broad that he can see (or is able to imagine by extension) that everyone is in fact related to everyone else: that people are just one vast related family. It is marriage, then, which separates people, because it *creates* the 'difference' that is necessary for marriage to occur. Like Sary's father who *became* her father-in-law in consequence of her marriage with Lefo, so all related people *become* 'different' through the act of marriage.[6] And yet, this difference is established only to be retransformed into *filongoa* at the next generation.

The Vezo emphasize that marriage does not erase the 'difference' between oneself, one's partner and the partner's kin. Hence, in-laws do not become kin. On the other hand, if 'different people' generate children they establish new *filongoa*. Since both parents are kin of their offspring, all those who are 'different people' in respect of the parents become kin with respect of the children: parents-in-law become grandparents, sisters- and brothers-in-law become mothers and fathers (*laha latsaky anaky teña, rafozanteña manjary longon' anakinteña*, 'if one has children, one's parents-in-law become one's children's kin').[7] This transformation of 'difference' into *filongoa* explains why 'people's kin increase all the time' (*longon'olom-belo mihamaro isanandro isanandro*).

Vezo marriage can thus be said to oscillate between the creation of 'difference' and the creation of kinship. In the first instance, marriage is the artifice whereby 'difference' is created within the universe of kinship; in the second instance, marriage transforms the 'difference' created at one point in time into new kinship for the generation at the next remove. This recursive feedback allows one to emphasize one of the two elements while ignoring the other, for each of the two poles (kinship and 'difference') logically includes the other. It is for this reason that *dadilahy* can place so much emphasis on the *creative* aspect of marriage, for it is this that provides the Vezo with their very many *longo*.

When *dadilahy* looks at *filongoa* he tends to disregard the 'difference' that exists between the people who have generated his descendants through marriage; he disregards the fact that his children's, grandchildren's, great-grandchildren's spouses are *not* his descendants, and includes them in his sight as if they were his own people. Thus, when he talks to them and about them, he insists that they are *not* his children-in-law, but rather his children (*tsy vinantoko ty, fa anako, zafiko*). He emphasizes that marriage is an exchange of a woman for a man (*ampela takalo johary*), in which the two sides say to each other: 'here is my child, it is not mine but it is yours' (*anako ty tsy anako, fa anakinao*) (see above, pp. 67–8). Hence, a son-in-law becomes like a son, a daughter-in-law becomes like a daughter.

For *dadilahy*, therefore, marriage is a way of acquiring other people's children. He is far less anxious to surrender his own; despite the alleged equality of the exchange, he takes without ever giving any away. *Dadilahy*, of course, is not alone in carrying out this act of plunder. Those from whom he takes are simultaneously taking his children from him: they insist, just like him, that marriage has transformed their children-in-law into their children.

Such multiple claims of kinship over the same people are a characteristic feature of *filongoa*. Let us return to the crowd that gathers in the evening around *dadilahy*, and to the many grandchildren that bring him scraps of iron for his knives. I remarked above that in order to recognize *dadilahy* as one of the sources from which they have been generated, his descendants look upwards along the same paths that *dadilahy* follows to recognize them as grandchildren. By contrast with *dadilahy*, however, the path that leads them to and past *dadilahy* is only *one* of the many that they could draw up to their ascendants.[8] Their view branches out and expands in all directions: it moves upwards on both their father's and their mother's side, and moves back through their four grandparents, their eight great-grandparents, and so on. For them, *dadilahy* is only *one* of the many grandparents who helped generate the grandchildren who gather around him at night and bring him scraps of iron. Although it pleases *dadilahy* to look down at his grandchildren as if they all 'belonged' to him – 'look, these are all *my* children (*anako*), grandchildren (*zafiko*), great-grandchildren' (*kitroko*) – his grandchildren do not in fact 'belong' to him any more than they 'belong' to any other of their grandparents.

When grandchildren look upwards (and sideways) at *filongoa*, they do not choose or privilege *one* path of ascendancy over the many that are available. Each person in *dadilahy*'s audience – including those who are actually his children-in-law – embodies a plurality of relations that can be enacted in different contexts and at different times. As the Vezo like to state, these relations are innumerable because people like *dadilahy* and his grandchildren keep all of them open, at all times, and draw no distinctions of gender. No choice is made to channel and order them: they all come together in the same, 'plurally' constituted person, a person who can thus be imagined as expanding and branching out in all directions.

Kinship of a different kind

A seemingly less laborious way of describing *dadilahy*'s and his grandchildren's ungendered vision of *filongoa* would have been to define Vezo kinship as cognatic. I chose not to do so because I wished to avoid the questions associated with the concept of cognatic kinship. How do the Vezo *limit* the tracing of their kinship relations (Radcliffe-Brown 1950: 13)? What are the non-kinship institutions used to generate the structural *boundaries* that kinship itself is unable to provide (Fortes 1969: 122)? Or, with direct reference to the literature on the west coast of Madagascar to which I shall return shortly, through what principle are the multiple 'clan memberships' of a person *reduced* to one (Lavondès 1967: 41)?

To ask these questions would be misleading. The Vezo are not preoccupied with limiting *filongoa* (although they may happily forget some of it), with creating boundaries that define the person as part of a group (Strathern 1992: 78ff.), or with reducing their paths of ascendancy from many to one. To be more precise, the Vezo *are* preoccupied with these issues, but only as matters pertaining to a domain of experience of a very different kind from the one explored with the aid of *dadilahy* and his grandchildren. In approaching this other domain, I shall first of all introduce a new term – *raza* – and explain its different meanings. These depend on whether *raza* is employed in the plural (*valo raza*, eight *raza*) or in the singular sense (*raza raiky*, one *raza*).

The Vezo, like other people in Madagascar, say that 'living human beings have eight *raza*' (*olom-belo valo raza*). When I asked what the word '*raza*' meant I was given a superficially simple definition: 'people of the past who are dead' (*olo taloha fa nimaty*). To state therefore that living people have eight *raza* means that they have eight (dead) great-grandparents, four on their mother's and four on their father's side; *olom-belo valo raza* is thus a statement about *filongoa*, and about people's multiple and ungendered sources of generation.

In another context, however, the term *raza* is used to define a *single* entity. This occurs when the Vezo refer to dead people who are buried in the same tomb; in this instance, a plurality of individuals ('people of the past who are dead') who in life possessed *many raza* come together as '*one raza*', as '*one* kind of people' (*raza raiky*). Membership by the dead of this *raza* is exclusive: one can only belong to *one raza* at a time, for one's corpse can only be buried inside one tomb. Hence, as my Vezo friends often remarked, 'corpses are what make people fight' (*faty ro mampialy olo*); as someone once pointed out, corpses cannot be cut up into pieces, one party taking the head and the other the feet (*tapa roe, raiky mahazo lohany, raiky mahazo tombokiny*). In sum, whereas 'living human beings have *eight raza*', the dead can only be part of *one*.

In the past, the existence of a plurality of *raza* and the need to choose one among the many has been read in terms of an interplay between cognatic and patrilineal kinship (cf. Southall 1971).[9] The clearest example of this interpretation is Lavondès' study of Masikoro kinship, which aims to prove the existence of 'an Indonesian [i.e. cognatic] base with strong

African [i.e. unilineal] tints' (1967: 167). Lavondès took the statement that people have eight *raza* to mean that they have eight (if not innumerable) clanic affiliations ('appartenances claniques') (pp. 40–1); he therefore attempted to show how the interplay between unilineal and cognatic descent leads people to choose affiliation of *one* descent group among the theoretically infinite number which can be claimed. It is worth quoting this passage in full:

> There must surely exist a principle by which the seven great-grandparents' clan memberships which are in surplus are eliminated. At least in theory, the patrilineal principle solves the difficulty, because among the eight clan memberships of a man, there is only *one* which is more important than the others, and this is the one which comes to him from his father, and it is only this *one*, always in theory, which will be transmitted from the great-grandparents to their great-grandchildren.
>
> (1967: 41, my emphasis)

Even so, the preference for patrilineality is only 'theoretical', because people can choose to affiliate themselves to their maternal *raza* if this happens to be more prestigious.[10] Nonetheless, despite the flexibility of the system in allowing a choice of *raza* membership, Lavondès' assumption that one cannot belong to more than one descent group at a time, that therefore one can only be a member of *one raza*, led him to postulate the need to make the choice itself.

Like Lavondès, I also began by assuming that people belonged to one *raza*, and I would therefore ask (as Lavondès had asked his Masikoro informants), 'what is your *raza*?' (*ino razanao?*). And every time I would detect unease and slight embarrassment, and I would elicit always the same answer: 'living human beings have *eight raza*' (*olom-belo valo raza*). I found this puzzling and incongruous: to a request to identify a single *raza* of their choice, people responded by invoking the plurality of their *raza*; their answer reflected a *refusal* to make the choice which Lavondès and I were postulating as the basis of our analysis. Eventually, I understood that it was my question rather than the answer that was out of place.

We saw above that the Vezo refer to the 'single' *raza* (*raza raiky*) as the 'one kind of people' buried inside the same tomb, and that dead people cannot belong to more than *one raza* because they cannot be buried in more than one tomb. As long as they live, however, people do not need to make a choice of *one raza* among the many they are related to; as *living people* (*olom-belo*) they do not yet belong to any *one raza*. The experience of the living is confined to the domain of *filongoa*; in this domain, their *raza* – the great-grandparents from which they were generated – are multiple. Only in the future, when people are dead, will they belong to *one raza*, for their bodies will be buried inside *one* tomb.

'Plural' *raza* (*valo raza*) become 'single' (*raza raiky*) as people move out of *filongoa* and enter a different kind of kinship order: unilineal descent. This order is only experienced by the dead. In this domain, in the domain of the dead, *filongoa* must be 'limited', it must be 'bounded', it must be 'reduced'; for whereas a *living* human being can be related to many different *raza* on both the mother's and the father's side, the dead cannot belong to eight 'single' *raza* at once. The Vezo would thus agree with Lavondès' statement that 'there must surely exist a principle by which the seven great-grandparents' clan memberships which are in surplus are eliminated'; but they would agree only if by 'clan membership' was meant membership of the *one raza* (*raza raiky*) that exists in death, inside a tomb.[11]

Death imposes the choice of one among the many *raza* of the living. This explains why to ask 'what is your *raza*?' was out of place and why it caused such discomfort: to ask a person to discuss the choice of her 'single' *raza* is akin to asking her about the prospect of her own death.[12] My friends' assertion that they had eight *raza*, not one, was thus an assertion of life over death; they were telling me that *as living beings* the *choice* of one *raza* was not yet of their concern. They were telling me, at the same time, that the only people who could answer my importunate question were the dead, those fenced inside one tomb who constitute one *raza*.

Descent created by death

In analysing Merina kinship, Bloch (1971) has used the notion of *regrouping* to illustrate how the Merina accommodate their image of the past with the reality of the present. While people, land and ancestors in the past are imagined to have been one and the same thing, in the present people live, work and die away from the 'land of the ancestors' (*tanin-drazana*). The living, however, have a way of regrouping those whom history, life and work has dispersed by reuniting them in the same tomb. A 'group' that did not exist in life is thus 'regrouped' in the tomb. Through the tomb, a physically massive object, the Merina create what otherwise would not exist: 'there are no descent groups of the living, but there is a notion of descent groups in relation to the dead in the tomb' (Bloch 1971: 165).

Vezo tombs are not massive constructions like Merina tombs (see below, pp. 125–7); but like Merina tombs, they also create groups – the 'single' *raza* – that otherwise, elsewhere and at a different time would not exist. There is, however, an important difference. Whereas Merina tombs *regroup* people who were divided in life, Vezo tombs *divide* people who were together in *filongoa*. The origin of this difference (which translates, as we shall see in chapter 8 below, in the way the living Vezo imagine the experience of the dead inside their tombs) lies in the endogamic preference of the Merina as opposed to the prescribed exogamy of the Vezo. The difference is expressed in the different 'ideals' held by the Merina and the Vezo respectively. The Merina ideal (the ideal past before dispersal, and the ideal made present inside the tomb) can be described as follows: *to be one and the same* with one land, one tomb, and the same people you marry; namely, to direct oneself and one's relations *inwards*. The Vezo ideal is the opposite: *to become many by transforming difference*, or else to project oneself and one's relations *outwards*. The Merina's ideal is compromised by the necessities and disturbances of *life*: as people move and look for work or new land to cultivate, they find themselves dislocated, outside 'the land of the ancestors' and involved with kin who should be, but are not, 'one and the same'. The Vezo's ideal, on the contrary, is compromised by the inevitability of *death*: death interrupts the growth of *filongoa* and imposes a constraining choice of the '*one* kind of people' with whom a person must be buried. Whereas the ideal of the Merina can only exist in death, that of the Vezo can only exist in life.

Let me return briefly to *dadilahy* to illustrate this point. *Dadilahy* is an old man who is reaching the end of his life; he has come to acquire during his lifetime an ever increasing number of descendants, gathered indistinctly from all sides including his descendants' spouses. When he looks down at them, *dadilahy* imagines that they are all 'his' grandchildren; he imagines himself at the head of a sort of bilateral, all-inclusive descent group. He does so by ignoring that other old men and women like himself are also looking down at their descendants and are enjoying the same vision of growth and expansion that occurred in the generations that followed them; he ignores the fact also that many of these men and women embrace within their own bilateral, all-inclusive descent group the *same* grandchildren that *dadilahy* includes in his. This overlapping is, of course, inevitable, because in the realm of *filongoa* people are not divided into discrete groups, but are plurally related on all sides. This overlap is not only inevitable, it is also unproblematic: because as long as people are alive (as *dadilahy* and his grandchildren are), they can 'belong' simultaneously to many bilateral, all-inclusive descent groups. They 'belong' to all of them because they are related to all of them; in *filongoa*, relatedness is not and need not be exclusive.

Death (*dadilahy*'s death and the death of his grandchildren) engenders a radical transformation. As he is lowered in his tomb, *dadilahy*'s vision is suddenly curtailed. He now enters an exclusive group, a group made up of only '*one* kind of people' (*raza raiky*). As he enters the 'single' *raza*, *dadilahy* loses sight of the many descendants who will *not* be buried with him. Thus, whereas in life he could pretend that all the grandchildren he included in his vision were 'his', in death he has to surrender many of them to other tombs and to other 'kinds of people'. Death, in other words, brings to an end the Vezo's ideal of *filongoa* – a kinship domain in which the person is multiply related and undivided.

Death among the Vezo divides what was undivided. Burial engenders the separation of *one raza* out of the many that the living person used to be related to. This process of division and separation *creates* discrete descent groups that did not exist in the present, a creation in some respects analogous to that of matrilineages in the Massim region (cf., for example, Macintyre 1989, Thune 1989 and Fortune 1963). The creation of 'pure descent' in the Massim is construed as a liberating and triumphalistic process of disengagement of the deceased person from the necessary but alienating involvement of oneself with other matrilineages (most especially through affinal relations, and through all other ties of friendship, *kula* partnership and so on). Death, in other words, engenders a positive process of 'distillation', at the end of which the person is at last constituted only by pure matrilineal substance. Death, in this context, is the realization of the 'phantasy of a world without exchange' (Bloch and Parry 1982: 31), a world in which the integrity of the matrilineage is ritually reconstructed through acts of closures and exclusions aimed at disposing of a person's intrusive affinal ties (Macintyre 1989: 135ff.)

For the Vezo, the creation of the 'single *raza*' does not realize an ideal phantasy, a utopian condition in which the person can finally achieve its integrity. On the contrary, as we have seen above with the aid of *dadilahy*, and as the following chapters will show through the analysis of mortuary rituals, the Vezo construe the realization of descent as a *loss*, the loss of *all but one* kind of relations that constituted the living person. If death and burial could thus be said to engender a process of 'distillation' as they do in the Massim, the phantasy of the Vezo does not consist in what remains after death (pure descent), but in all that which is thrown away (the plurality of non-exclusive relations experienced in *filongoa*).

Behind the Massim ideal of pure descent and the Vezo ideal of *filongoa* lie two different notions of how the person is constituted in life, hence of what is engendered by death. In the Massim, the living person is made up of two elements: an enduring matrilineal substance and an ephemeral patrilineal substance (see, for example, Thune 1989 and Macintyre 1989). Although the two elements have to be brought together in life for reproduction to occur, the emphasis remains on difference, on the distinction between the two separate sources of one's blood and of one's intelligence (Thune 1989: 155), of one's bones and of one's flesh (Macintyre 1989: 138). Among the Vezo, instead, the emphasis is on the sameness of the many sources of generation that constitute the living person; although women and men differ in procreation, 'mother's side' and 'father's side' are the same in *filongoa* (see above and Astuti 1993). As a result, the makeup of the person is not gendered and divided into matrilineal *versus* patrilineal substance; although the person is plurally constituted (through its many sources of generation and its many relations enacted in the present), it remains whole and undivided: a plurality of sames that produces wholeness, rather than a combination of differences that produces partibility (M. Strathern 1988).

The contrast I have drawn here is intended to emphasize how among the Vezo the realization of descent is *not* inscribed in the living person, in the sense that what is 'distilled' and created at death (the 'single' *raza*) is not singled out during life as *one distinct* component of the person; on the contrary, the 'single' *raza* (*raza raiky*) remains merged within the *eight raza* (*valo raza*) of living human beings. Descent, in this respect, not only is not yet realized or realizable in the present, but is not even immanent in the Vezo person (as blood or bones are in the Massim examples quoted above).

And yet, the realization of descent in death is anticipated and prepared during a person's lifetime; what needs to be prepared and anticipated is the *choice* of the 'single' *raza*, a choice that the living as such do not yet make. This is accomplished through a ritual – the ritual of *soro* – which establishes where people will be buried, hence which *raza* they will belong to. When the ritual is performed, it is as if the 'single' *raza* momentarily cast a shadow over the living person, transforming it into a lifeless body which can enter only one tomb and can belong to only one *raza*. This same shadow is cast more permanently over the *hazomanga*, the person who mediates between the 'single' *raza* and the living. It is to this shadow that I now turn.

Soron'anake
Soro is a ritual offering to the dead. *Soron'anake* (the *soro* of the child) is the offering of a head of cattle or of rice by a father to the *raza* of his children's mother[13] (*soro* is performed only for the first-born child, but it affects all the subsequent children borne by the couple). I have never seen this ritual performed, and I shall therefore not attempt to describe it. I shall analyse instead what the ritual (or the lack of a ritual) accomplishes. In fact, I heard people discuss this issue so often that I found myself asking whether *soro*[14] had been performed for such and such a person before I even realized what the question meant.

People ask whether *soro* has been performed by Iano's father when Iano[15] dies. The answer tells people where Iano's body will be kept before burial, who will be the 'master of the corpse' (*tompom-paty*; see below, pp. 99, 110), and above all where Iano will be buried. If Iano's father has performed *soro* (*laha vita soro*), Iano is buried in the father's tomb,[16] the father's elders[17] are the 'masters of the corpse', and the body is kept at Iano's father's home before being taken to the tomb, where the *raza* is informed about the newcomer. By contrast, if Iano's father has *not* performed *soro* (*laha tsy vita soro*) he has no rights over the corpse; the mother's elders are the 'masters of the corpse', Iano is buried in the mother's tomb,[18] and he therefore joins the *raza* contained in it.

If *soro* is delayed, but is expected to be performed some time in the future, people say that '*soro* has not been done *yet*' (*mbo tsy vita soro*).[19] In this situation, if Iano dies without *soro* his father can nonetheless 'beg for the corpse' (*mangataky faty*) from his in-laws. If they give it to him (*laha manome faty*), it is *as if* Iano's father had performed *soro*, and the father becomes Iano's new 'master' (*tompo*). At the same time, however, by begging for, and receiving, the body Iano's father recognizes that his in-laws are the true 'masters of the corpse' (*rafozany ro tena tompom-paty*).

What Iano's father begs from his in-laws when Iano is dead is identical to what he would have asked had he performed *soro* when Iano was still alive. In both instances, Iano's father asks to 'buy the *raza*' (*mivily raza*). When Iano is dead, the request means, literally, to buy Iano as a corpse (dead bodies, especially of older people, are often referred to as *raza*). But what does the father acquire when the children are still alive? One person put it this way:

From this moment [the moment when *soro* is performed], the man *has* the children. If he hasn't performed *soro*, the man doesn't have them; it is the woman, the mother who gave birth to them, who is the children's 'mistress'. But if the man has performed *soro*, it is he who is the children's 'master'. [pause] For example: one of the children dies; if the father has not performed *soro* yet, the child is buried in the mother's tomb. But if the child dies and *soro* has been performed, the child is buried in the father's tomb.[20]

The most notable aspect of this passage is that the example that follows the pause recurred in every conversation I had or heard on the topic of *soro*.

What a father 'buys' by doing *soro* can be stated even more clearly. I once overheard a discussion about whether some people might think that it makes no difference if they perform *soro* or not, because a father is not barred from having his children live with him even if *soro* has not been done. But this, a man explained very firmly, is a wrong way of looking at things, because through *soro* 'one doesn't buy the child's mouth or the child's flesh; what one buys is the child's bones' (*tsy mivily vavany, tsy mivily nofotsiny, fa taola iny ro nivilin'olo*).[21] This argument put paid to the discussion, as everyone agreed.

If *soro* 'buys' the child's dead body, the ritual could be imagined as anticipating the child's funeral. It would be interesting to analyse the performance of the ritual from this perspective to see whether the close association between *soro* and death is expressed; but I lack the data to address this point. There are nonetheless two aspects of the ritual's broader organization which support the view that *soro* concerns people's allocation to tombs and *raza* which occurs only after death.

In the first place, the Vezo perform *soro* at the elders' of the child's mother. The maternal *raza* is informed that the child is being 'given' (*manome*) to the father, who from now on will be the child's 'master' (*tompon'ajà*). Lavondès reports that among the Masikoro a second *soro* is performed at the father's elders': 'the purpose of the sacrifice is to inform the ancestors of *the entry into the lineage of a new member*' (1967: 65; my emphasis). In both instances, the offering is provided by the child's father.

Most of my informants claimed that among the Vezo the second *soro* is never enacted.[22] Some of them suggested that this was because the Vezo are too poor to afford the two cattle necessary for the two rituals; the Masikoro, by contrast, raise cattle and therefore can afford to do so. Others argued instead that the second *soro* is a specific Masikoro custom (*fomban'i Masikoro avao, tsy fombam-Bezo*), whose significance they found hard to understand (*ino dikany?*, 'what's the point?', 'what does it mean?').

One man even asserted that there could not possibly be two *soro* (*soro tsy roe*, lit. 'the *soro* aren't two'): if a second *soro* were performed, who would be the 'master' of the child? (*ia ro tompon'anaky ty?*). My friend could only imagine that the second *soro* repeated the first one, and thereby inverted it: with the first *soro*, the mother's group surrenders the child and the father 'buys' it; with the second one, it is the father's group that surrenders the child and the mother who buys it. The outcome would be that no-one would know whom the child belonged to. Although this man misunderstood the meaning of the two Masikoro *soro*, since the second ritual is meant to restate (rather than reverse) the child's acquisition by the father, his mistake provides an interesting clue to why the Vezo perform only the first *soro* and do without the second.

Lavondès suggests that the second *soro* among the Masikoro is an acquisitive ritual, in which the paternal ancestors are informed that the child is being 'bought'. The first *soro* is instead a ritual of surrender, in which the maternal ancestors are informed that the child has been 'sold'. The fact that my Vezo informants consider it necessary to perform the first *soro*, whereas they are unsure about the need for a second one, suggests that they consider *soro* primarily as a means of surrendering rights over children, rather than of acquiring them. This belief can be attributed to the fact that the ritual actually concerns the allocation of corpses to tombs, rather than the allocation of living persons to groups. The first *soro* is indispensable to mark the maternal *raza*'s surrender of its rights over children's future dead bodies. By contrast, there is no need for a second *soro* marking 'the entry into the lineage of a new member' to take place because acquisition occurs only when the children die, at which moment they join the paternal *raza*. For the Vezo, therefore, a second *soro* is redundant, because the paternal *raza* will be informed anyhow that it is acquiring a new member when the person is buried in the *raza*'s tomb (see below, pp. 116–17).

The second aspect of the ritual to be discussed is the existence of two types of *soro*. These are distinguished by the kind of offering that is presented to the *raza* of the child's mother. On the one hand, if the woman is still pregnant with the first child of the man who wants to perform *soro*, the father-to-be can perform *soron-tsoky* (lit. 'the *soro* of the belly'). In this case, he must provide twenty or thirty *kapoaky* (a tin of Nestlé condensed milk) of rice.[23] On the other hand, if the child is already born, the father must perform *soron'aomby* (lit. 'the *soro* of cattle'), in which case he must present his in-laws with a head of cattle.

Popular recognition that *soron-tsoky* is far cheaper than *soron'aomby* is reflected in the fact that an increasing number of people try to perform *soro* when the woman is still pregnant in order to avoid having to buy an *aomby* later on. This implies that my informants considered *soron-tsoky* to be a valid substitute of *soron'aomby*. When I suggested that the Masikoro seem to believe differently,[24] my interlocutors initially justified this once again with the fact that the Vezo are too poor to buy cattle. They also offered a more interesting explanation, however, which is that if the mother is still pregnant one can get by with something cheaper than cattle because the unborn child 'is not a human being yet, it's an "animal"' (*mbo tsy olo, fa biby*).[25] The fact that a live child is worth more than an unborn *biby* was considered self-evident, and the matter was not discussed any further. It seems reasonable to suppose, however, that the cheaper rate is a way of compensating the father for the risk that the *biby* he acquires with *soron-tsoky* may not become a real person.

The recognition of the difference between acquiring a *biby* and acquiring a person does not contrast, as might at first appear, with the argument that *soro* entails acquiring the child as a corpse-to-be rather than as a living person. The phrase 'it's not yet a human being, it's a *biby*' is used to explain why babies of less than a year are given an unmarked burial,[26] typically under a large tree in the forest, rather than being buried in tombs (*tsy milevy an-dolo*). Little babies are 'water children' (*zazarano*), they are 'soft' (*malemy*) and are therefore unable to stay upright. Only when they start sitting up (*fa mahay mipetsaky*) do they become 'people' (*fa olo*). 'Water children' are not buried in tombs, I was once told, because they lack bones (*taola tsy misy*):[27] for burial is 'the gathering and the preservation of bones' (*fanajaria taola*). This explains the risk a man incurs when he performs *soron-tsoky*. The risk is not, in fact, that he acquires a *biby* instead of a baby, but that he acquires a corpse that will be too soft to be buried with the other bones in his tomb. I mentioned above the frequently made remark that 'corpses are what make people fight' (*faty ro mampialy olo*); that is, that people fight over where a dead person will be buried.[28] The fact that this decision should be contested at all seems strange, given that the performance of *soro* (or lack thereof) is supposed to establish the choice of tomb and *raza* before a person's death. All that people should need to know after someone's death (and indeed this is what is always asked) is whether *soro* was performed or not. If the answer is yes, the person will be buried in their father's tomb; if the answer is no, burial will take place in the mother's tomb.

In fact, the indication of a person's place of burial provided by *soro* remains open to negotiation. In the first place, as we already saw, a father who has not *yet* performed *soro* can 'beg the corpse' (*mangataky faty*) of his child from his in-laws, and he 'may or may not obtain it' (*misy mahazo, misy tsy mahazo*). Similarly, a husband who has performed *soro* for his children can 'beg the corpse' of his wife from his father-in-law; in this instance, the father-in-law 'may or may not give it' (*misy manome, misy tsy manome*). On the principle that 'women follow their husbands if they're alive; if they're dead they are buried with the father who has done *soro* for them' (*ampela manaraky valy laha velo; laha maty milevy am-babany nisoro azy*), the father-in-law will probably refuse his daughter's corpse for burial in her husband's tomb. If this occurs, however, the husband-father may send the dead woman's children to beg that their *mother* be buried where *they* would be buried also, namely in their father's tomb. If this occurs, the grandfather (the mother's father) will most probably agree, thereby granting not the body of a wife to her husband but that of a mother to her children.[29] In both cases, the possibility of begging, giving, refusing and receiving the corpse can give rise to conflict, dissent and resentment.

A further potential source of conflict is the fact that the right, conferred by *soro* to the father over his children's bones, can be contested on grounds of his lack of commitment towards the children's 'mouth and flesh' during their lifetime. Let us take the case of a man whose father had performed *soro* for him many years before, and who, when his parents divorced, had followed his mother and had lived with her and her kin ever since. When the man fell sick and the severity of his illness became clear, the elders on his father's side were informed. However, contrary to custom, they did not visit the dying man. This was later recalled by the dead man's mother in support of her refusal to relinquish the body to her son's paternal *raza*. Only after lengthy negotiations was it agreed that the mother could keep the body during the funeral, but that it would then be buried in the paternal tomb 'with the father who did *soro* for him' (*amin'ny baba nisoro azy*).

These examples suggest that *soro* leaves the actual decision as to the place of burial relatively open and ill defined. One thing it does establish very clearly, and that is that dead people's bones can only enter *one* tomb and *one raza*. If nothing else, *soro* establishes that a choice must be made, a choice that has to be exclusive and hence divisive. In death, people are either here or there. The 'here' or 'there' between which people must choose in the context of *soro* are defined along lines of gender, by distinguishing between the mother's and the father's tomb.[30] The impossibility of burial in both tombs calls for a clear and absolute distinction between mothers and fathers; it calls, in other words, for an absolute definition of gender difference. The ritual of *soro* is instrumental in creating and defining such difference.

I mentioned previously, that women are regarded as 'the real source – origin – hence the owners of the children' (*ampela ro tena tompony*) because of their role in procreation (cf. Astuti 1993). This is the reason adduced to explain why mothers do not need to perform *soro* for their children: in recognition of women's hard labour as mothers, children whose father has failed to perform *soro* are buried in their mother's tomb and enter their mother's *raza*. By contrast, in order to become 'masters of the children' (*tompon'ajà*) and to bury them in their tomb, fathers have to perform *soro*. Thus, while being a father is insufficient to win the children into membership of the 'single' *raza*, being a mother is sufficient by default. Gender difference, in this context, is defined as the difference between those who acquire their children's bones by performing *soro*, and those who acquire them simply through generation.

This difference is clearly illustrated by the way relations between children

and their parents are described. Because of the extensive use of classificatory terms, an individual addresses many people as 'mother' and 'father'; if
one wishes to specify that the 'mother' or 'father' concerned is actually the
person's parent, the relationship is described as 'the mother/father who
generated it' (*neny/baba niteraky azy*).[31] A man, however, can also be
described as 'the father who did *soro* for him/her' (*baba nisoro azy*), and this
is the formula customarily used during funerals, when the *raza* is told in
front of its tomb that someone is going to be buried 'with the father who did
soro for him/her' (*am-babany nisoro azy*).[32] By contrast, when someone
whose father did not perform *soro* is buried in her mother's tomb, the link
with her tomb and her *raza* is never described in terms of *soro*. The elder
who informs the *raza* about the newcomer cannot say that the person is
buried 'with the *mother* who did *soro* for him/her, because mothers do not
perform *soro* for their children – they only generate them.[33]

The ritual of *soro* thus establishes an absolute difference between men
and women as fathers and mothers, as well as a difference between the
relation engendered by *soro* between a child and its father, and that
engendered by procreation between a child and its mother. This difference
is and must be absolute because it determines a choice that is and must be
absolute – the choice of *one* tomb and *one raza*. But the difference so
established is significant only in the context of this choice, which involves
people's bones rather than their 'mouth and flesh'. Their 'mouth and flesh'
remain within the scope of *filongoa*, a domain in which gender difference
makes no difference. Thus, while children's bones can only be buried either
in mother's or in father's tomb, their 'mouth and flesh' are equally related
to both mother's and father's side.

The ritual of *soro* and the gender difference it establishes has no effect on
people's *filongoa*, in that it does not discriminate between their mother's
and father's side and does not choose one of the eight *raza* they are related
to as living people. Despite the performance of *soro*, *dadilahy's* vision of
filongoa remains blind to gender difference as he sits admiring the multitude
of grandchildren who come to him from all sides. During the ritual,
however, people are treated as if they were already bones. At this moment,
it is as if a shadow – the shadow of the 'single' *raza* – is laid upon them, like
an imprint marking their final destination to *one* tomb and *one raza*. At this
moment, when the shadow of the single *raza* is cast, *dadilahy* is cured of his
blindness. Through the shadow, he sees gender difference, and in so doing,
he loses sight of all but *one* 'kind' of grandchildren who will follow him into
his tomb and *raza*.

The *hazomanga*

There is one person among those living who become members of the same *raza* for whom its shadow is rather more invasive. This person is the *hazomanga*.[34] The *hazomanga* is usually defined by the literature as the 'clan chief' or 'lineage chief' (see for example Lavondès 1967 and Schlemmer 1983), or as 'the eldest of the senior generation' (Ottino 1963: 43). The *hazomanga*, in other words, is defined as the eldest living member of a descent group. However, since the group of which the *hazomanga* is allegedly the 'chief' (what I have called the 'single' *raza*) only exists after death, the *hazomanga* is more correctly viewed as someone who, though still among the living, is the most likely (because of his age) to be the first to join a tomb, hence also one *raza*.[35] From this perspective, the *hazomanga* is both the eldest of the living members-to-be of a *raza* and the youngest of the ancestors because he has not yet joined them.[36]

By being both a senior among the living and a junior among the dead, the *hazomanga* is in a position to mediate between the 'single' *raza* and the living. He talks to the *raza* (*mañambara an-draza*), offers food to the dead when they are hungry (*misoron-dolo*), and presides over the ritual of *soro* (*misoro an-kazomanga*). Last but not least, the *hazomanga* is the 'master of the tomb' (*tompom-dolo*) that contains the *raza*, and the 'master of the corpses' (*tompom-paty*) that are to be buried in his tomb. He is responsible for informing the *raza* that a newcomer is entering the tomb (see below, p. 116), and that the living are planning to build a new tomb (see below, p. 130).

As a mediator between the living and the 'single' *raza*, the *hazomanga* is in a very dangerous and difficult position (*sarotsy mare*); as is frequently noted, he is in constant danger of death (*homaty*). If the ancestors are unhappy or upset by the wrongdoings (*hadisoa*) of the living, their response will most probably fall on the *hazomanga*; the consequence of the ancestors' anger is graphically described as *maty 'sur place'*, 'dead on the spot'. The *hazomanga* is also in an intrinsically dangerous position because he is the closest living person to the 'single' *raza*, and therefore also the closest to the tomb and to death. In the latter, of course, lies also the most paradoxical aspect of the *hazomanga*'s condition, for the fact that the *hazomanga* is chosen for being closest to death is defied each time he presides over a burial, for that person must be younger than himself. As 'master of the corpse', the *hazomanga* leads into the tomb and the *raza* people who should have died after him. When the *hazomanga* buries a young child, he states that it is 'not right' (*tsy mety*) for him to bury a grandchild (*zafy*). Although this statement expresses the grief of an old man who has seen too many people die too young, it also demonstrates that the *hazomanga* recognizes his paradoxical position with respect to the living on the one hand and to the *raza* on the other: if things were 'right', he would be the first to join the *raza* and he could only preside over his own funeral.[37]

The living need the *hazomanga* to communicate with the dead of a particular 'single' *raza*. In this respect, it is useful to draw a distinction between the *hazomanga* that a person uses, and the *hazomanga* that the same person has, namely the *hazomanga* that is named if asked 'who is your *hazomanga*?' (*iha hazomanganao?*).

People use as many *hazomanga* as they need to communicate with all their ancestors, who are divided into separate tombs, belong to different *raza* and need to be approached by different 'masters of the tomb'. Thus, if an offer of food has to be made to a maternal grandmother who is troubling her granddaughter's dreams, the *hazomanga* who is master of the tomb where the grandmother is buried will be approached; but if the offer is due to a paternal great-grandfather, the same granddaughter will approach a different *hazomanga*. In principle, since living people have eight *raza* (eight great-grandparents), they use eight *hazomanga* to communicate with them; in practice, some of the eight ancestors may be buried in the same tomb as spouses, and others may no longer have any direct contact with their descendants. Both in principle and in practice one makes use of at least two *hazomanga*, one's mother's and one's father's. By contrast, if one is asked 'who is your *hazomanga*' one will refer to one *hazomanga* alone, to the man who communicates with the 'single' *raza* one will join at death, who will be the 'master' of one's corpse and will preside over one's funeral. Thus, whereas living people *use* several *hazomanga* to communicate with their ancestors, they only *have* one *hazomanga* because in death they join only one tomb and one *raza*.

So far I have referred to the *hazomanga* as a person. More accurately, however, the *hazomanga* is a sharpened wooden pole sticking upright in the sand; the person is known as the 'holder of the *hazomanga*' (*mpitan-kazomanga*). The distinction between the *hazomanga* (pole) and the *mpitan-kazomanga* (person) is recorded throughout the literature: the wooden poles are raised to commemorate an offering to the ancestors, whereas the person who holds the *hazomanga* is the head of the descent group.[38]

After I arrived in Betania (but the same applies to Belo), I wandered around the village searching for the sharp wooden poles. I found none. At first I assumed that there were no *hazomanga* in this village, and I took this to be a sign of the Vezo's peripheral position in the Sakalava kingdoms.[39] But as soon as I began to master the language I noticed the word *hazomanga* cropping up frequently in conversations: so and so had approached the *hazomanga* (*namonjy ny hazomanga zahay*); meetings were held at the *hazomanga*'s place (*mivory an-kazomanga*); messages were sent to it (*mañambara any hazomanga tse zahay*). It dawned on me that people made no distinction between *hazomanga* and *mpitan-kazomanga*, between the object and the person, and that when my friends in Betania mentioned the *hazomanga* they referred to a person rather than to an object. The first time I asked an *hazomanga* where the wooden poles were, he paused, straightened up, and with a dramatic flourish pointed to his chest: his *body* was the *hazomanga* (*vatako ro hazomanga*).

The fact that there was no *hazomanga*-object in Betania was seen as the result of intense migration:

among the Vezo there exist only a few of these sharpened *hazomanga*; what makes them a difficult and dangerous thing is that people here are not really their 'master', but are substituting someone who is far away [in the immigrants' place of origin]. This is why people don't have the standing *hazomanga*. If one were the 'master' like those Masikoro over there . . . they are 'masters' of the *hazomanga*, their *raza* is there and nowhere else, they don't come from afar, and when one [*mpitan-kazomanga*] dies another replaces him, when one dies another one replaces him. But the Vezo are people coming from far away and the 'master' of their *raza*, their *hazomanga*, is not here but has been left there, there, there [pointing to the south]. Only the children, only the grandchildren move over here, and so people cannot raise the sharpened pole over here because its real 'master' is still there, is still far away over there.[40]

Everyone in Betania referred to the south as the direction from which they or their forefathers had originally come. This is why the first piece of meat or handful of rice in an offering to the ancestors is thrown southwards. The south, as the previous excerpt suggests, is also where the sharpened *hazomanga* stand. But the interest of this account does not lie in its factual content or in the question of its accuracy. Whether or not Vezo further to the south make offerings to the ancestors in front of sharpened poles and whether or not they have maintained a distinction between *hazomanga*-object and *hazomanga*-person is not at issue.[41] The interest of the account lies in the gesture of an old man (and of all other Vezo *hazomanga* I met) who states that his *body* is the *hazomanga*.

Bloch's recent analysis (in press) of the process whereby the Zafimaniry gradually merge into places and become features of the landscape provides significant analogies and contrasts with the Vezo. The Zafimaniry, a group of shifting cultivators who live in western Madagascar, view the forest as an amoral, uncaring, uncontrollable environment. Human life within it is fragile and impermanent, but it can acquire permanence by leaving a mark on the landscape. One of the ways to do this is through successful human reproduction, which establishes houses made of the hardest and most durable wood. Following the death of the couple which founded the house, the latter lives on, is beautified and is made increasingly permanent by the couple's descendants; slowly the house becomes a 'holy house' and replaces the original couple, or more precisely, the original couple *becomes* the house. The ancestors undergo an analogous albeit more permanent transformation into megalithic stone monuments erected in the forest. In both instances, the ancestors become long-lasting objects merged into the landscape.

Similarly, Bloch (unpublished) has described the hard and straight walking sticks carried by Zafimaniry elders. Hardness and straightness are associated with ancestorhood: the walking sticks *are* the hardness and straightness that the shrivelled and bent bodies of the elders visibly lack. Thus, when the Zafimaniry talk about the hardness and straightness of an elder, they are not actually speaking about him but about the walking stick that he carries: the elder has *become* the walking stick.

We can contrast this transformation of the Zafimaniry elders into walking sticks with the Vezo *hazomanga*. On the one hand, the Zafimaniry project the elder's body onto an object that displays the characteristics of ancestorhood; by carrying and identifying with the walking stick, the elder anticipates his disappearance as a living person and emphasizes his transformation into an ancestor. The Vezo, on the other hand, having left their *hazomanga* far away in the south, have projected the object onto the body of the elder. Although the Vezo elder's body is just as bent and frail as that of the Zafimaniry elder, it is also, more significantly, a body that is *still alive* rather than in the process of dying and becoming an ancestor. Instead of a process in which elders become objects and thereby adhere to the hard and straight order of ancestorhood, as is the case among the Zafimaniry, we find that among the Vezo the object that stands for the hard and straight order of ancestorhood is made to coincide with impermanent, mobile people. Whereas the Zafimaniry seem to be trying to insinuate the ancestors' permanence into life, the Vezo aim to introduce the fluidity of life into the fixity of ancestorhood.

Both solutions to the tension between life and death are problematic. Bloch has pointed to the paradox of the Zafimaniry's attempt to fix people

into places, namely that in the process of transforming people into objects –
houses, stones and walking sticks – the people lose their 'peopleness'. The
solution adopted by the Vezo is less paradoxical but more dangerous: if life
in the form of the *hazomanga*'s body insinuates itself into the fixity of
ancestorhood, it follows also that in the body of the *hazomanga* the fixity
and permanency of descent becomes contiguous to life. As a result, the old
Vezo man carries the shadow of the 'single' *raza* inside his body: when the
shadow takes over completely and descent comes to be realized, the
hazomanga is 'dead on the spot'.

My use of a localized transformation (the merging of the *hazomanga*-
object with the *hazomanga*-person) to draw general conclusions about how
the Vezo construe the relationship between life and death, between
impermanence and permanence, between living people and the *raza* they
will only join at death, is supported by the preceding analysis of *soro*. In
both cases the shadow of the 'single' *raza* can be seen to linger over people's
life while remaining outside it. By establishing people's place of burial, the
ritual of *soro* treats people *as if* they were already dead, and thus prepares
their membership of *one raza*; and yet, living people do not become
members of any *raza* until their bones are buried in the tomb that contains
one raza. For the *hazomanga* who mediates between the living and the
'single' *raza*, the realization of descent has come closer – the shadow, as it
were, has grown thicker inside his body. But even in his case, the shadow is
never cast fully so long as he holds on to life and while his body, no matter
how bent and frail, remains outside his *raza*'s tomb.

Kinship and identity in life and death

This chapter has described two different types of kinship, one which
operates in the present among living people, and one which takes effect in
the future when people are dead and lie inside a tomb. The transition from
one type of kinship to the other (from undifferentiated *filongoa* to the
'single' *raza*) occurs only at death, but it is prepared and anticipated
through the ritual of *soro* which determines a person's place of burial; when
the choice of one tomb and one *raza* is made, people become as if they were
already bones, and the future is momentarily made present.

The transition from *filongoa* to the 'single' *raza*, from life to death, from
the present to the future, marks a radical transformation in the nature of
the person. In *filongoa*, the person embodies a variety of relationships
which can be enacted in different contexts and at different times; no choice
is needed to discriminate between them, for they can all come together in
the same plurally related and plurally constituted person. Membership of

the 'single' *raza*, on the contrary, strips the person of all but one kind of relationship; as the person enters the tomb that contains 'one kind of people', she must become the same as all the other members of that kind – the same, unitary person. In the process of operating this closure – from plural to singular – people are made to lose their gender blindness: gender becomes an absolute difference.

I mentioned above that *filongoa* could be described as a system of cognatic kinship. I also suggested that to use this term would be misleading, for the Vezo are not concerned with the 'problems' traditionally associated with cognatic systems of reckoning. In particular, the Vezo are not concerned with the fact that *filongoa* does not establish which descent group a person belongs to, but leaves open innumerable possibilities as to which 'group' (the kind of bilateral, all-inclusive descent group that *dadilahy* looks down at) a person draws her connections to. Similarly, they are not concerned that *filongoa* does not provide the person with a unique, individuating history, but provides many alternative histories (i.e. paths of ascendancy) that she can map out onto the past, all of which are worth remembering not because they provide a genealogy, but because they create relatedness in the present. Finally, they are not concerned that *filongoa* does not determine who the person is, but only who she is related to (or more exactly, who she has the potential to be related to), at different times and in different contexts. The Vezo are not concerned with these 'problems' because, contrary to what Fortes' unilineal descent theory predicated, they are *not* 'made aware of who and what they are as persons' (1987: 281) by their place in a descent group. Thus, while cognatic kinship was problematic for Fortes because it failed to define bounded groups, and thereby failed to define the person as a member of one of such groups (cf. Strathern 1992: 79–80), *filongoa* is *not* problematic for the Vezo precisely because it is a type of kinship that does *not* define and determine the person by placing it into *one* group, *one* kind of people, *one* particular history. *Filongoa* is not problematic because it preserves and enhances the transparency (the lack of residues from the past) of the Vezo person, who knows and is made aware of who and what she is through what she does contextually in the present, rather than through what she is (was and will be) inherently through time.

Filongoa becomes problematic only for the dead. Once a person is transformed into bones, a definite, determining and definitive choice is needed as to which group, which tomb, which kind of people, which particular history it is to be part of. As bones, the Vezo person cannot be both here and there; it cannot be related to both mother's and father's side; it cannot be simultaneously part of eight *raza*. The choice that death forces on the Vezo person clouds its transparency and indeterminacy. Through membership of the 'single' *raza*, the dead become fixed into one immutable identity, as they join one kind of people who share one and the same ancestry, one and the same history, one and the same tomb. While in *filongoa* people's identity is flexible and contextual as they trace different relations with one another in different contexts of time and space, inside the 'single' *raza* the identity of the dead loses its flexibility and contextuality and becomes fixed and categorical. When the dead are placed inside their tomb, they acquire a new identity, different from that of the living: for now it is only their place in *one* tomb and *one raza* that can make them aware of who and what they are.

7

Separating life from death

For the living Vezo, the 'single' *raza* is only a shadow that lingers over them. For the dead, membership of the *raza* has become their permanent and only form of identity. The transition from life to death, from *filongoa* to the *raza*, transforms the living person profoundly; as a result of this transformation, 'the dead and the living are not together, they are not the same' (*ny maty ny velo tsy miaraky, tsy mitovy*). This otherness of the dead was conveyed most starkly in the statement that 'the dead aren't people, they're "animals",[1] they aren't related to the living' (*lolo reo tsy olo fa biby, tsy longon' olom-belo*). The dead are bad tempered, wild and aggressive (*masiake*), and must be prevented, for this reason, from interfering in the life of their descendants; the living must therefore create a barrier (*hefitsy*) to keep themselves separate (*miavaky*) from the dead.

The new, alien and dangerous identity of the dead is created by the living through acts of separation and division. During funerals and mortuary rituals, the living expel death from life, creating and recreating the barrier that keeps the dead separate from them. As the dead are separated from life and from their living descendants, they are also divided among themselves by being placed in different tombs. Thus, when the living bury the dead and when they build tombs for them (something they regard as their duty), they also enact the transition from *filongoa* to the 'single' *raza* –they transform what in life was only a shadow into a new and fixed state of being of the deceased person.

This and the following chapter will be examining funerals and mortuary rituals. Since the main theme elaborated by these rituals is the separation of the living and the dead, I shall begin by looking at the clearest manifestation of this separation, the contrast drawn by the Vezo between two distinct spaces: cemetery and village.

106

Hot cemeteries and cold villages

Cemeteries lie in the forest (*añala any*), far away from the villages (*lavitsy mare*) and well hidden in the vegetation (*tsy hita maso*). People say that cemeteries are hidden like this because the Vezo dislike seeing the tombs, which make them sad and unhappy (*mampalahelo*); people would also be afraid (*mahatahotsy*) if the tombs lay too near or inside the village, as is known to be the custom among the Merina. In any case, as was often pointed out, cemeteries are not places that one visits very often; one hardly goes there just for a stroll (*mitsangatsanga*). The living only visit the cemeteries when they carry a corpse (*laha manday faty*), or build a tomb (*lafa miasa lolo*).

In Belo, the cemetery lies far away in a deserted area of shrubby forest across the lagoon. When I first took part in a funeral there, I was warned that the cemetery lay at a great distance and that the long walk under the scorching sun would be very tiring; I soon found out that the march was indeed exhausting. If it were not for what I had learnt previously in Betania, however, I might have overlooked the fact that the cemetery in Belo stood where it did not as a matter of chance but in respect of a norm. At the same time, my experience in Betania suggested that the cemetery's perceived distance can sometimes be defined by desired norms rather than responding to actual fact.

The area around Betania has two cemeteries, one to the south of the village (*an-dolo raiky*) and one to the east (*an-dolo be*). The southern cemetery is strikingly close to the village itself, the reason being that in the early seventies Betania was 'broken' in half (*kopaky tana*) by the incoming ocean, and the inhabitants of the northern half had to move to the south of the village. Since then Betania has been forced to expand to the south in the direction of the cemetery; as a result, the house at the southernmost tip of the village now nearly borders on the northern end of the cemetery.

A major worry in Betania is the process of marine erosion, which affects the entire coastal area near Morondava and which is advancing at such a rate that the villagers fear that the strip of land on which Betania lies, with the ocean to the west and the swamps to the east, will eventually be entirely washed away. As the sea pushes southwards and eastwards, however, people's main concern seems to be the village's increasing proximity to its cemeteries. On one occasion, observing my dismay at seeing the water at high tide coming so close to the inhabited area, an old woman explained the dramatic changes in the recent past. She claimed that what is nowadays the closest fishing location, Berenzea, which lies some 5 km offshore, was not very long before a Vezo village, whereas Betania itself had been an area of rice-fields inhabited by Masikoro. For the people who lived in Berenzea, the cemetery (which lay where it still lies now) was 'really far' (*lavitsy tokoa*), so far in fact that when they went to bury someone, they had to sleep outdoors for a night because they could not get back home on the same day. The woman asked me what I thought would happen if the sea keeps pushing inland: will people end up living among the tombs?

Although I did not know the answer to my friend's question, I soon discovered that each funeral I witnessed in Betania provided an opportunity for denying the actual proximity of the village and its cemeteries. The distance between them was recreated by asserting the *experience* of a long and exhausting journey, even if in fact the distance was covered in a short and untaxing walk. After every burial, as I headed back towards my house, there would always be someone in the crowd who would suggest that I felt, like everyone else, exhausted by the walk. Although distance and tiredness are, of course, a matter of personal judgement, at stake was rather a shared appreciation that the distance between village and cemetery *must* be long and exhausting to travel.

Cemeteries and villages are distant because they differ irreducibly from one another. Cemeteries are 'hot' (*mafana*), villages are 'cold' (*manintsy*). But although heat and cold are attributes of the earth (*tany*) where the dead and the living respectively reside, the two qualities express the categorical difference between cemeteries and villages rather than denoting features inherent to either location.

I came across the notion that the village earth is cold while discussing the meaning of a formula, *sañatsia tany manintsy*, that people seem often to mumble almost to themselves. *Sañatsia* can be translated as 'forgive me', *tany* means 'earth' or 'land', and *manintsy* means 'cold'. The expression therefore means to beg the cold earth (the land where the earth is cold) for forgiveness. I first became aware of this formula when a man uttered it before sketching his family's tomb on the sand to tell me about a plan to build an extension to it. He later explained that he had asked the cold earth of the village to forgive him for using it as if it were the hot earth of the cemetery.[2]

I tried to argue with my Vezo friends that the association between heat and cemeteries is counter-intuitive. I used Bloch's ethnography (1986) to describe the coldness of Merina tombs, suggested that ancestors and all that is associated with them ought to be cold, and stated my surprise that the Vezo should think otherwise.[3] Most of my interlocutors were unmoved by my reaction; some were positively annoyed by my insistence; a few however explained that cemeteries are hot because 'in cemeteries there is no breath' (*an-dolo tsy misy ay*).

Breathing connotes life.[4] A baby in the mother's womb that moves, eats and is alive (*fa velo*) must 'already have its breath' (*ainy fa misy*); the moment when someone dies is described as 'his breath has departed' (*fa roso ny ainy*). Cemeteries are breathless, therefore, because they are lifeless. But why should the lack of life make cemeteries hot? After pestering my friends for days, one finally volunteered that the expression is a 'matter of speech' (*fomba firesake*). Living people desire coolness and try to achieve it (*nintsy ro ilain'olom-belo*), because coolness stands for calm, lack of worries and an unproblematic life (*laha tsy misy probléme, laha tsy misy heritseritsy hafa, de manintsinintsy soa teña*). To say that cemeteries are hot is not descriptive, but is a way of stressing their difference (*sambihafa mare*) with respect to villages. According to my friend, the heat of the dead is merely a figure of speech that is contrasted with the (desired) coolness of the living.[5]

One evening, around the time I was enquiring about the contrast between heat and cold, *dadilahy* volunteered the statement that when people sit outside their homes and chat while waiting for their meal, and eat, and chat a little longer before going to sleep, everything is 'nicely cool' (*manintsinintsy soa*). When there is a death in the village (*laha misy faty*), however, everyone is hot (*mafana*).

The occurrence of death in the village breaks down the separation between life (in the village) and death (in the cemetery). Funerals are the process through which the barrier is recreated. First, death is allowed to disrupt people's life, as productive activities are halted, and cooking, eating and sleeping are moved close to the corpse. Then, death is expelled from the village and taken to the cemetery. When the body has been laid in the tomb and is covered with sand, an elder gives a short speech to thank the funeral's participants, following this by declaring: 'The funeral is over' (*fa vita*). The crowd disperses and everyone returns home. On leaving the cemetery to re-enter the village, people experience the barrier that the funeral has created anew. What follows aims to re-evoke this experience.

For ease of exposition, I shall begin by describing funerals as if they followed an unchanging routine, despite the fact that they vary significantly according to the status of the deceased and the emotional involvement of the living.[6] I begin by what my Vezo friends taught me to recognize as a 'normal' funeral: an occasion of sadness caused by an unexpected and untimely death. I turn then to the funeral of the very old, for whom death is less unexpected and untimely because the deceased has 'lasted a long time' (*naharitsy*). In this kind of funeral, the living are expected to rejoice as they celebrate the dead person, while at the same time they force on the deceased the traumatic transition away from *filongoa* and into the 'single' *raza*.

Duty and disruption: the funerary wake and the communal meals

A death in the village is first revealed by cries suddenly erupting from a house. Anyone close enough to hear runs in their direction. The door of the house where the corpse is lying stays shut, while a few people of the same gender as the deceased wash the body, tie its feet, arms and jaw, comb or plait its hair and dress it. When the door is opened, the people who sit closest to the entrance go inside the house, cry and sit there for a while; they then move out and sit in silence nearby. The crowd then slowly disperses; only few people stay inside and around the house. Among them is the deceased's *hazomanga*, the 'master of the corpse' (*tompom-paty*), who will preside over the funeral and in particular over delivering the body to the tomb and *raza*.

Later on a formal announcement (*fañambara*) of the death is made to every house in the village. Two boys go from house to house and mutter in a low voice that they have come to announce so and so's death. On this occasion the dead person's first name is used, even if the person was addressed with a tekno-name during her lifetime; I was told that this is so because that is the name that will be written on the dead person's cross (see below and ch. 8, p. 139). Messengers are also sent to inform relatives in other villages close enough to come before the burial; those who are too distant will get a brief letter with the essential facts: who died, when, and their date of burial.

As long as the dead body stays at the village, people will gather at night around the house where it lies and sing until dawn (*miaritory*); each day, a crowd gathers to eat the two communal meals (*sakafo am-paty*) provided by the dead person's family. Both activities are described as a process of moving from every house in the village to 'approach the deceased' (*mamonjy faty*).

Miaritory means 'to endure the absence of sleep'. Soon after dark, men, women and children gather around the dead person's home. Two Petromax lamps owned by the village community illuminate the area around the house. People slowly emerge from the darkness in small groups and sit down in a place of their choosing. Women are usually surrounded by children, who soon lie down on the sand and fall asleep wrapped up in their blankets. Although adults also try to get some sleep during the night, everyone complains the next day that the mosquitoes or the humidity made it impossible to have a proper rest. Some will attend the wake only until the early hours of the morning and then go home for some sleep; others go to sleep early in the evening and join the wake from the first hours of the morning until dawn. Younger people will be very active throughout the night, although not necessarily in anything directly concerning the wake; groups of young men play dominoes in a corner or move in small groups in search of new sexual encounters. The area of darkness around the wake is filled with ceaseless comings and goings.

The purpose of the wake is to produce 'ripe singing' (*hira masake*) of church hymns that everyone knows by heart.[7] The singing lasts from early night until daybreak (*vaky andro*). For the first couple of hours people sing together with little order, everyone performing at the top of their voices. The singing intensifies in order to drown out the wails of those sitting inside the house with the corpse; singing should always be energetic so that the deceased's relatives and friends do not feel unhappy (*tsy mampalahelo*). Slowly, as people tire or get bored, they divide into two groups, often of no more than four or five people each, and take turns singing. There is a core number of people who will sing throughout the night at every funeral, and who are known to be good singers (*mahay mihira rozy*). There is a tacit understanding that people who sing, particularly those who 'sing hard' (*mihira mare*), must be rewarded with rum; if the dead person's relatives provide no rum, the singing will not be 'ripe'. But although such stinginess is criticized, so are those singers who 'play politics' (*manao politiky*) by holding back their 'hard singing' so as to get more rum. Thanks to the rum, by daybreak the night-singers are usually so drunk that they will continue wailing through sheer inertia until they lose their voices entirely.

Attendance of the wake implies different things for different people according to what they are engaged in during the night. Ideally, everyone should contribute loudly to the common songs; yet the fact that most people do not do so is not considered especially significant. The main expectation, and what people will be thanked for, is that they be present at the wake rather than being asleep in their houses. At dawn, when the crowd disperses, everyone feels completely exhausted; it is through such tiredness, as we shall see, that people participate in the heat caused by death.

During the communal meals men and women are assigned to different tasks. Women are in charge of cooking; men are responsible for building the coffin (*tamango*) and the cross (*lakroa*) which will bear the dead person's name. But whereas only a small number of men are needed for this second task, which is usually completed in an afternoon,[8] preparing the meal involves a far larger contingent of women to fetch wood and water, cook, distribute the food and clean up, and their cooperation is needed for as many days as the funeral lasts. And since even if they do not participate actively in any of the work, the villagers are expected to participate in the day's gathering, all other village activities come grinding to a halt.

The focus of the daily gathering is the eating of the meal called 'meal at the deceased' (*sakafo am-paty*) or 'food at the deceased' (*hany am-paty*). Both providers and consumers state emphatically that the food tastes bad (*tsy soa*). One woman suggested that this was because the meat is boiled in water with no onions and tomatoes (*ketsiky am-paty tsy soa . . . tsy misy tongolo, tsy misy tamatese*). Another reason that seems implied by the insistence that it is food eaten at, or close to the dead person, is that the food tastes bad because it is cooked and eaten in proximity with death. The lack of onions and tomatoes signals that this food is something different from, and cannot taste like, everyday food.[9]

Although I was told that the dead person's family distributes food to the crowd because people have to interrupt their normal activities and therefore cannot provide for their day's meal, participants also emphasize that what they eat at the funeral should not substitute for their normal meal. The food at the funeral is not meant to make one full (*tsy mahavintsy*), for to do so would be far too expensive for the dead person's family. Therefore, participants in the meal take care not to seem to be stuffing themselves; it is also improper (*tsy mety*) to leave the gathering as soon as one has finished eating, for this would show that one has 'approached the deceased' only with the intention to be fed. When the crowd disperses after eating the 'food at the deceased', everyone is meant to eat another meal cooked by someone left at home for this purpose.

At this point, one might suggest that if people are worried about seeming greedy, the food cannot be as bad as they say. In fact, the women do not aim to cook poorly. Although they will readily discuss the food's shortcomings (the rice was cooked in too little water, the meat was too salty, or there was not enough broth to go with the rice), the women make an effort to cook well, and the failure to do so is strongly criticized. Similarly, the dead person's family is expected to provide enough ingredients for a decent or even enjoyable meal. And yet eating at funerals must by definition *not* be enjoyable, for otherwise it would mean that the living are enjoying death and conviviality with the deceased. Consequently the more a meal is to people's taste, the more important it is to emphasize that the 'food at the deceased' is bad by avoiding eating much and with greed. One eats in order to demonstrate one's closeness to the dead person and to participate in the disruption caused by death, not for the food itself.

People give a simple answer to the question why they attend funerals: if they didn't, they couldn't expect other people to attend their own and those of their kin.[10] By contrast, when I tried to understand the 'meaning' (*ino dikany?*) of the actions performed while the dead person is still in the village, I drew a blank. It gradually dawned on me, after witnessing five or six funerals, that when a death occurs it is as if the whole village put itself into motion through a routine that is acted out and experienced as such, and that might have little 'meaning' once it is taken up. At the same time, I was aware that to participate in the routine is a matter of choice: as soon as a death was formally announced, people became engrossed in the discussion whether or not to 'approach the deceased', pitting their reluctance to do so against their sense of duty and reciprocity.[11]

At every funeral in Betania, my adoptive mother would engage the entire family in a discussion as to whether she should attend the wake, given that her health was very poor and she could not afford to catch flu. Although she nearly always decided to attend, on the grounds that if she did not she would feel ashamed (*mahamenatse*) and no-one would come to her funeral, she would unfailingly complain about the damp sand and sometimes would cough for days after the event. Since I refused to take up the excuses she provided me with for not attending the communal meal, she expected me to complain of a stomach-ache for having had to eat what she firmly stated was uncooked rice. The family discussions, the mother's cough and my own stomach-ache were all essential parts of the funerary routine.

As *dadilahy* explained, when death is present in the village everyone is hot. Death, however, does not produce heat of itself: people must deliberately give up their coolness by abandoning their ordinary lives and food to 'approach the deceased'. The wake and the communal meals cause a loss of coolness through lack of sleep, tiredness, drunkenness and eating 'bad' food. As my adoptive mother repeatedly demonstrated, this disruption – the transition from coolness to heat – is enhanced and accentuated by people's open discussion of the possibility that they might *not* participate in the funerary ritual, thereby transforming a routine into a choice of duty.[12]

'When one's dead, one's dead'

As I mentioned in chapter 4, the Vezo have 'easy customs' because they are soft and gentle people. A 'difficult custom' (*fomba sarosty*) the Vezo could not endure is to have funerals that last a long time, like those of the Masikoro or the Antandroy. Death, and the disruption that it causes in the village, are not allowed to remain there for long.

Some of my friends admitted that funerals lasting weeks or even months would simply be unaffordable by the Vezo, who do not own cattle and therefore could not feed the village for such a long time. Expense, however, is not the main reason for keeping funerals short. The most pressing reason is that the Vezo abhor keeping dead bodies in the village for more than a few days because the sight of a decomposing body 'makes people sad' (*mampalahelo*). Accordingly, they employ various devices to keep the corpse cool and delay putrefaction. Little openings are made in the walls of the house so as to create a gentle breeze around the body; the leaves of a special tree (*ravin-kinana*) said to keep the body cool are collected; formalin, when it can be afforded, is considered a 'very good thing' (*raha soa mare*). When the body begins to decompose, measures are taken to avoid contact with it. If the body 'breaks' (*vaky manta*), it is immediately put inside the coffin so as to avoid handling it as putrefaction advances; nylon sacks are carefully placed under and around the body to prevent fluids from dripping out of the coffin. If the smell becomes too powerful or the dead person's features begin to alter, the coffin is closed and the lid is nailed down.

Rightly or not, the Vezo consider these acts to be peculiar to themselves. They inject formalin or put plastic bags inside the coffin with the awareness that other people have different, 'difficult' customs which force them to endure the sight of and contact with putrefaction. The Vezo refer constantly to these alternative forms of behaviour. When a coffin is nailed down because the sight of the swelling corpse can no longer be endured, people comment on the Vezo's 'easiness' compared to the 'hardness' of the Masikoro, who allegedly have the strength of character to observe the decomposing body of their beloved. One way the Vezo seem to rationalize their 'easiness' and contrast themselves to other Malagasy groups is by repeating the vaguely Keynesian saying, 'when one's dead, one's dead' (*lafa maty, maty*). This motto refers to two related issues, the first one concerning the corpse and the second one the separation of the living and the dead.

When a body is lifeless (i.e. 'breathless') it no longer has any bodily sensations: 'it doesn't feel or hear anything' (*tsy mahare raha*). Once, when formalin was used to preserve the body of a very old woman, someone gave a detailed description of how hard it had been for the doctor, who had arrived very late, to inject the liquid in the corpse; others remarked that it made no difference because the old woman was dead and no longer felt anything. Similar comments were made when a gold tooth was extracted with great difficulty from the corpse of a young woman.

By insisting on the fact that a corpse lacks all sensitivity and is doomed to putrefaction it is possible to argue that it makes no sense (*tsy misy dikany*) to keep dead bodies in the village where they no longer belong. To some extent, people's reiteration during funerals that there is no point in keeping the corpse in the village for long suggests that some may feel the temptation, if not the desire, to do so. The removal of the corpse from the village is, in fact, recognized as being emotionally traumatic for those closest to the deceased. These people are the most affected by the sight of decomposition, and at the same time they are the most inclined to hold on to the deceased so as to postpone its departure. Thus, it is the role of 'wise people' (*olo mahihitsy*), particularly of the village elders (*olo be*), to remind everyone that 'when one's dead, one's dead', that 'she won't come back to life but will begin to stink', and that 'when one's dead one must be buried' (*lafa maty maty . . . tsy mihavelo fa mansty . . . tsy maintsy mandevy lafa maty*).

The burial

There is only one appropriate place for a dead body, and that is the cemetery. The decision about when to bury it is taken by 'the master of the corpse' and is announced during the wake, usually when people gather the first night. Children's funerals generally include only one night's wake; adults' funerals, especially those of old people, may last three or four nights. Some unfavourable days, or half days, must be avoided by delaying or anticipating the burial.

Burial effectively starts with the removal of the body from the house. If this has yet to be done, the corpse is laid in the coffin, the lid is nailed down and covered with a white cloth, and the coffin is carried out of the house through a door or a window in an easterly direction (east is where the dead dwell and where the *hazomanga* turns to when he addresses the *raza*).

The separation at this point between the dead person and what it leaves behind as it moves out of the house and village is differently marked according to the dead person's status. A child's separation is cried out by its mother who, from inside the house, sees the coffin go; she is not allowed to join the procession because people say that she would cry too much at the cemetery and would be unable to face the burial. If the dead person was married, the spouse must stand outside the house on one side of the coffin opposite to a close kin of the deceased (normally a sibling, and always a person of the same gender as the deceased). The two hold over the coffin a string called *fañitoa*, loosely knotted in the middle, and pull it until it breaks, at which point the coffin begins to move towards the cemetery. In the case of an old widow, whose funeral I describe further below, the separation was acted out by her grandchildren (*zafy*) who were called into the house just before the coffin-lid was nailed down. They walked past their grandmother and were told to look at her: 'There's your grandmother, she's dead!' (*io dadinao, fa maty io!*). Outside the doorway, the coffin was laid down and the grandchildren stepped across it; the procession then moved towards the cemetery.

Once the body has left the house and the act of separation has been accomplished, it cannot re-enter it (*fa faly*). Hence, if the funeral takes place in one village, let us say in Betania, and the body is buried elsewhere, for example in Belo, the coffin cannot be put back inside a house when it gets to Belo; if it is not buried immediately, it will be kept outdoors. The reason for this prohibition is that when the coffin is removed from the house and heads eastwards towards the *raza*, it cannot change direction, its destination *must* be the tomb.

The act of separation when the coffin leaves the house marks death's departure; the body's destination is irreversible. But although delivering the corpse to its tomb solves the problem of harbouring death within the village, as the body arrives at the cemetery the focus of attention shifts to the dead person's entry into its tomb. Leading the procession to the cemetery is the dead person's *hazomanga*, who will be the first to get there together with a few other men. On arriving at the tomb of which he is the 'master' (*tompon-dolo*), the *hazomanga* sprinkles some rum over it and announces (*mañambara*) to the *raza* that so and so is coming and is about to enter their 'house' (see below, p. 123). Having just been informed about the new burial, the ancestors are exhorted not to be surprised (*tsy hotseriky nareo*); they are told that in the future they should have no reason to enquire about the body they are about to receive, and they are asked not to do so (*ka hañontanianareo*). Finally, they are exhorted to behave well (*mipetsara soa nareo*). The ancestors must be kept informed, I was told, because otherwise they will visit the living to enquire about the alien body buried in their tomb. The problem with this is that if the dead have to ask questions of the living, the latter fall seriously ill and may even die. By informing the ancestors of the new arrival, therefore, the *hazomanga* ensures that the dead will not step across the barrier that separates them from the living.

By informing the ancestors about the newcomer, the *hazomanga* also opens the way for the dead person into the tomb and the *raza*. As I remarked in chapter 6, the announcement to the dead by the 'master of the corpse' makes a second *soro* at the paternal *hazomanga* unnecessary and redundant. The 'acquisition' of a new member by the paternal *raza*, which was established by the first *soro* but had remained suspended thereafter, finally comes into effect when the *hazomanga* stands in front of the tomb and the men who accompany him begin digging the grave. Only at this moment is descent fully realized, as the deceased moves out of *filongoa* to enter the 'single' *raza*.

The procession itself, as it slowly moves from the village towards the cemetery, is led by a young man carrying the cross and is followed by the coffin carried by four men who take turns with others who stay close by. The crowd follows, men and women together, who resume the singing that had ended at daybreak; children are left at home, for they are forbidden from visiting the tombs during a funeral. Normally, by the time the procession reaches the tomb the grave has been dug. The coffin is lowered into the grave, lying with the head to the east and even and flat; the wood cross is placed at the head. The crowd gathers around to watch. Once the coffin is in place, the women are asked to throw a handful of sand from inside the tomb over the grave; they then move slowly away to a place a small distance away in the shade. The men left standing inside the tomb begin to shovel sand over the coffin. The noise of wet sand hitting the wood alternates with the wails of the dead person's kin and friends, who are moved to a distance and urged to stop because crying at cemeteries is forbidden (*fa faly*).

As the sand inside the tomb is swept even and clean, a man 'who knows how to speak in public' (*mahay mivola am-bahoake*) asks for people's attention and delivers a brief speech on behalf of the dead person's family. He thanks the people who have attended wakes and communal meals and who have carried the dead person to the cemetery. He recalls when the death occurred and the succession of days people have 'approached the deceased'. Finally, he says, the deceased has arrived where she belongs (*farany, fa avy an-plasy misy azy*, lit. 'she has arrived in the place where she is'). Membership of the 'single' *raza* starts at this moment, as the dead person arrives in *this* place.

Once the dead body is interred where it belongs, the living have completed the removal of death from the village. However, something quite remarkable has occurred as they did so: in order to put an end to death's intrusion in the village, the living have intruded into death. When the *hazomanga* exhorts the ancestors to behave well, he is concerned that this intrusion do no harm to the living. But above all, as soon as the burial is over people *must* move out of the cemetery, in order to re-create a similar but inverse separation to that when the deceased was removed from the village. Hence, the speech of thanksgiving ends with an exhortation to the crowd to disperse and return quietly home. The final words are uttered as a command: 'It is over; let us return home' (*fa vita, tsika holy*). Women are the first to stand up and repeat: 'It is over, let us return home.'

I suggested above that when people return from the cemetery to the village they experience the separation that their involvement in the funeral has created. When the villagers are ordered to go home and are told that everything is over, the process of disruption they had previously joined in – actively, even purposefully and out of a sense of duty – acquires its full meaning. As they walk back to the village, they return to normal food, normal nights of sleep, normally productive activities; in other words, they walk back to coolness.[13] Coolness, however, is meaningful only in so far as people know what heat feels like; the village feels cold only because the cemetery was hot, and vice versa. The living enjoy and desire coolness; they would gladly do without heat. When death occurs, however, the entire village joins in the heat (for as long as people with 'easy' customs can endure) in order to experience what coolness feels like when death is finally expelled.

What I have just described has the appearance of a simple logical exercise. But when people participate in funerals, stay awake and sing through the night, eat food that may be good but must taste bad, smell the sickly smell of decomposition, hear cries and wails of despair, enter the cemetery, see a grave and throw handfuls of sand over a coffin, the logical exercise is experienced rather than being apprehended. Through this experience, the coolness of the village, the heat of the cemetery and the restored barrier between the two become real and meaningful.

Dadikoroko's death

Funerals are not performed for everyone in the same manner. As I mentioned in the preceding chapter, the death of a small baby (*zazamena, zazarano*) does not lead to a funeral because the baby is not yet a proper human being (*mbo tsy olo*). Since the baby has no bones, burial in the cemetery (which is where bones are kept) makes no sense, and the body is therefore buried in an unmarked grave in the forest. By contrast, children old enough to sit up straight are human beings (*fa olo*) and have bones, and consequently are buried in the cemetery. Their funeral lasts only one night's wake, and whereas everyone in the village is duty-bound to participate, the crowd is expected to remain unmoved by such a death. This lack of emotion is in stark contrast with the funerals of people who are 'still young' (*mbo tanora*), a loosely defined category of people who are no longer children but are not yet old. Their death is a 'waste' (*mosera*); the younger they are, the greater the waste caused by their death. Their funeral lasts longer than that of a child, and collective display of grief is common; especially at night, an outburst of crying close to the dead person may suddenly spread to the whole crowd, whose singing turns into a wail, while a few older people try to get things again under control.

Finally, when an old person (*olo fantitra*) dies, people are expected to be joyful (*sambatsy*), and the funeral must express this happiness. In what follows, I begin by briefly describing how the funerary routine of an old person is affected by the joy of the living, taking the example of the funeral of Dadikoroko, an old woman of Betania. I follow this by exploring why people are joyful, what it is that they celebrate and the broader significance of their celebration.

Dadikoroko died of old age. She was very tired (*rerake mare*); she stopped eating and slept all day. One day she was told that Safy, another very old woman in Betania, had died. Dadikoroko went back to sleep. As the crowd returning home from Safy's burial dispersed, her breath left her. The village was summoned for another funeral.[14]

When Dadikoro was young, she liked to dance. She was a 'great devil' (*devoly be*): she was uninterested in the religion of the white people and never went to church to sing; she preferred dancing to singing hymns. Her funeral reflected her lifetime's tastes, as the crowd produced increasingly 'ripe' feasts (*fisa masake*) during the three nights of her wake.[15] Each night part of the crowd would begin to intone some hymns, trying hard to sound happy rather than sad. But each night, a few hours into the wake, a different kind of humming would join the hymns, growing somewhere in the darkness, and a group of young men would start to dance *gañaky*: wrapped up in their blankets, head and face wholly covered, they jumped up and down, holding tightly on to each other and panting loudly in increasing paroxysms of sound and movement. More and more people would join in, at first outside the lighted area around the house and then gradually moving into the light. Lined up in a long, winding snake, men, women and children danced near and around the house. As the excitement mounted up, the crowd called upon Dadikoroko, challenging her to join them. A tall, very skinny woman, almost as old as Dadikoroko, stood on the threshold of the house where Dadikoroko lay, dancing and looking sideways into the house; her stiff body was slowly transformed as she began to sway her hips and mimic her friend's seduction. Dadikoroko, however, did not respond.

Dadikoroko's funeral lasted four days and three nights. When an old person dies, it is important that as many children, grandchildren and great-grandchildren as possible arrive in time to participate in the burial (*ho tsatsy faty*, lit. 'catching the deceased'). Hence, the funeral is made to last three or four days – but never any longer. In order to feed the mourners for such a long time, the dead person's family buys a live head of cattle instead of buying meat at the market. When the animal is taken to the mourners gathered around the deceased, a mock bull-fight will usually ensue; the animal, tied securely by the horns, is forced to run, to stop suddenly and to run again towards the crowd. Since the bull bought for Dadikoroko's funeral had lived nearly wild in the forest, finding and capturing it was a long and exacting job involving a number of men; people waited for the bull for half a day. The delay added to the crowd's excitement when the bull, which had been shot down with a rifle but was still alive, was carried into the village on a wooden stretcher. As the carriers' singing began to be heard in the distance, the mourners ran to meet the men with their prey. The carriers acted out a bull-fight with the animal immobilized on the stretcher, running in circles and coming to a sudden halt. Women waved their sarongs in praise of the hunters, and surrounded the stretcher, dancing and singing more and more loudly and frenziedly. The bull was paraded around the house where Dadikoroko lay, and Dadikoroko was called upon; jokes were shouted at her as a man hit the bull's testicles hard. Once more, Dadikoroko gave no reply.

When the dead person is old, the funeral should give them renown (*malaza*); distributing lots of fat meat at the communal meals ensures that people remember the deceased. Participants are encouraged to eat plentifully and they do so without hesitation, contrary to custom when the dead person is young. Since the crowd is expected to be joyful, the meal can be enjoyed and becomes a moment of celebration, of cheerful conviviality with the deceased. But while people banqueted in Dadikoroko's name all around her house, Dadikoroko's body began to smell of the sweet stench of decay.

I mentioned above that just before the coffin was nailed shut, Dadikoroko's grandchildren were summoned into the house. They were told, rather aggressively, to see that she was dead (*io dadinao, fa maty io*). As Dadikoroko was taken out of the house, the crowd was so excited and anxious to move on that the 'master of the corpse' nearly forgot to ask the grandchildren to step across the coffin. This was hurriedly done, and the procession set off towards the cemetery.

It was midday and it was very hot. Dadikoroko was to be buried in the cemetery east of the village. Since at high tide the area between the village and the cemetery is flooded, when the tide ebbs it leaves a vast expanse of mud through which people had to walk knee-high to take Dadikoroko to her tomb. This did not prevent the procession from being wild and 'ripe' (*masake*); wading through the mud and the effort of running through the swampy plain added to the crowd's excitement. Men struggled to squeeze a shoulder under Dadikoroko's coffin, those at the nether end pushing forward and the others pushing backwards. Under such contrasting pressures, the coffin often came to a halt, swinging wildly while its bearers skidded and teetered in the mud. Around them, women roused the men in their efforts, or rather aroused them by dancing provocatively and swinging their hips against the men's pelvis. As soon as some bearers reacted to the provocation and began to dance with the women, other men took their place at the coffin.

In this instance the *hazomanga* was left to wait for a long time at the tombs. Eventually Dadikoroko got there, the white cloth over the coffin covered in mud and the coffin lid loosened at one side. As the coffin moved closer to the tomb, the dancing, singing and writhing of bodies reached its acme. Finally Dadikoroko was handed over to the men standing inside the tomb who laid her in the grave, a speech like the one I described above was delivered to the crowd, and suddenly it was all over. On the way back to Betania, everyone took care to walk on the firmer patches of ground to avoid sinking in the mud; life had returned to normal.

People rejoiced when Dadikoroko died because, like everyone who dies when they are old, she had 'lasted a long time' (*fa naharitsy*). Her death was not a 'waste' like that of people who died when they are 'still young'. Old age comes after a life of growth and transformation; death stops this process by causing lack of breath and stillness. The main result of old age is that an old person, both man and woman, has many children (*anaky*), grandchildren (*zafy*) and great-grandchildren (*kitro*).[16] By 'lasting for a long time', an old person sees and enjoys the branching out of *filongoa*, of the generation of new life from the life she originally generated (see above, pp. 80–6). On dying, Dadikoroko left behind the outcome of this generative chain. The 'ripe' feast organized for her funeral – the dances, bull-fights, abundant meals[17] and wild procession – celebrated this outcome. People expressed joy because of Dadikoroko's long and successful life, not because of her death.

Dadikoroko nonetheless was dead. People danced around her and called on her to join what she used to like and was good at, and she never joined in. A bull-fight took place around her house, and she did not react. People ate in her honour and her body began to decay. Her coffin swung up and down amidst erotic dances, but at the end of it all she lay flat and still in her grave. Dadikoroko was proved dead by the display of life around her.

And yet the vitality displayed all around her also proved that Dadikoroko was *not* wholly dead. The crowd acted out the liveliness that she had produced, whose source Dadikoroko was. Dadikoroko may have been unable to dance herself, but in the course of the funeral she danced *through* her children, her grandchildren and her great-grandchildren. A highly pleasing spectacle took shape as more and more people joined in. For a time, it seemed as if everyone in the dancing and singing crowd was one of Dadikoroko's descendants – for the last time, Dadikoroko was at the head of a large, all-inclusive descent group made up of all her descendants, coming to her from all sides; for the last time she was able to enjoy the undividedness of *filongoa*. Thanks to this spectacle, the funeral became a celebration that moved people to happiness.

Like all funerals, however, Dadikoroko's had to accomplish something quite different from the celebration of the good life of an aged grandmother. It had to separate Dadikoroko from the life she had generated, and had to force her into her *raza*; thus, at the end, the vast crowd of people who danced with her, placed her dead body inside *one* tomb, *one raza*, with only *one* kind of people. As Dadikoroko was laid in the sand, her vision of *filongoa* was brought to an end.

The funeral staged a complex, contradictory and emotional play whose parts proved both that Dadikoroko was dead and that she was not wholly so. At the end, however, the funeral was declared over and people were told to return home. As the crowd dispersed, Dadikoroko remained motionless in her grave, while the life that she had generated walked away from her and headed back towards the village. As life withdrew from the cemetery, Dadikoroko settled down in her new, permanent and unitary identity as a member of her *raza*.

8

Working for the dead

The tombs in which the dead are buried and through which they become members of the 'single' *raza* are built by living people through work (*asa*) which they perform because the dead desire nice, clean, proper 'houses' (*trano*).[1] If the living fail to carry out the work, the ancestors will make known their discontent. This will begin with a visitation of dreams and minor illnesses, in response to which the *hazomanga* may try to talk to the ancestors to reassure them that the desired work will be undertaken soon. If the promise is not kept, however, the ancestors may get very angry (*meloke mare*) and 'make people die' (*mahafaty*).

Although the living work for the dead out of a sense of duty and under duress, the desires of the dead coincide in a subtle way with those of the living. For the dead, the performance of the work is a way to be remembered and be taken care of by their descendants; for the living, working for the dead provides a form of blessing (*asantsika ro tsipiranontsika*, our work is our blessing), because when the ancestors are happy they stop interfering with the life, dreams and health of their descendants. In other words, working for the dead is another way of *separating* life from death.

In the previous chapter, we saw how the intrusion of death into the village is dealt with: by joining the disruption and 'hotness' caused by the presence of death, the living restore coolness in the village as they deliver the deceased to its tomb and *raza*. Having successfully separated death from life, however, the living are still faced with a problem, which is that 'the dead feel a longing for the living' (*olo maty manino an'olom-belo*). This is a very dangerous kind of longing, which may prompt the dead to come back to trouble their descendants, causing them to die (*mahafaty*); the greatest danger comes from those with the strongest longing, people who, like Dadikoroko, died in old age and left behind them large numbers of children, grandchildren and great-grandchildren. These older people long for all that which they have lost as they entered the 'single' *raza*; as they lie with only '*one* kind of people', they long for all the other 'kinds' they left outside their tomb; they long for the undividedness of *filongoa* which they experienced when they were alive, and which they enjoyed for the last time during their funeral (see pp. 121–2 above).

From inside their tombs, therefore, the dead not only want to be remembered and looked after by the living; they also want to remember life.[2] As we shall see below, the work that the living perform for the dead is not simply a way of showing that they remember and honour them, but is just as much a means of appeasing, if only momentarily, their longing for life and for their living descendants: during the work, the dead are brought back in contact with life and are offered a spectacle of the life they have left behind.

As the living entertain their dead ancestors in this manner, however, they also create those material objects – the tombs – which divide the dead among themselves and make them into members of separate, 'single' *raza*. Like the act of burial, therefore, the work performed by the living creates and realizes descent among the dead. It therefore seems paradoxical that the moment when the dead are brought back in contact with life and are offered the possibility of enjoying once more an unrestricted sight of *filongoa* should also be the moment when the transition from life to death and from *filongoa* to the 'single' *raza* is re-enacted. A further paradox comes from the fact that when the living work for the dead in order to make them enjoy the undividedness of *filongoa*, they are forced to experience the divisiveness of the *raza* – the same divisiveness that the tombs create among the dead. This is because the work for the dead is the responsibility of people of a specific 'kind', the living people who will be buried in the tomb under construction and will join the *raza* there. These people are known as the 'masters of the work' (*tompon'asa*), whose leader is the *hazomanga*. Although as living people they are not members of the *raza* yet, as 'masters of the work' they act collectively as those who will join it.[3] When the 'masters of the work' are planning the work and putting aside money for it, their reference to '*our* work' (*asantsika, asanay*)[4] draws a clear distinction between themselves and everyone else. It is a distinction that is not normally made, because membership of the *raza* is not yet relevant for the living; but when people act as 'masters of the work', they recognize and activate the shadow of the 'single' *raza*. Not surprisingly, the organization of the work makes the 'masters of the work' hot (*mafana*), whereas those who are not involved stay nicely cool (*manintsinintsy*).

This chapter analyses the work that the living perform for the dead, and describes the complex interplay between the desires of the dead and those of their living descendants, between the task of bringing the dead close to life and that of separating life from death, between recreating the undividedness of *filongoa* for the dead while casting the shadow of the 'single' *raza* over the living. These complexities are acted out on two separate ritual occasions. I introduce these acts with a brief description of the objects that the living build when they work for the dead. I follow this with a few remarks on those aspects of the two rituals that are similar. I then proceed to examine each ritual in its own right.

Betania's eastern cemetery (*an-dolo-be*) is surrounded by a thick and thorny forest crossed by several narrow paths leading to the tombs. The paths are protected by a number of taboos or restrictions (*faly*); for example, they cannot be cleared of any obstruction, not even of the many thorny branches that make walking difficult and painful. The tombs are therefore invisible until they emerge suddenly a few metres away from among the vegetation. Although they are ordered along a north–south axis on a narrow and slightly hilly strip of sand, the cemetery has a chaotic and crowded appearance and there is hardly any room to move around in. Forest shrubbery encroaches on the tombs, sometimes even growing inside them.

Tombs come in different styles. Some are simple fences (*vala*) bounding some land where the dead bodies are buried, not very deep; a number of crosses with the name of the deceased are stuck in the sand. The fence and the cross are made of either wood or cement. The fence measures approximately 3 m by 5 m and is about 1 m high. Alternatively, there are large concrete 'boxes' (*sasapoa*) half-sunk in the sand and surrounded by a concrete fence. Elsewhere the tomb is a heap of stones covering some coffins, with crosses sticking up between the rocks.

On the basis of my informants' statements and explanations of Vezo customs (*fombam-Bezo*), the typical Vezo tomb (at least in the area where I lived) appears to be the *vala*.[5] *Sasapoa*, which seem to be a recent innovation, are considered a 'good thing' (*raha soa*) because they allow many people to be buried together; the bodies are laid inside the 'box' without a coffin and therefore take up much less space. However, to start a *sasapoa* implies exhuming previously buried bodies, and since exhumation is taboo for most Vezo this kind of tomb is rarely built. Heaping stones over the dead is considered unusual in Betania, but is more commonly practised in Belo (where a fence is nonetheless built around the stone mound) and is said to be quite common in Tulear; people in Betania see it as the practice of outsiders (*vahiny*).

Although I came to consider whitewashed concrete fences as the cemetery's most prominent feature, such fences are in fact built to replace pre-existing wood fences, and wood is therefore as much or more a part of the landscape. Besides the wood fences that are still in place, wooden remains of dismantled tombs are scattered along the cemetery borders, and other wood fences are in the process of collapsing. Wood fences can be made with roughly cut poles hewn directly in the surrounding forest, or with boards and carved poles that are built into elaborate structures, sometimes with sculptures standing on top of four or six of the main poles.[6] Fences of the first kind are temporary structures, built at the time of burial if a place in an already established (concrete) tomb is unavailable; in due course, the temporary fence is dismantled and the concrete one is built in its place. The same occurs for the crosses; a first, temporary wooden cross will later be replaced by a concrete one. Fences of the second kind are regarded instead as a feature of the past before concrete came into use; they are thought to belong to people whose descendants have moved away, for otherwise the wood would have been replaced.

As this description suggests, the work performed by the living for the dead consists in substituting concrete for wood. First, the concrete fence is built (*asa lolo*); then, all the wooden crosses contained in that tomb are replaced with concrete ones (*asa lakroa*). Although the two rituals are sometimes performed within a short interval of one another, they constitute distinct enterprises, and it will usually take many years after the fence is built for the wood crosses inside it to be replaced with concrete ones. The completion of the work, when the tomb has been cleared of all the rotting wood, produces a strong sense of accomplishment. The dead are imagined to be pleased with their new, nice and clean house, while the living can also be said to appreciate the aesthetic values of the tombs and crosses they build for the dead. Each of the three times I took part in an *asa lolo*, and once the work had been completed and people began to disperse to go home, I was called over by some men and urged to admire the result: I was expected to agree that the fence was beautiful and good (*soa*); to ask why a concrete fence is *soa* would have been offensive. In fact, on observing the effort and care with which men dug the sand to lay solid foundations, I realized that the beauty of concrete fences is that they stand straight, firm and even on loose and shapeless sand. Concrete crosses are similarly admired for being big, heavy, solid objects, in stark contrast with the flimsy wood crosses they replace.

Concrete is considered a 'good thing' (*raha soa*) because it lasts a long time (*maharitsy*).[7] The dead are thought to like it because it extends their material presence in the cemetery. Older people would often point to a small baby, a grandchild or great-grandchild: thanks to concrete, they would say, when the child was grown up and they were long dead, she would still be able to see her grandparents' tomb and the crosses with their names. The living, however, appreciate the durability of concrete because it allows them to build an even firmer barrier between themselves and the dead: their expectation is that, once wooden fence and crosses have been replaced, the dead will have no reason to complain about their 'house' for a very long time, and so keep at a distance from their living descendants. The durability of concrete can thus be seen as articulating the paradox between the dead's desire to be remembered by the living, and the latter's desire to be forgotten by the dead.[8]

The only drawback of concrete is that it is very expensive (*sarotsy mare*), and therefore adds considerably to the already notable costs of organizing the work for the dead. Cash is needed not only to buy building materials but also to provide food and plenty of rum for the participants and to pay for the diviner's counsel. Although the cost of building materials is normally higher for building the fence, the cost of food and drink is considerably greater for the cross ritual because many more people are invited to attend.

The 'masters of the work' begin to collect money among themselves by subscription (*cotisacion*, Fr. subscription, quota, share) months before the ritual is performed.[9] Each person's contribution is carefully annotated in a notebook, as are (or should be) all expenses. Contributions (*enga*) of money, cattle, rum or beer are also expected from everyone invited to attend the last stage of the cross ritual, when the crosses are taken to the cemetery. In one case, total expenditure for the two rituals was 707.620 FMG,[10] plus two head of cattle and one case of beer. Of this sum, 151.000 FMG, the cattle and the case of beer were received as *enga*; the contribution of the 'masters of the work' was therefore just over 550.000 FMG.[11]

This huge sum of money (approximately the value of 1100 kg of Spanish mackerel, nine canoes, four large bulls or 600 kg of rice) 'comes from the sea' (*vola bakan-drano*) (see above, p. 53). Although one contribution to the *cotisacion* came from Marofasy, a young Antandroy man employed by a local retailer, the work's success was always stated to depend on fishing. In fact, such 'big work' (*asa ,bevata*) could only be accomplished by very successful fishing. This is the reason why the rituals are performed towards the end of the cold season during September and October,[12] for the best fishing period occurs during the preceding months when earnings are likely to be high. When my family began to plan the two rituals, everyone repeated, as if to ward off bad luck, that the work would be done at a certain time if *Ndrañahary* (the creator) protected them and helped them to 'see' a lot of fish (*mahita fia maro*); family members who failed to contribute to the *cotisacion* were told disapprovingly: 'And yet you catch plenty of fish every day' (*kanefa, mahazo fia maro isanandro isanandro nareo*).

The willingness and ability to gather such large sums of money may seem surprising if we remember that a fundamental trait of Vezo identity is the inability to 'manage money' (see above, ch. 3). While the work was still in its preparatory stages, my family endlessly discussed the best way to achieve the necessary savings. They finally agreed that the five brothers and sisters, their mother and older sons and daughters would pay their quotas in small instalments; the cash was to be collected and kept at the *hazomanga*'s, the eldest brother's house. Many of them failed to contribute, however, claiming that they were keeping the money at home and would hand it over once they had saved the full amount. Although they never said so to his face, it appeared that they did not trust the *hazomanga*, or rather that they took it for granted that in need he would be willing to use the collective fund for private purposes.[13] One of his sisters, however, dismissed this apparent suspicion as an excuse by her relatives to shirk their duties, and told them that she doubted that they would ever succeed in saving any money if they kept it at their own home. The only way to save the necessary sum, she said, was to set aside 1000, 500 or even as little as 200 FMG from their daily earnings and to remove it immediately from their house, this being the only way to avoid spending the money on food, snacks, rum or clothes. Although this woman often exhorted her relatives to be wise, most of the time she charged them with being the opposite (*tsy mahihitsy nareo!*).

Discussions in my family suggest that people are aware that in order to meet their responsibilities towards the dead, they are forced to plan and save. While it was taken for granted that the 1000, 500 or 200 FMG to be set aside daily for the work on the tombs would otherwise have been spent in immediate gratification, people also recognized that to spend money in such a way is incompatible with their duty towards the dead. In other words, in order to succeed in building a permanent and lasting tomb the living have to abandon their customary Vezo behaviour.

Although in practical terms this argument is straightforward (tombs are expensive and people must save money in order to build them), its ideological implications are more interesting, for it appears to be drawing a clear distinction between two opposite 'transactional orders'.[14] The first order is the concern and defining feature of the Vezo as living people; the second pertains to relations between the living and the ancestors. By stressing that they *must* save money only when they have to build tombs and crosses, the Vezo draw a sharp contrast between 'working for the dead' and 'keeping themselves alive'. This contrast is yet another way of formulating and creating the separation between the living and the dead. The difference between life and death can be understood in no better way than by looking at the outcome of the two 'transactional orders': permanent, lasting concrete fences and crosses on the one hand, transitory, sensual gratification on the other.

As with all other major undertakings, a favourable day (*andro soa*) must be chosen for things to go smoothly and safely during the ritual's performance, and a diviner (*ombiasa*) is consulted for this purpose (*mila andro*, 'to ask for the day'). Although people will often hazard a guess whether a day is favourable or not, the matter is so 'difficult' (*raha sarotsy*) that no-one wishes to hazard a mistake. In fact, while it is advisable to undertake all activities concerning the ritual and its preparation on 'good days', it is crucial to do so for the more 'difficult' acts. For the *asa lolo*, for example, the bricks for the fence can either be moulded at the village or can be bought ready made. In the first case, the diviner will certainly be consulted; in the second, people may trust their own judgement as to the right day for buying the bricks and carrying them to the village. If the building materials are taken near the cemetery before the ritual, however, the day for doing so must be chosen by a diviner.

A further essential requisite for the ritual's success is a specially prepared medicine called *fanintsina*. The medicine, which is prepared by the diviner a few days before the work is done, is used in both rituals prior to leaving for and on the way to the cemetery; it is made each time with a special combination of ingredients dissolved in water. The fact that the medicine's effectiveness may vary is often commented on at the end of the ritual: if no fights break out, no accidents occur and everything goes smoothly, people say that the *fanintsina* was good (*soa*) and strong (*mahery*).

The root of the term *fanintsina* is *nintsy*, which means 'cold'. When I asked whether *fanintsina* is meant to keep people 'cool', my friends would explain that *fanintsina* is meant to prevent fights among the participants and to counter people being silly (*adaladala*) when they drink too much rum. Hence, large amounts of *fanintsina* are sprayed over the crowd when the dancing and singing gets too excited or when arguments between drunk men flare up. *Fanintsina* is also used by the 'masters of the work' just before they leave for the cemetery. Everyone – man, woman and child – must get their share; following the diviner's instructions, people either sip the medicine a set number of times or smooth their hair back with it, or do both. The ancestors also get a share of *fanintsina* when the *hazomanga* sprinkles it over their tomb to ensure that they behave well while the work is under way.

The *asa lolo*

The day when the work at the tombs takes place must begin with informing the ancestors. On one occasion the announcement was made first in the *hazomanga*'s house at the village and was then briefly repeated at the cemetery; but usually it was uttered only in front of the fence that had to be rebuilt. The main purpose of the announcement is to inform the ancestors about what will happen so they will not be surprised (*tsy hotseriky nareo*).[15] At the same time, the *hazomanga* asks the ancestors to recognize their descendants' merits for not forgetting them and for looking after them. Finally, the *hazomanga* asks the ancestors to protect the living as they approach the ancestors' home in order to dismantle it and build a new and better one.

Once a tape-recorder was taken to the cemetery to make the dancing 'riper'. The *hazomanga* was especially concerned that the ancestors should be given due warning, telling them that

they [the ancestors' descendants] are really happy because they have got this thing, this 'electrophone', a thing of whites; they're showing it to you because they're happy. We're informing you, the ancient *raza*, so that you won't be surprised and won't say: 'How is it that when these grandchildren, when these children get something, they don't remember us?' [As you can see] this is not true, because we are now calling you and informing you.[16]

The *hazomanga* was not worried that the ancestors might dislike the tape-recorder; rather, he was concerned that they might think that they had been forgotten and were being excluded from the living people's fun.

On arriving at the cemetery, the *hazomanga* sprinkles a few drops of *fanintsina* inside the tomb where the work is to be done. The old wood fence is dismantled and the men begin to discuss the building of the new one; they estimate how large a fence can be made with the number of available bricks and how to design holes in the walls so as to save on materials and make a larger or taller fence; they jot the figures down by scratching white marks on their skin with a twig. Most men just carry the building materials, for only a small number in the village (always the same individuals at each ritual I witnessed) have the necessary building skills and stay sober enough to raise a straight wall. Meantime, some young boys clear a shaded area under the trees, where the elderly and those who early on stop pretending to be of any use in the work can sit. Most men will eat their meal in the shade, whereas the few employed in building the fence tend to eat where they are, sitting on the top of the dead and leaning over the crosses.

The women's task is to help cook and distribute the meal. They usually arrive at the cemetery later than the men because they have to wait at the village for the women who, first thing in the morning, leave for the market to buy rice, meat, onions, tomatoes and *tsaka* (green, pungent leaves) for the communal repast. When the women accompanied by children arrive at the tombs carrying pots, buckets, plates, spoons and food, they clear an area and transform it into a kitchen. When the food is ready, the women dish out rice and meat on big plates, the number of spoons on each plate indicating how many people should eat out of each dish. The men, who are served first, often hide a spoon so as to increase their individual portions, and send a young boy over to the women to show that their plate is still full of rice but has no more meat or broth in it. The women give generous portions, but they also make sure that enough food is left for themselves. On one occasion, when the men were overly insistent in asking for more food, the women hid a small pot of meat and broth under a basket; when the men demanded more broth they were shown the big, nearly empty pot and were told to be content with what they had.

The food cooked at the cemetery is meant to make people full and should be good, tasty (the meat is cooked with onions, tomatoes and *tsaka*) and plentiful. At one *asa lolo*, the main attraction and source of amusement and laughter was a woman who, holding a spoon in each hand, stuffed herself with rice and meat, screwed up her eyes and made silly faces.

If food is an important element of the ritual, rum is essential. The work cannot be accomplished without rum because, as I was told, Malagasy people can work very hard but they need to be supplied with liquor. Although the 'masters of the work' are expected not to drink much before the work is finished, there will always be some members in the family, both men and women, who drink heavily from the start and get scolded by their 'wiser' relatives.

Much of the interaction between women and children on the one hand and men on the other concerns rum. In theory at least, the source of drink should be only one, a few plastic canisters supervised by a trustworthy man and kept where men sit and work. Only one bottle is passed around, and is refilled from time to time. The bottle tends to be monopolized by the men;

only rarely is a young boy sent to offer a round of drinks to the women. The latter complain strongly and make a great fuss over how much each of them gets when the bottle finally reaches them. After a while, however, those men who are too drunk to get more drink from the 'official' source come over to the women to beg for a little more, for everyone knows that the women always have a small supply hidden among their pots and buckets. For my family's *asa lolo*, the women's secret reserve was bought by the *hazomanga*'s wife with money I had contributed to a last-minute *cotisacion*; since the *hazomanga* was absent, his wife took the money without registering it among the official contributions, at the same time asking for my assent and complicity in this little bit of fun the women were going to have.

Having fun at the tombs is important. Although the Vezo say that they are not very good at making 'ripe' feasts, people do not find it hard to amuse themselves. Above all, they enjoy dancing, and they found that having a tape-recorder helped a lot. Their favourite dance is *minotsoky*, which consists of rotating and thrusting the pelvis back and forth, faster and faster, preferably against and in unison with someone else's. Its sexual overtones are too obvious to be dwelt upon, and partly for this reason, adults have few opportunities when dancing *minotsoky* is considered appropriate.[17] The *asa lolo* is one.

People stay at the cemetery, dancing and drinking, until the building of the fence is completed. After the meal, having cleared up and packed the cutlery and utensils brought from the village, the women have time to look more closely at the new fence together with the rest of the crowd. The few men still at work are pressed to join the dance, and the others dance next to them inside the fence. When the construction is finally over, the sand inside the fence is swept even and clean and the tools have been gathered together, someone asks for silence and attention. As the noise of the crowd slowly dies down, someone who is known to be a good orator gives a short speech. After announcing that he speaks in the *hazomanga*'s stead, he thanks the crowd for their contribution to the completion of such a 'big work' (*asa bevata io*); had it not been for their help the work could not have been successfully undertaken. *Ndrañahary* (the creator) is also thanked, for without *Ndrañahary*'s help people would not have been strong enough. There have been no obstacles to the work, everything has gone well and has been done well from morning to eve; there have been no fights or disagreements, only play and banter. Now it is time to disperse and return home (*dia ravo tsika zao holy*).

The crowd now breaks up and heads back to the village; some people are so drunk that they need help to do so, others have to be dragged back home.

Back at the village, all feasting, dancing and drinking must normally stop. On one occasion, however, things were not called off, the *hazomanga* himself encouraging people to look for new batteries for the tape-recorder and giving money to buy more rum; the crowd regrouped around his house. But later that evening people came to announce that a young man, a classificatory son of the *hazomanga*'s wife, had died of tetanus in Belo. Since both the *hazomanga* and his wife were too drunk to receive the messengers, the *hazomanga*'s eldest sister, who had disapproved of her brother's behaviour all along, forced the feast to an end: she took the batteries out of the tape-recorder and shouted that people were to return home, for things were now over (*fa vita*). In the aftermath of this incident, she found countless opportunities to recriminate over her brother's behaviour. That his wife had been unfit to listen to the announcement of the death of a son showed unmistakably how wrongly he had behaved. In particular, he had been unwise (*tsy mahihitsy*) in bringing back to the village what should have ended at the cemetery: 'once it's over it's over' (*lafa vita, fa vita*). In her view, it was no coincidence that the news of the boy's death had come when it had.

Let us briefly summarize the sequence of events of the *asa lolo*. The living, who are responsible for building nice tombs for the dead, must enter the cemetery to do so. Several precautions are taken to do it safely, by choosing a favourable day for the work and by using *fanintsina*. The ancestors must also be informed about what is going to happen to their 'home'; in addition, they are asked to protect the living who prove, by looking after them, their remembrance and care. Many people are invited to the *asa lolo*, more than are needed to carry out the work itself. When the men arrive at the cemetery, they dismantle the old wood fence and proceed to build a new concrete one; the women follow them a while later with food for the communal meal. People eat and enjoy large quantities of tasty food; there is plenty of rum. While the fence is being built, most people (in a state of lesser or greater drunkenness) dance around it and have fun. Once the work is completed, people are thanked for their help in undertaking such a 'big work' and everyone returns home. The ritual is over.

The core of the ritual occurs between the dismantling of the old fence and the completion of the new one. Having ensured that a favourable day has been chosen, that the ancestors have been informed and that the tomb has been sprinkled with *fanintsina*, when the fence is dismantled the living seemingly suspend all the caution, hesitance or reticence that they normally feel in coming into contact with the heat of the cemetery. They walk, dance, stamp their feet, drink and eat inside the tomb and over the corpses of the dead.

People are aware that this behaviour is 'surprising' (*mahatseriky*). Not only did they tell me that my friends abroad would be surprised to see pictures of the *asa lolo* and hear that the people I had lived with in Madagascar dance and eat inside the tombs; they also warn and exhort their own ancestors not to be surprised by this behaviour. Indeed, they often seemed as surprised themselves by what they did as they expected my friends and feared their ancestors would be.

The cause of the 'surprise' can be seen to be that the *asa lolo* upsets and temporarily destroys the normal distinction between the cemetery and the village, between the dead and the living. During the *asa lolo* the living bring within the bounds of the cemetery what is normally outside it. They take life, and with life they take breathing, cooking, eating, drinking, dancing and a large crowd of people. They invade the cemetery with life.

Although the ostensible reason for doing this is that the living must provide the dead with a new and clean house, by invading the cemetery the living also respond to the dead's desire to remember life. Thus, when the participants stamp their feet as hard as they can and dance erotic dances on top of the dead, they imagine that the dead underneath them enjoy the feast – indeed, if they did not, the living would be 'dead on the spot' (*maty sur place*). Similarly, they imagine that the dead like having the tape-recorder blast music over their heads for they desire to share in live people's activities and fun, and it is for this reason that the *hazomanga* made sure that they did not feel excluded. As long as the old fence is down and the new one has not been raised yet, the dead can also be tantalized with a glimpse of *filongoa*; for a brief lapse of time, their sight can extend once more to include *all* the people who participate in the work as their descendants.

But while the moment when the old, flimsy fence is dismantled marks for the dead the beginning of their spectacle of life, for the living it marks the beginning of an emotionally charged contiguity with the dead. When the fence is removed, no barrier is left to separate the living from the dead.[18] By taking down the barrier which marks the boundary between death and life, the dead are allowed to enjoy life and a sight of *filongoa*; at the same time and for the same reason, the living run the risk of 'enjoying' death and entering the 'single' *raza*. The living endure this frightening prospect because they hope that by pleasing the dead they will be left alone and will not be pursued by the dead people's longing for life. But they also actively respond to their proximity with death by devoting all energies to making themselves as alive as they possibly can.

During the *asa lolo*, what the living perform over the dead persons' bodies and inside their tomb is more a parody of life than a representation of its 'coolness'. Thus, for example, although live people in their village homes eat food that is as tasty and satisfying as that which is eaten around the tombs, they do not deliberately make fools of themselves by stuffing their mouths with two spoons and making comic faces. When people invade the cemetery, they seem to be doing something more than simply staging a spectacle of life for the dead: they exaggerate their liveliness, they overstate the fact that they are 'living people' (*olom-belo*) rather than dead. This fact is crucial. In the same way as Dadikoroko was proved dead by the contrast with the vitality enacted around her during her funeral (see above, pp. 119–22), during the *asa lolo* the living demonstrate that the ancestors are dead by contrasting the latter with their liveliness, at the moment when their customary distance and separation is temporarily transformed into frightening and 'surprising' proximity. When the living eat their food inside the tomb and stamp their feet over the corpses, the dead underneath are proved to be dead: they cannot partake in the meal, join in the dance, or respond to the rhythm of the music and to the provocations of *minotsoky*. They remain silent and motionless, listening to life filtering through the sand.

The spectacle of life for the dead and the near hysterical display of super-vitality by the living last only as long as it takes to complete the new fence. Then the living, carrying their pots, buckets and empty canisters, return home, to the 'real' coolness of their village. The dead are left behind inside a new, firmer and more permanent barrier, once again contained and constrained inside their 'single' *raza*.

The *asa lakroa*

Building the concrete fence is only the first stage of the work the living perform for the ancestors. It is followed by the cross ritual, in which all the wooden crosses inside one tomb – the tomb of 'one kind of people' (*raza raiky*) – are replaced with concrete crosses. The *asa lakroa* lasts longer, involves more people, costs more and is more elaborate than the building of the fence.

The ritual (see Fig. 4) lasts between five and seven days according to the diviner's instructions on favourable days. It starts when the crosses are moulded at the village (*manily lakroa*) by a small crowd which is invited to undertake the work and is fed by the organizers. On the following days, the names of the deceased are engraved on the crosses, the wood moulds are removed and the crosses are painted. On the afternoon before the day they

Fig. 4 The cross ritual

Day 1	Day 2	Day 3	Day 4	Day 5	Day 6
MANILY LAKROA				guests begin to gather	**ATERY AN-DOLO**
moulding of crosses at the village	crosses are left to dry	crosses are left to dry	wood moulds are removed	3 o'clock **MANANGA LAKROA**	processions carry crosses to the cemetery
		names are engraved on crosses	crosses are painted	crosses are raised	**FA VITA** ritual is over people disperse and return to village
				ENGA	
				contributions paid to 'masters of the work'	
				SAKAFO	
				communal meal	
NIGHT	NIGHT	NIGHT	NIGHT	NIGHT	
MIARITORY	**MIARITORY**	**MIARITORY**	**MIARITORY**	**MIARITORY FISA**	
wake with few people (only 'masters')	wake with few people (only 'masters')	wake with few people (only 'masters')	wake with a few more people ('masters' and friends)	wake and feast with huge crowd	

are carried to the cemetery, the crosses are raised (*mananga lakroa*); immediately after, the participants' contributions (*enga*) to the ritual are presented to the 'masters of the work'. In the meantime, women cook huge amounts of food for the crowd. Between the day when the crosses are first moulded and the day when they are removed from the village, wakes are held near them. To begin with, the wakes are held only by the 'masters of the work', but on the last night the wake becomes a major event that is meant to entertain a large crowd. At dawn of the final day the crosses are carried to the cemetery (*atery an-dolo*). The procession can either be very quiet and uneventful or frenzied and wild, according to the status of the dead person whose cross it is. When the crosses reach the cemetery and are placed inside the fence, the crowd is thanked and asked to go home. The ritual is over.

The work starts with the building of the crosses (*manily lakroa*). The building materials and tools are collected in advance next to the house that will provide the stage for the entire process before the crosses are carried to the cemetery. Although the crosses are usually built at the *hazomanga*'s house in virtue of his role as 'master of the crosses' (*tompon'lakroa*), other people can beg (*mangataky*) and obtain (*mahazo*) the cross or crosses[19] from him. In one instance, a son begged his half-brother (same father but different mothers) for his mother's cross. The *hazomanga* replied that had it been someone else, he would not have surrendered the cross, but that since the request came from someone who had been generated (*anaky naterany*) by the woman whose cross was being built, he would give his assent and his blessing.

The people invited to take part in the work arrive in a trickle early in the morning. Men and women gather in different areas near the house where they will perform their different tasks, the women cooking and the men building the crosses. Under the shade of an improvised awning, the men divide into small working groups, each of whom is responsible for making a wooden mould. Although I never followed the men's work closely, I overheard them discussing the crosses' plan and design. Shapes range from a traditional Latin cross to a diamond-shaped object with quite elaborate ornaments; sometimes bold and innovative designs are rejected because of their technical impracticality. The main consideration, however, is that the dead person's seniority be reflected in the shape and size of their cross. Children's crosses should be short, narrow and with few frills; the children's grandparents' and the parents' crosses must be much taller, wider and heavily decorated. The identification between the cross and the person it represents is made explicitly when the crosses are built, and we shall see in fact that the crosses *become* these people during the ritual, their size, weight and beauty re-creating the bodily presence of the dead among the living.

When people reach general agreement about the crosses' dimensions each party starts on its own work. Due to the limited number of tools available and the small number of skilled carpenters, most work is done rather confusedly by sharing out both tools and skills between the different groups. When the frames are finished, concrete is poured inside and is reinforced with metal rods. Although many more people are involved in this work compared with the building of the fence, just as in the *asa lolo* a large number of them gradually drop out of the task.

As usual, the women are in charge of cooking the meal. When those who have been to the market return with the ingredients, the other women begin to winnow rice, cut up meat, dice tomatoes and onions, and clean bunches of *tsaka*. Fires are lit and pots of rice and one with meat are lined up under the sun; women have their own awning to which they retreat after tending the fire and supervising the cooking. The cooked food is served to the men, who stop working, eat and send back their empty dishes. It is now the women's turn to be fed.

Once, owing to the late return of the women who had gone to the market, the crosses were almost finished by the time the meal was over, and most people dispersed immediately after eating. Another time things were better organized and the meal was served much earlier. A record-player had been set up under the men's awning and, after the meal, women and children began to dance; the men were clearly shy, and only a few of them danced following pressing invitations by some of the women.

Although rum is available, it is not provided in the same quantities as for the *asa lolo* and it would seem that no-one expects it to be plentiful. Once, when the crosses were being moulded at my family's *hazomanga*'s, I volunteered to buy some extra rum; later I was privately asked by one person to do so a second time. After this I realized that the 'wiser' members of my family had disapproved of my initiative, since they did not think it necessary for anyone to get drunk.

My impression during this first stage of the cross ritual was that work, food, dancing and rum were 'neutral' and no different from normal life. The reason for this is that the crosses are still unfinished and what they will become is still absent. The crosses are yet to be 'activated', they are yet to acquire the double imagery of dead bodies and live ancestors that I discuss below.

Once the crosses are ready, they are carefully moved to a central point of the yard east of the *hazomanga*'s house. They are lined up on the ground next to each other, with the senior person's cross to the north and the others ranked southwards in descending order of seniority. The point of the cross is always oriented eastwards and its base westwards, which is how dead bodies lie during funerals and inside the tombs. Sometimes a kind of protective fencing is built around the crosses with a few wooden poles and coconut palm branches; during the hottest hours of the day, canoe sails are raised as an awning so as to avoid the concrete cracking in the sun. After a day of drying, the names and, if known, the dates of birth and death are engraved on the crosses, preceded by French expressions like *ici gît*, *ici repose*. The inscriptions are made by a relative of the dead person, typically by young people known for their good calligraphy, and are not set off in a ritual manner.[20]

As far as I could understand, the choice of when the wood frames are to be removed is determined solely by the time it takes for the concrete to dry thoroughly. Although no formal gathering is called for this occasion, all the family members try to be present when the frames are removed and the operation's success or failure becomes manifest. If a part of a cross breaks or cracks, this is interpreted as a sign that the deceased is unhappy and angry about the living people's doings (*hadisoa*). In the case of a woman whose body was 'begged' by her husband and was then granted to her children (see above, p. 96), one of her cross's decorations broke off. Her father and brothers, who were all extant, had previously expressed their discontent for the fact that the woman's husband had taken more than fifteen years to build the concrete cross for her, and the crack in the cross (which was later carefully repaired) demonstrated to the onlookers that the woman herself was also unhappy about the delay.[21]

After the frames have been removed, the crosses are given two coats of paint: front and back white, the sides a light blue or green, the lettering in black. While they stay at the village the crosses will thus be shiny, bright and clean; some will loose much of their paint during 'ripe' processions on the way to the tombs, when they will get covered with dirty hand-prints. If there is any fresh paint left over, the cross may be given a quick coat as it stands inside the tomb; otherwise it is left as it is. Although people complain that, as with everything else they buy, the quality of the paint has deteriorated while increasing in price, they do not seem to mind about the cross's appearance at the tombs, nor do they think the dead mind either – probably because the dead are more interested in the dancing and are prepared to put up with cheap paint that does not dry properly and peels off too easily.

When the paint is dry the crosses are left lying on the sand; the fencing built to protect them when the concrete was still soft and the paint wet is dismantled. Everything is ready for the final stage of the ritual.

At three o'clock in the afternoon of the day indicated by the diviner, the 'crosses are raised' (*mananga lakroa*) in descending order of seniority to a standing position with the help of a wooden framework built previously for this purpose behind and east of the crosses themselves; the side of the cross bearing the dead person's name faces westwards. This operation is performed by men. A small crowd gathers in a semi-circle around the crosses as they are raised up; when they are all standing they begin to sing church hymns.

The raising of the crosses arouses intense emotions among the onlookers. The people most closely related to the persons represented by the crosses are often moved to tears; if this occurs, they will immediately be exhorted to stop. As the cross of the woman who had died giving birth to her eleventh child was raised, more than fifteen years after her death, her children were visibly moved. The woman's husband later explained to me that raising dead people's crosses in this way is a 'very good thing' (*raha soa mare*) for two reasons: first, because people who were unable to get to the funeral in time – who 'did not catch the corpse' (*tsy tsatsy ny faty*) – can compensate for this by seeing the dead person's cross; second, because the children who have not known their mother in life now have the opportunity of seeing her (*farany fa hitan-drozy nenin-drozy*, 'at last they see their mother').

The reasons this man gave that render the cross ritual a good thing (*mahasoa azy*) indicate that the ritual rests on a fundamental paradox. The first justification implies that the ritual re-enacts the funeral; in this context, the cross is a substitute for the corpse. The second justification, however, is that the children see not their mother's corpse but their mother (*nenin-drozy*). In other words, the man was stating that the cross not only substitutes the woman's *dead body*, but also recalls her presence as a living *person*. This paradox is expressed in the process of raising the crosses from a flat to a vertical position. Lying flat on the sand, the crosses are substitutes of dead bodies; as such, it would make little sense to raise them from that position. By raising them to a standing position, they and those they represent are brought back to life: hence the emotionally charged atmosphere among their living kin.

The dimension of life incorporated in the crosses is crucial to the cross ritual's general understanding. Two seemingly incompatible performances are going on at the same time: the dead are brought back to life, and their funeral is re-enacted with a mock corpse. One reading of this is that the

Plate 4 The raising of the crosses (*mananga lakroa*)

living can be moved to perform mock funerals for mock corpses only if they have first re-created the image of live bodies and lively lives; the case of *Be-nono* (the cross with concrete breasts) which I discuss below lends support to this interpretation. A second, complementary reading is that the contrasting imagery conveyed by the cross – both live ancestor and mock corpse – accommodates the contrasting desires of the dead and the living. Whereas the dead are given an opportunity to savour and remember life as part of the service they expect from the living, this opportunity is granted by re-enacting a funeral which ends, as all funerals do, with the dead within their tombs and the living in the village.

Before developing these ideas any further, however, let us briefly return to the course of events that follow the raising of the crosses. Through a description of the wake and of the processions which convey the crosses to the cemetery, we shall get a clearer understanding of how the dual, conflicting imagery of the cross is expressed and confronted.

After the crosses have been raised, the onlookers present their contributions to the 'masters of the work'. The *hazomanga* and one or two other senior men, usually his brothers, sit in his house, while small parties of men (women are seldom included) queue up outside waiting for their turn. As one group leaves, another asks for permission to enter and is invited inside. The visitors sit down, chat a few moments about the weather or about their journey; then, with a sudden change in his tone of voice, the senior visitor hands an envelope with some money to the *hazomanga*, who receives it with thanks. After some further small talk, the group leaves and another one comes in. A deep sense of boredom transpires from the entire procedure.

As soon as one lot of visitors leaves the house, the envelope is opened, the money is counted and the sum is written down in a notebook together with the donor's name. Contributions can vary considerably, from a minimum of 500 or 1000 FMG to sums in the range of 20,000–30,000 FMG. *Enga* can also be in kind: a head of cattle, one or more canisters of rum, or one or more cases of beer. Their value differs considerably,[22] but they share the manner in which they are given to the 'masters of the work'.

The giving of *enga* in kind gives rise to a frenzied procession, similar to the bull-fights that occur during funerals of old people. If the *enga* is an animal, it is forced to stage a mock bull-fight with a long rope tied securely around its horns, while the crowd runs, dances, sings, claps, laughs, shouts and screams around it. If the *enga* is a case of beer or a jerrycan of rum, it is secured to a pole and is carried by an excited group of youngsters who will also act out mock bull charges and feints against the crowd. This game will begin at some distance from the house where the *hazomanga* is receiving the *enga* and will make long detours before finally reaching its destination. To begin with, the procession includes only the *enga*'s contributors, but soon more and more people (including many of the 'masters of the work') are drawn into it. As the crowd approaches the *hazomanga*'s house and the crosses, a leading member of the group presenting the *enga* is borne in triumph waving two sticks with paper notes stuck on them; this money is also part of the *enga*.

Who contributes what and how much plays an important role in defining relationships among the living. In the context of this discussion, it is important to note that the moment when the *enga* are handed over establishes the distinction between the 'masters of the work' and the rest of the crowd. I pointed out earlier the divisiveness of this distinction, which is forced on the living by the work they perform for the dead. Through this distinction the 'masters of the work' constitute themselves as the 'kind' of people who will be buried in one tomb and will join the same *raza*, and contrast themselves with the people who will be excluded from that tomb and *raza*. By paying *enga* participants in the ritual differentiate themselves from the 'masters of the work' who contributed instead to the *cotisacion*. The people who pay *enga* are further distinguished by the fact that the *enga* in kind are customarily paid by the 'masters of the work's' in-laws ('sons-in-law', *vinanto*, and 'fathers-in-law', *rafoza*). As was discussed above (see pp. 69–70), this is a very delicate moment in the relations between wife-givers and wife-takers; and although the end result is equality ('no-one is below, no-one is above'), the actual handing over of the *enga* expresses in an acute, even aggressive form the (contextual) hierarchy between the two sides.

The aggressiveness and divisiveness that are experienced by the living are concealed from the sight of the dead. The *enga* in kind, which for the living are the most divisive kind of offering, are those the dead who are being brought back to life are imagined to enjoy most, for the mock bull-fights enacted for the *enga* in kind are the first act in the spectacle of life that the dead are there to receive. The divisiveness experienced by the living is transformed into a loud and irresistible occasion to sing, dance and to parade in front of the crosses a crowd of undifferentiated people which includes even the 'masters of the work'. Thus, while the living experience differentiation because of the dead, it is to fulfil the dead's desire to be brought back to life that the divisiveness that the dead and the *raza* momentarily impose on life must be concealed from their sight.

While the *enga* are being handed over, the women begin to cook large quantities of rice and meat. Although the 'masters of the work' achieve fame through lavish consumption, the success of the occasion is shared by all the participants through their contribution of *enga*; the sharing of the food neutralizes the distinction between the 'masters' and the rest. By the time the food has been distributed the paying of the *enga* is over. The distinctions among the living are no longer visible; standing erect in the middle of the crowd, the living-dead-as-crosses are able to enjoy the sight of what can be imagined to be an undifferentiated, undivided, immense crowd of descendants. It is this view over the living's *filongoa* that the dead miss from inside their tomb and their 'single' *raza*.

Each night, between the day when the crosses are moulded and the day they leave the village, wakes are held at the place where the crosses are kept. Except for the last night, only the 'masters of the work' are expected to attend; friends, neighbours and good singers are welcome to join, but no formal invitation is issued. The first days, people gather for the wake and pretend very hard that they are 'enduring the absence of sleep' (*miaritory*; see above, pp. 110–11). They sing a few songs, but the crowd soon falls silent; most people eventually tiptoe back home, leaving only a few to stay sleeping outdoors. However, activity picks up as the final wake approaches. The night before the last is usually a true wake, including the customary singing and a fairly generous distribution of rum. Finally, the last wake is a major social event involving a considerable crowd, far exceeding any funeral gathering. People coming to the wake have high expectations, for it is understood that the 'masters of the work' are responsible for providing a good night's entertainment, typically by distributing large quantities of rum and by renting a *baffle*, a huge tape-recorder fully equipped with screeching loudspeakers and a limited number of tapes.

Within the general context of the ritual, the cross wakes appear to be a replica of funeral wakes. Despite this similarity, which people freely recognize, the two events also differ fundamentally. Early in my fieldwork, I was warned never to take a recording of the singing at funerals but to wait to do so at the cross ritual, for whereas people at funerals are sad (*malahelo*) and it would therefore be improper (*tsy mety*) to record their voices and cries, people at the cross wakes are happy (*falifaly*) and thus it does not matter (*tsy mañahy*) if one records their songs. Despite this, however, and despite the presence of the *baffle* at the cross wake, I was reassured that 'people's singing doesn't change, it's just the same' (*fihiran' olo tsy miova, fa mitovy avao*) at the two types of wake.

What this implies, that the cross wake transforms the funerary wake into its opposite, a sad occasion into a happy one, is not in fact entirely accurate.

On the one hand, as we have seen, not all funerals are sad occasions. During the funerary wake for Dadikoroko (the old woman whose funeral moved people to happiness; see above, pp. 118–22), for example, I asked whether I could record the singing, clapping and yelling that accompanied the dances; after some thought, it was agreed that I could do so because the crowd was happy. On the other hand, not all cross wakes are happy events. In the same way that sadness and happiness during a funeral depend on the dead person's status, the mood that prevails during a cross wake depends on the status of the cross. This status is always intrinsically ambiguous.

At one level, the status of the cross is that of the dead person that the cross represents and personifies. At a more abstract level, the status of the cross derives from which of the cross's two images, of a live ancestor and of a corpse, the organizers and participants of the ritual wish or are asked to emphasize during the ritual itself. In order to understand how the choice between the two images is formulated, we must return to the final wake's entertainment and to the *baffle*.

During the months leading up to the cross ritual, my adoptive family held endless meetings to discuss, and often to argue about, the renting of the *baffle*. I soon grew tired of listening to the discussions; besides dreading the screech of the loudspeakers, I did not think that a night of Malagasy pop music at full blast could be regarded as a feature of note of the cross ritual. Only later did it occur to me that if so many meetings were being held to discuss the issue of the *baffle* there must have been something of interest about it. The renting of the *baffle* was highly controversial. Some people were opposed because they thought that it was too expensive, but this argument was curtly dismissed as a manifestation of stinginess. One woman's objections were rather more interesting. As the mother of the only child buried in the family tomb, she voiced the opinion that it was improper to have music and dancing when one of the crosses was that of a small child (*aja mbo kelikely*); since remembering her child made her sad (*malahelo*), she wanted people to sing hymns rather than dance during the wake. This objection was clearly taken seriously, and supporters of the *baffle* had to resort to the argument that a wake without music was in danger of being deserted. In the end, the family decided to rent the *baffle*, one of the brothers managed to get a bargain price for it, the crowd was large and the wake loud and successful.

On another occasion a similar argument to that of the child's mother met more understanding, possibly because four out of six crosses were for small children, and the wake was held without any music. As a result, the participants complained loudly of boredom and lack of rum; but although the crowd was listless, the singing lasted the whole night. The reasons for holding such a quiet wake were similar to those adduced by the woman in my first example. On this occasion, the organizers chose to emphasize the second image of the cross representing the children's corpses, and participants in the cross wake were accordingly asked to perform a *de facto* funerary wake.

Yet this is only one side of the story. The other image of the cross, that of a live ancestor, was allowed to take shape in a second, 'alternative' wake held alongside the 'official' one I just described. The protagonist of this alternative wake was a cross representing an old woman. Her name inscribed on the cross was Nentiko, but throughout the ritual she was called *Be-nono* (big breasts), for the cross was adorned with concrete breasts, the size of the halved coconut shell with which they had been shaped, with the areola carefully painted black and the nipples red.[23]

The final wake was to be held on Friday, and the formal invitation to it was sent out late on Thursday afternoon. Since it was rumoured that the Friday wake would be a quiet affair, with no music and dancing, some friends suggested that if I wanted to see a 'ripe' wake I should go to the Thursday wake and avoid the one on Friday. That Thursday night far more people than is customary for a penultimate wake gathered at the house where the crosses were. They had come to have fun with *Be-nono*.

Because it was only the eve of the final wake, there was no Petromax lamp lighting the yard; people gathered in the darkness and appeared to be restless as they waited for something to happen. Eventually some women began to sing church hymns, and this seemed to break the ice. Groups of young men began to dance *gañaky* among themselves (see above, p. 119), but as soon as some women started a dance of *minotsoky*, they broke off to join them. Some of the refrains (*antsa*) that accompanied the dances were invented for the occasion and were dedicated to *Be-nono*. The dancing, singing and drinking continued the whole night.

Although the crosses were still in a corner of the yard and would be moved to a more central position only the following day, that Thursday night people found them already standing. This fact is very significant. I suggested previously that crosses lying flat on the sand represent the dead corpses, whereas by raising them the dead person is brought back to life; consequently, had *Be-nono* still been lying on the sand on the eve of the final wake, she would have missed the dances and singing in her honour. By raising the crosses a day earlier, furthermore, the organizers divided the wake (if not the entire ritual) into two separate events, one centred on *Be-nono* and the other centred on the children's crosses. On this occasion, the duality of the cross's imagery was formally and explicitly acted out by confining the two contrasting images, that of a live ancestor and that of a corpse, to two separate wakes – one in which people were asked to be sad, and the other in which they were expected to have fun.

Carrying *Be-nono* to the cemetery was the most frenzied part of the ritual. I explained above how the wake on the final night had been very quiet and boring, entirely devoted to the crosses of small children. At about two o'clock in the morning, however, it was rumoured that *Be-nono* might be taken away to the sand hills just west of the village in order to have some 'ripe' celebrations. Although this expedition was forbidden by the *hazomanga*, who feared that people might get too excited and drunk and that 'big trouble' (*istoara bevata*) might ensue in the dark, he granted that *Be-nono* be carried to the sand hills at dawn.

At the break of dawn *Be-nono* was taken away. She left the courtyard heading westwards in the opposite direction to that of the cemetery. A smallish crowd accompanied her, mainly young men, children and a few women, said to be in a joking relation (*ampiziva*) with the 'masters of the work', hence with Nentiko too; among people linked by this relationship everything is allowed and everything must be endured. Initially at least, only these people were thought to dare (*mahasaky*) taking Nentiko on her eventful tour, suggesting that the treatment Nentiko was going to receive raised a certain degree of apprehension and fear;[24] once the initiative was taken by the *ampiziva*, however, many more people joined in, including some of the 'masters of the work' and, as we shall see, including Nentiko herself who was thought to have taken over the living to have them do what she used to like when she was alive.

Be-nono's procession was frenzied from the start, and became increasingly so each time the men carrying the cross on a run stopped and stuck *Be-nono* in the sand: with the crowd pressing around them, they danced *minotsoky* with her, rubbing themselves against her and tweaking her nipples. When *Be-nono* reached the top of the hill, the crowd stopped. The dancing went on, but something was clearly missing. The crowd had kidnapped *Be-nono* and was waiting for ransom in the form of rum. Eventually, one of the *hazomanga*'s younger brothers came with a group of relatives to rescue the cross and the crowd. He came balancing a bottle of rum on his head in triumph. The first nip of rum was poured over the cross's breasts; everyone else then had a share. *Be-nono* could then return to the village and start her long and tortuous journey to the cemetery accompanied by what was now a very large crowd of people.

If one allows for the difference between a cross and a coffin, *Be-nono*'s procession to the tombs was analogous to that of Dadikoroko's corpse (see above, pp. 120–1).[25] *Be-nono*'s journey progressed as a series of spurts and sharp jolts; each stop was the pretext for more rum and for a new round of erotic dances and performances. As the cross moved on, the carriers battled for *Be-nono*, pushing and pulling for leverage and a hold.

Those people who had carried the children's crosses in quiet, straight and uninterrupted procession to the tombs had to wait for a long time before *Be-nono* finally arrived. After a few final stops at the edge of the cemetery, *Be-nono* moved close to her fence and in a last, frantic run was delivered to her tomb. The young men who took her inside the fence to stick her upright in the sand gave her a final go of *minotsoky* and some more rum. The *hazomanga* then asked them to leave. The usual thanksgiving speech praised the crowd because no fights or accidents had occurred and exhorted it to return home peacefully and quietly. The ritual was declared over. As the living headed back home, *Be-nono* and the other crosses were left behind inside their fence.

A few days after the ritual was concluded, I asked the *hazomanga* and his wife who had organized it about the 'meaning' (*ino dikany?*) of the breasts on Nentiko's cross. They answered that Nentiko was a 'great-grandparent' (*dady-be*) who had 'brought up many people' (*namelo olo maro ie*); she had had many children, grandchildren and great-grandchildren; the breasts were a 'playful joke' (*kisaky*).[26] When I asked whether Nentiko had actually had big breasts, they laughed and told me that that was beside the point. So, what was the point?

We saw earlier that the dead feel a longing for the living. I argued above that during the *asa lolo* the living respond to this longing by bringing life into the cemetery. In the course of the cross ritual, in a different spatial context and through different ritual devices, the living similarly stage for the dead a spectacle of the life they have lost but still long for. In Nentiko's case, her grandchildren and great-grandchildren decided that she deserved a special treatment, because she had been such a wonderful parent. And so, on the cross that was to bring Nentiko back to life, they stuck concrete breasts, which represented Nentiko as the prolific source and support of many descendants. While it is hard to surmise what Nentiko would have thought of the breasts herself, it is easy to say what effect they had on the crowd that surrounded her. Like the pop music that usually accompanies a final wake, *Be-nono*'s breasts gave additional zest to the dances, clapping and inebriation, and became the main focus of attraction for the large crowd that closed in around the cross. This crowd is what Nentiko longs for

Plate 5 *Be-nono*, the breasted cross, has finally been delivered inside her fence

inside her fence: it is the life that she left behind her when she died, and which has since then reproduced, increased and multiplied itself. The breasts were a means, a highly successful one, of offering Nentiko a particularly pleasurable sight of life and of the undividedness of *filongoa*.

Yet in the end, after a long, wild night of amusement, Nentiko's cross was taken out of the village and away from life; Nentiko was carried to the cemetery and back into her fence. After opening a window on life in the village, that window was shut. The spectacle of life reverted to a funeral in which Nentiko was proved once more to be dead, and *Be-nono*'s concrete breasts were proved to be only a 'playful joke'.

Nentiko was thought to have enjoyed the feast and to be happy as a result; the living had visibly enjoyed it too. We can now see that the force of this ritual lies in the fact that it draws together the dead and the living, pleasing the former without forcing the latter to feel the fear raised by the *asa lolo*. Indeed, we can assume that the cross ritual makes the ancestors even happier, for instead of hearing the display of life from inside their tomb, they are brought back to life right inside the village where they can dance with the living; the living in turn are less fearful, because they dance in the village with concrete crosses rather than at the tombs over the bodies of the dead.[27]

The dead are so involved in the celebration that they direct the living people's performance, their dancing, running and singing. In response to my admiration for the crowd's behaviour, I would be told that the dead person whose cross was being carried had liked to dance and drink and that she had been very good at both. I mentioned in chapter 7 that Dadikoroko also had been a very good dancer in her lifetime and that she had been a 'great devil'. When her cross left the courtyard on its journey towards the cemetery, people found it almost impossible to carry. Because of its unusually large size, the cross had been tied to a wooden stretcher to allow more people to carry it, but the poles kept breaking and the ropes coming loose. Large amounts of medicine (*fanintsina*) were sprinkled on the crowd and cross. Yet even after the stretcher had been repaired the procession did not increase its pace, obstinately making detours, pushing and tugging the stretcher, and stopping for more rum. I was told with great satisfaction that all these delays went to prove what a 'great devil' Dadikoroko had been and still was (*devoly be ie*).

If the ancestors are able both to affect and to enjoy the dancing, drinking and delivery of their cross to the cemetery, it remains to be explained how the living manage to bring their spectacle of life to an end by fencing the crosses inside the tomb and abandoning the dead in the cemetery. To do this, we must return to the dual image of the cross and to the presence within the same ritual of crosses that project different images.

I have argued above that the cross projects two images, that of a corpse and that of an ancestor brought back to life. The image and the feeling of life first take shape when the cross is raised up and people see the person the cross represents; and then when people are taken over by the deceased who makes them dance, run and drink with its cross. The image of the corpse is established instead by means of the ritual's structure, which follows step by step the structure of a funeral; right from the start, when the crosses first appear in the village and people around them begin to 'endure the absence of sleep', the crosses are treated as substitutes of dead bodies.

In the example I just recalled, these two images were separated into two distinct events. Despite this separation, the two events reacted on each other. On the one hand, the devices whereby *Be-nono* was endowed with life also established, by contrast, the image of death which upheld the performance of her and of the other crosses' mock funeral; as noted earlier, people must first be able to imagine that a concrete cross is a live person before they can be moved to perform a mock funeral for it. On the other hand, the presence of the children's crosses and the special emphasis on their representation of corpses forced *Be-nono* to her final destination in the tomb. *Be-nono* could enjoy such an extreme degree of vitality, because the representation of death through the children's crosses ensured that Nentiko be brought back to life *in the context of a funeral*, thus ultimately ensuring that the cross be delivered to Nentiko's tomb and her life be brought to an end. Although there exists no doubt in people's minds that a cross's only destination is inside the tomb, the cross ritual plays on the possibility of bringing the dead back to the village and to life, and at the same time establishes a device for sending, or returning, the dead and their crosses to where they belong.

While the image of the cross as a mock corpse and the overall structure of the ritual are important features for prescribing the crosses' final destination, one should also bear in mind that the procession leading *Be-nono* (or the cross of any old person such as Dadikoroko) to the cemetery was strikingly similar to the *funerary* procession for old people. I suggested this similarity above, but I wish to add a few comments.

Although it is undoubtedly more comfortable, both physically and emotionally, for the living to carry a piece of concrete than a decomposing corpse,[28] the dead person whose cross is carried in triumph years after her death passes through a very similar experience to that which she had when she left the village for the cemetery the first time. As argued in chapter 7, the joyful funeral held for old people is meant to celebrate their life, rather than their death; the living celebrate the fact that the dead person has lived long enough to see a great growth in the number of descendants, generation after generation. In the course of the cross ritual, these ancestors – the old people – are offered a new, updated vision of the life they left behind when they died, a life that has increased and multiplied ever since their death. In order to please the ancestors, as many people as possible must attend the wake and participate actively in the procession (it is often pointed out that far more people attend the cross ritual than the funeral). The great, wild crowd surrounding Nentiko's and Dadikoroko's crosses proved that both of them had been and are still 'great-grandparents', who gave life to many descendants whose number keeps expanding. It becomes clear then why the crosses of dead children receive such a different treatment. If the cross ritual is an occasion for the dead to remember life, children have seen too little to have anything to long for and to want to remember – they can thus be carried fast, with little fuss and excitement, straight into their tomb.

The analysis of the cross ritual has shown how the ancestors are offered an opportunity to remember and to enjoy life, and how they inevitably get pushed back and are abandoned, lifeless, in their tombs at the cemetery. The cross ritual has the same plot as the *asa lolo*, except that the spatial opposition within which the plot unfolds is inverted. In the *asa lolo*, the living bring the village into the cemetery, and then leave taking life back with them; the ancestors are spectators who can play only a limited role as active participants, for at most, they hear the stamping of feet above their dead bodies. In the cross ritual, the ancestors return to the village, stand upright, dance, run and drink rum; they take over the living so that they can do what they used to like as living people. Both rituals respond to the longing that the dead feel for life, but in doing so they also create the very source of this longing: they realize descent and the division that descent engenders among the dead, they create the 'single' *raza*. Both rituals act out the contrast between life and death, between the village and the cemetery, between *filongoa* and the *raza*. Both rituals provide the same solution, that the two worlds that are brought together for a while ultimately be kept separate.

The solution, however, is not conclusive. The longing of the dead for life is never fully and permanently appeased; it could be so only if the rituals, instead of a 'playful joke', actually gave life back to the dead. It is the dead's lifelessness and the divisions established by the rituals which endlessly draw the dead back to the living.

9

Conclusion

In this book I have explored the identity of the Vezo, a group which defines itself as 'people who struggle with the sea and live on the coast' (*olo mitolo rano, olo mipetsaky andriaky*). In order to study Vezo-ness, I have not looked at who the Vezo are, but rather I have immersed myself and the reader in the ways of doing that render people Vezo. I have described men, women and children becoming Vezo by sailing skilfully, by selling fish for a profit, or by carrying the canoe paddle in a certain way on their shoulder; I have described people losing their Vezo-ness (and thus becoming Masikoro) by making a blunder while they change the position of the canoe masts, by choking on a crab's heart, or by feeling sick on a sailing expedition.

I have shown how Vezo-ness is experienced contextually as an activity, rather than inherently as a state of being: people 'are' Vezo when they perform Vezo-ness. Vezo-ness is an identity that binds people to the present, the only temporal dimension in which a person can 'be' Vezo by acting Vezo. The past, by contrast, does not determine what a person 'is' at any point in time. The past does not turn into 'history' – a chain of events that explain how the present has come to be what it is – for it is constantly shed as people move from one context to another, from one moment to the next. We have seen some of the manners whereby the Vezo deny that the present is determined by the past: by construing the process of learning Vezo-ness as a sharp and easy 'jump' from a state of not-yet-knowing to a state of full knowledge; by claiming to be 'unwise' and prone to be surprised in the pursuit of their livelihood; by describing themselves as 'soft' people who dislike ties and bonds.

Vezo-ness shapes both in mind and flesh, for it inscribes the body with the 'signs that one is Vezo' (*famantaram-Bezo*). Yet this shape and its signs remain contingent on the performance of Vezo-ness in the present: if one stops acting, one stops being shaped. Neither in mind nor in flesh is Vezo-ness a lasting and determining feature of the person. Thus the Vezo person appears transparent, lacking an inherent, permanent core within.

A similar transparency is manifest in Vezo kinship (*filongoa*). *Filongoa* is a field of innumerable relations of kinship embodied simultaneously by the same person. Here, the past is remembered as the source of many alternative histories (paths of ascendancy) through which people come to be related to one another in the present. In *filongoa*, all these histories are equally important, for they all serve to establish to whom one is related, rather than to determine what kind of person one is. The past, in other words, does not fix the person into an identity that lasts through time; rather, it provides the person with relations that expand and branch out in all directions, and which can all be enacted in different contexts and at different times. In its indeterminacy, *filongoa* is analogous to Vezo-ness; it is a domain of kinship which preserves and enhances the transparency of the Vezo person.

Having come this far in the study of Vezo-ness, we encountered a different kind of identity; to use the Vezo's idiom, we saw 'kindedness' protruding out of 'un-kindedness'. Thus, whereas the Vezo state that they are 'not a kind of people' (*Vezo tsy karazan'olo*), or in other words, that their identity is not determined by descent, I also found that they *are* divided into kinds of people (*raza*) constituted through unilineal descent. *Raza* identity is the opposite of Vezo-ness: it is a state of being which lasts unchanged through time; it is inherent in the person and cannot be acquired through practice; it does not fade away, like the marks of Vezo-ness on the body; it provides the person with only one kind of history that is divisive and exclusive.

How can these two seemingly opposite, indeed incompatible principles of identity – 'kindedness' and 'un-kindedness' – co-exist? My answer to this question came in the second part of the book, which followed the Vezo's efforts to keep the dead separate from the living. The Vezo act to raise a barrier (*hefitsy*) dividing (*miavaky*) two different types of existence, two utterly different types of person, and two different temporalities: on one side, there are people who breathe and move, are cool and soft, and enjoy the undividedness of *filongoa*; on the other, there are the dead, who are breathless (*tsy misy hay*), hot (*mafana*), bad-tempered, wild and aggressive (*masiake*), and are divided into 'kinds' (*raza*) by the solid walls of the tombs. 'Un-kindedness' exists on the side where life unfolds in the present; whereas 'kindedness' prevails only on the other side, in the fixity of death which lies only in the future. This barrier between life and death, between 'coolness' and 'hotness', between the village and the cemetery, allows 'un-kindedness' and 'kindedness' to be kept separate and *not* to co-exist: 'the dead and the living are not together, they are not the same' (*ny maty ny velo tsy miaraky, tsy mitovy*).

The transition from life to death, from the coolness of the village to the heat of the cemetery, effects a loss of identity: the dead 'are' not, because they 'act' not. *The dead are not and cannot be Vezo*, because they can no longer 'be' what they did (as living) in the present. They no longer act in the present and are thus outside time. They cannot be Vezo because their identity can no longer be contextually defined in time and space; they cannot be Vezo because their body can no longer take on the 'signs that one is Vezo'; the signs inscribed in their flesh have long disappeared as their body, which feels and hears nothing, turns into dry bones. Breathless and motionless, the dead are fixed both in time and space.

The dead cannot share the identity of the living because they can no longer disregard the past and deny its determination; outside Vezo-ness, the past – a single and individuating history provided by descent – is their only source of identity. In order to *be*, the dead must be 'kinded', because for them *raza* membership has become the only available means to be 'made aware of who and what they are as persons' (Fortes 1987: 281): members of descent groups that have a fixed centre and a fixed locus, that always remain the same and which embody both the past and the future (cf. Fortes 1970: 41). Thus, when the living place the dead inside their divisive tombs, they *create* an identity for them: a form of individuation through descent.

If the dead must be 'kinded' because they cannot be Vezo, the Vezo cannot be dead, because they are 'un-kinded'. This is to say that while Vezo identity shapes people's lives, it cannot cope with their deaths. Vezo-ness ends when people stop acting, when they stop being surprised in a world that appears to have no past and no future, when they lose the ability to avoid 'ties and bonds' by transforming the past or by fleeing from it. The fixity of death challenges the identity of the living Vezo, by setting the limits beyond which their 'un-kindedness' must be transformed into 'kindedness'.

By separating life from death, the Vezo preserve their 'un-kindedness', while at the same time through 'kindedness' they provide an identity to the dead. The barrier they raise marks a discontinuity: once on the other side, the dead become so different that they cease to be human (*lolo reo tsy olo fa biby*, 'they aren't people, they are "animals"'), and cease also to be relatives of the living (*tsy longon' olom-belo*). It is of course the case that if the barrier were impermeable and these statements were held to be unconditionally true, the Vezo would be effectively denying that the living and the dead are the same people; they would be denying that 'un-kinded' people die, and that the dead, now 'kinded', were once Vezo. They would similarly deny that the people lying in the cemetery divided into 'single' *raza* are also the eight *raza*, the eight great-grandparents, through whom the living trace their networks of *filongoa*. In sum, if the Vezo conceived of the barrier as impassable they would thereby deny the continuity between life and death, between the past and the present, between 'un-kindedness' and 'kindedness'.

Needless to say, the barrier is not entirely impermeable. Although the Vezo stress separation and otherness between the two sides, they also acknowledge their continuity and sameness; they recognize that the living are affected by death and by 'kindedness', just as the dead are affected by life and by 'un-kindedness'. I have described the effect that death has on the living with the image of a shadow: a shadow that seeps through the barrier erected between life and death, between the village and the cemetery, between coolness and hotness. This is the shadow of death over life, that which the 'single' *raza* casts over the living in anticipation and preparation of their death. In the ritual of *soro*, in the body of the *hazomanga*, in the acts of the 'masters of the work', death takes hold of the living and transforms them into members of *one raza*, future occupants of *one* tomb. The effect of death, however, is only transient, and as superficial as the darkness cast by a shadow: *raza* membership remains imminent, as yet unrealized; descent is something in the future, not a permanent and fixed state of being in the present.

The same image can be applied to the effect of life on the dead, as the shadow of life over death seeping through the barrier that divides them. Although far from the village and its inhabitants, the dead are not indifferent to life; they still feel a strong longing from within the cemetery for their living descendants, for the fun and pleasure they had in their lifetime, and for the extended view of *filongoa* which is a prerogative of the living and is lost to the dead. To appease their longing, the dead demand to be remembered and looked after by the living; they demand to be brought back to life from time to time, and to be entertained with music, dance and drink amidst a large and undifferentiated crowd of descendants. But like the effect that death has over the living, the effect of life over the dead is transient: like a shadow, life remains out of the dead's reach. The mortuary rituals can give the dead a taste of life, of the coolness of the village, and of the undifferentiation of *filongoa*; but the dead are doomed to further, unsated longing as soon as they are left once more alone inside and behind the solid, concrete walls of their tombs.

The existence of the shadows of death over life and of life over death marks a continuity between the identity of the living and the identity of the dead. Although the Vezo deny it, they are also forced to recognize this continuity by the undisputable fact that living people die, and that the dead were once alive; that the living were generated by those who are now dead; and that the past does impinge on the present, and the present on the future. It is by labouring to establish the discontinuity that the living Vezo also acknowledge that a continuity exists: the one is achieved dialectically by denying the other.

The analysis of Vezo 'un-kindedness' reveals a person – a living person (*olom-belo*) – undergoing a constant process of making and becoming; an identity that is performative, a way of doing that is learnt and acquired; and a form of kinship which creates undifferentiated and expanding networks of relatedness that are enacted contextually in the present. The analysis of 'kindedness', on the other hand, reveals a person – a person of the past who is dead (*olo taloha fa nimaty*) – which no longer acts, hence is no longer Vezo; an identity that is fixed through time, as an unchangeable and intrinsic state of being; and a type of kinship which provides the person with one, individuating history that attaches its identity to the past.

The analytical challenge has been to account, in this particular ethnographic context, for the articulation of these two opposed configurations of the person, of these two contradictory principles of identity, of these two different forms of relatedness between people. In more general terms, the challenge has been to bring together two of anthropology's 'localizing strategies', namely 'regional concerns in ethnographic writing' (see Fardon 1990). Written from a purely Austronesian perspective, the book's main concern would have been to show how the Vezo, through their 'un-kindedness', are part of a world where persons and groups are fluid and boundless, and where identities are non-primordialist and non-essentialist; written from a purely African perspective, the main concern would have been instead to show how, through their 'kindedness', the Vezo are part of a world where the person is determined by membership of bounded and divisive descent groups (see Fox 1987). In more 'traditional' terms, the issue would have been to prove that Vezo kinship is either predominantly cognatic or predominantly agnatic (see Southall 1986: 417).

To a certain extent, the distinction between Austronesian and African ethnographic concerns could seem to reflect the separation that the Vezo endeavour to establish between themselves and the dead, the discontinuity between 'un-kindedness' and 'kindedness', between the undifferentiation of *filongoa* and the divisiveness of the 'single' *raza*. The division of academic concerns, however, fails to render the continuity that exists between the indeterminacy of the living person and the determinacy of the dead, between the fluidity and malleability of Vezo-ness and the fixity of *raza* identity, between 'cognatic' kinship and unilineal descent. It fails, in other words, to reveal the complexity of a world in which the person is 'Austronesian' in the present and 'African' in the future; a world in which kinship is 'cognatic' among the living and is 'agnatic' among the dead; a world in which death casts a shadow over the living and life a shadow over the dead. The example of the Vezo suggests that the way to understand the complexities of this world is for Austronesian anthropology to be shadowed by African and African anthropology by Austronesian.

Notes

1 Introduction

1 Although this etymology may be technically mistaken, it is nonetheless significant for being employed by the Vezo to link their name to the canoe and to their activities in the sea. See Grandidier and Grandidier 1908–28, I:241 note 2, who note that the word 'vezo' means 'the people who paddle'. On this see also Poirier 1953:23; Faublée 1946:23; Faublée and Faublée 1950:432; Koechlin 1975:51.

2 Virtually all the authors who mention the Vezo define them as coastal fishing people. See Walen 1881–4:7, 12–13; Douliot 1893–6:119, 245; Marcuse 1914:39, 172; Petit 1930:26–7; Faublée 1946:23; Faublée and Faublée 1950:432–3; Dandouau and Chapus 1952:28; Battistini and Frère 1958:10; Condominas 1959:4–5; Deschamps 1960:153; Angot 1961:142, 145; Ottino 1963:279; Decary 1964:36 note 2, 53–4; Fauroux 1980:82. The only exception seems to be Noël 1843–4. For a more detailed analysis of the literature, see Astuti 1991.

3 'Ils ont seulement un genre de vie particulier', Decary 1964:54 note 2.

4 On the use of the Vezo/Masikoro distinction and its regional variations, see Lavondès 1967, Birkeli 1926 and Dina 1982.

5 For similar formulations of this point, cf. Decary 1964:36, 53–4; Douliot 1893–6:119; Grandidier and Grandidier 1908–28, I:214; Koechlin 1975:23–6. Cf. also Covell 1987 and especially Alvarez n.d., on the invention' of Malagasy ethnic groups to meet the needs of French colonial policies (the so-called 'politique des races', a precondition of which was the existence of discrete indigenous groups, whose leaders the French administration could use to gain control over the local population). For the problems involved in using these ethnic labels in Madagascar, see Southall 1971 and 1986 (on how to distinguish between common and differentiating features among Malagasy groups); Huntington 1973 (on varying degrees of discreteness of ethnic labels); Eggert 1981 and 1986 (on the Mahafaly); Lambek 1983 and 1992 (on negative definitions of group identities); Hurvitz 1986 (on the definition of 'embouchures' culture); Bloch in press (on the Zafimaniry).

6 One of the officially recognized 'ethnic groups' of Madagascar, occupying the western region between the Onilahy river to the south, and the island of Nosy Be to the north. The term Sakalava refers to the people who were subjects of the kingdoms established by the conquering Maroserana dynasty (and its various branches).

7 For a fuller discussion of this point, see Astuti in press a.

8 This is to suggest that the statement that the Vezo are *not* a kind of people should not be regarded as an instance of the widespread Malagasy practice of defining oneself by means of negation (recently discussed by Lambek 1992).

9 Marikandia 1991 is the first significant contribution on these issues.

10 'Fa Vezo tsy mana tompo, tsy mana tompo, fa añara ankapobe olo iaby. Ka ze mahatojo an'ny fila ty, Vezo lafa tia ny rano ty fa atao hoe Vezo. Tsy añ'olo raiky, zay tsy manan-tompo zay. Ny havezoa tsy añ'olo raiky, hoe iano raiky ro tompony. Aha! Zay olo iaby tompon' ny havezoa lafa tia azy manao azy.'

11 I estimated the adult population of Betania at the time of my stay at 335; I was told by the village head (*prezidan' fokonolo*) in Belo that the village numbered about 800 inhabitants.

2 Acting Vezo in the present

1 'Ndra iha zao lafa avy eto, hoe aha: madame io mitoa. Ha! maminta matetiky madame io, fa Vezo atoko: tsy fa Vezo iha? nefa vazaha baka lavitsy añy. Lafa maminta iha isanandro etoa: Ha! madame io Vezo, satsia fa mitolo rano, satsia fa mive laka, fa atao Vezo zay.'

2 'Hoatra zay laha misy Masikoro bakañy aminy faritany antety avy de mipetsaky eto a Betania ziska manambaly; jerevy fiveloman'olo eto tsy misy tanimbary raha tsy mandeha maminta, manarato, mandeha andriva. Farany ze mety hotongany velahiny reñy na rafozany anty amin'zao mandeha maminta añy; de eo miasa sainy aia atao amin'zao sy izao fandehany raha ty; kanefa raiamandreny tsy mahafantratra zany, tsy mahay amin'zay. Lasa amin'zao izy andesin' namany manahakan'zao manahakan'zao, farany mahay – manjary Vezo zany izy.'

3 'Aja kely kely mbo tsy azo atao Vezo, atao hoe anabezo. Reo zaza reo, io fianarandrozy, ao añaty rano ao, mianatsy mandaño reo, lafa miasa mandaño, miasa mandaño, mianatsy, lafa ie mahay mandaño, aha, fa mahasky rano zao, fa azo atao hoe Vezo.'

4 The outrigger canoe consists of a hull (*ain-daka*, lit. 'the breath of the canoe'), an outrigger (*fañary*), two booms (*varoña aloha, varoña afara*), a pole which lies parallel to and opposite the outrigger (*linga*), two masts (*tehy*) and a rectangular sail (*lay*). It is steered with a paddle called *five fañoria*. A medium-sized canoe is 7 m long and 0.65 m wide at its widest point; the two masts are 5 m long.

5 For other types of canoes, see Koechlin 1975:109; Ottino 1963:283; Faublée and Faublée 1950:438.

6 The tree's circumference is measured by embracing the trunk (*mañoho farafatse*). If the distance between the fingertips is more than two *zehy* (the

distance between thumb and forefinger) the trunk is considered suitable for building a canoe. The height of the tree is judged by sight and experience; no formal rules for measuring it exist.

7 The bottom half of the hull, which lies below the water-line, gradually gets waterlogged and rots; the upper part lasts much longer and is reused more than once as side-planking.

8 See also Koechlin 1975:73–86 and Faublée and Faublée 1950.

9 The felling of the *farafatse* is considered to be a difficult job (*raha sarotsy*, 'a difficult thing'; *asa bevata*, 'a big job'). For this reason, a number of prohibitions (*faly*) apply to the people involved. For example, neither the man who is cutting a tree in the forest nor his wife at the village can have sexual intercourse while the man is in the forest (on the other hand, if the pair are together in the forest they can have sex); a man whose wife is pregnant cannot fell a tree for a canoe, for the operation resembles that for preparing a coffin and would be inauspicious for the wife. If the felling is unsuccessful, the failure is not attributed to technical error or incompetence, but is viewed as a sign of worry or danger for the canoe owner's relatives, his wife or his ancestors. Faublée and Faublée (1950) report (quoting Julien 1925–9) that before felling the *farafatse* the Vezo address 'nature's spirits' and sacrifice to them, but I have no evidence of this.

10 Vezo who live in areas where *farafatse* does not grow or has become very scarce buy their canoes from other Vezo who live closer to the primary materials (Faublée and Faublée 1950:434–42). See Battistini 1964:113 on the supply of canoes in southern Madagascar.

11 Comparing canoes to cattle troughs has didactic purposes in a story reported by Koechlin (1975:63–5). A group of Vezo settle in a Mahafaly village and begin pursuing typically Vezo activities, which the Mahafaly observe with some surprise. When the Vezo say that they are going into the forest to fell a tree for a canoe, the Mahafaly ask what a canoe looks like. The Vezo reply that 'it is a dug-out trunk like one of your cattle troughs, but it is much bigger'.

12 Petit (1930:209) noted that Vezo children receive their first sailing lessons with these toys.

13 This is a generic term used on the west coast for the people from south-eastern Madagascar.

14 The fishing techniques described by Koechlin (1975) for Bevato, south of Morombe, differ from those I observed in Betania or in Belo. Near Morombe, the Vezo exploit the coral reef, while near Morondava, where there is no reef, the Vezo practise line fishing almost exclusively; in Belo, by contrast, people exploit the vast lagoon and its canals with a variety of techniques that depend on the kind of fishing net they employ.

15 The name of the fish does not always need to be specified. Kola, aged fourteen, was well known for his ability to avoid any task he was asked to do. His mother asked him to clean the fish she had brought back from the market. Kola called out to his younger sister, who however was not around; he tried to gain time and pretended to be fixing the sail of his toy canoe. His mother repeated her request to clean the fish. Kola looked at it and asked

her what kind of fish it was: '*ino karazam-pia io?*' At this point she lost her temper, shouting 'I don't know! That animal over there that comes from the sea' (*tsy hainteña biby io bakan-drano io*).

16 People may well eat only rice without an accompanying side-dish, but it is unthinkable to eat fish, or any other side–dish for that matter, without rice or one of its substitutes (maize or manioc). The only exception occurs during ritual occasions, including the consumption of sea-turtles, when rice is not consumed.

17 If large quantities of fresh fish are on sale in the evening, its price may be lower than that of smoked fish which is sold the next morning.

18 Cheating people who 'do not know fish' was reported by Petit (1930:250), who noted the poor quality of smoked fish exchanged with the Masikoro. According to Petit, the fish is imperfectly cured, but if this is pointed out to a Vezo 'he will not hesitate to reply: "It's good enough for a Masikoro."' According to Koechlin (1975:94), the Vezo customarily sell a kind of inedible octopus to the Masikoro; he also notes that the Masikoro cheat the Vezo in turn with an inferior quality of manioc.

19 In other words, I am not claiming to be doing what, for example, Borofsky (1987) has done for the Pukapukans (South Pacific).

20 '*Reo tsy ho Masikoro mifitaky antety añy, fa Bekoropoka antety tety? Masikoro reo.*'

21 '*De lafa niavy tety, nanjary Vezo zahay. Nianatsy lafa niavy taty, nianatsy ranomasina io, ehe, nanjary niha Vezo any.*'

22 '*Lafa niavy tatoy voalohany rozy, tany ty fa tanim-Bezo raha teo, taloha. Ka lafa niavy an-rozy, nandramby avao koa nianatse. Reo tsy raha sarotsy ianara, na zaza kelikeliky manahakan'zao, lafa mianatsy, malaky mahay, satsia tsy misy taratasy moa, raha ahazoa diplôme, fa io tsy raha misy diplôme. Fa lafa mianatsy mive, fa mahay mive, fa mahay manday laka. Zay ñy fianara laka zay. Ka razanay reo fa nahay, nianatsy koa zahay nandimby any reo, satsia raha nataon-draiamandreninteña any vo ataonteña arakaraky tenim-bazaha manao hoe: 'tel fils tel père'. Zay io, raha nataon' babanteña, ataon-teña koa. Zay fandehany. Nianatsy laka zahay, nahay laka; nianatsy laka koa zafinay retoa. Zay io fandehany io.*'

23 '*Olo mifitaky andriaky iaby atao hoe Vezo*'; '*mahatonga iñy moa, avy amin'ny fitondranteña hain-teña, amin'ny toerany misy an-teña.*'

24 The term *fomba* refers to ways of doing *anything*, including a certain way of fishing, cooking, eating, talking, offering food to the ancestors, marrying, giving birth, etc. On *fomba*, cf. also below, pp. 61–5.

25 My informants suggested that practices in Betania and Belo are representative of differences between the northern and southern coast as a whole.

26 The excitement and sense of achievement that accompanied my transformation into a Vezo person was followed by the somewhat difficult realization that, on leaving Betania to return home, I was going to 'drop' my Vezoness. As the time of my departure approached, I noticed that my friends began to make insistent comments on my ability to eat fish. I found this sudden interest in something I had learnt months earlier rather odd, until someone remarked that my parents in Italy would be astonished to see me eat

fish in this way; they would exlaim: 'You really are Vezo!' (*fa Vezo tokoa iha!*). I then realized that as far as my friends could judge, eating fish and spitting out the bones was the only Vezo activity I could engaged in back home, in the absence of canoes, a beach and fishing expeditions. But although the act of eating fish in a certain way renders me Vezo still, my friends were also perfectly aware that on returning home, I was going to become a *vazaha* (a white) again. If the identity with which I arrived in Betania was considered to be irrelevant to what I was about to become as I started to live on the coast, I felt that what I had experienced for eighteen months was similarly regarded as irrelevant to what I was about to become in England, where people imagined me engaged in the process of writing a book about them.

27 The Lamarckian model of identity elaborated by Linnekin and Poyer (1990) to account for cultural identity and difference in Oceania, is predicated on the principle that 'acquired characteristics are heritable'; this principle addresses two related issues. On the one hand, the fact that characteristics *are* acquirable means that the environment, broadly defined, determines people beyond their genetic substance; this in turn implies that people are malleable and transformable. On the other hand, the fact that acquired characteristics are heritable means that people pass on to future generations not their genetic substance, but rather their lived relationships with the environment. From this perspective, Lamarckianism provides a theory of ontogeny which postulates that people are not born what they are, but are made by what they do, by how they behave, and by the environment in which they live. Lamarckian cultural identities, like Sahlins' 'performative structures' (1987), 'are made as well as born'; they are constructed out of practice (Linnekin and Poyer 1990:8–9).

28 See Watson 1990:39–40 for his discussion of the 'ethnic' dimension of Kainantu identity; for a more general discussion of descent within Lamarckian models of identity, see Lieber 1990.

29 I could have made a similar point, using Pomponio's ethnography on the Mandok islanders (1990:43). Although people are made what they are by the place where they live (the sea as opposed to the bush), Mandok's perceptions of their '*essential* identity' is informed by the idea that 'despite the fact that they originally migrated from primarily bush locations, through subsequent generations the Mandok seem to have *absorbed* the autochthonous essence of a maritime habitat' (p. 52), elsewhere referred to by Pomponio as 'marigenic substance'.

30 My informants did not use this term; I employ it as short-hand for the kind of oppositions they drew between Vezo and Masikoro activities. One may note in passing that the incompatibility between Vezo and Masikoro modes of livelihood also establishes their mutual dependency: the Vezo need the Masikoro to provide them with agricultural products; the Masikoro need the Vezo to provide them with fish.

31 Individuals or groups who contradict this postulate by engaging in both kinds of economic pursuit are considered to 'be' Vezo or Masikoro contextually; cf. for example, above, the case of the Masikoro who can build

canoes.

32 I wish to thank Marilyn Strathern for suggesting this point to me.

3 People without wisdom

1 This was my informants' explanation of *mitindroke*. Dahl (1968:119) explains the term as follows: 'nourriture ramassée, cueillie; *mi-* chercher, cueil-
lir de la nourriture, picorer; *fitindroha* endroit où l'on en cherche habituelle-
ment'. Koechlin (1975) is slightly ambiguous about the meaning of the term
mihake. In one context, *mihake* is defined generically as 'the search for food
. . . hunting and gathering' (p. 23) and appears to be a synonym for *mitindroke*; elsewhere the term refers to the specific fishing technique of the Vezo
of Bevato (p. 69).

2 *Mitindroke* does not apply to pigs raised inside fences which are fed directly
by their owners.

3 'Io mahay olo Vezo reo mipetraky andriaky reo, reo nahay anio.
Voalohany, nataondrosy laka, misy hazo ataoe hoe mafay. Hazo, ka vinahy
io natao hoe, natao laka, natao sary sañan'io; vita nasay, nitoky raha io,
tsy nihafo. Nandeha amin'zao reo, nilitsy nandeha añala, mbao nahita an'i
farafatse io; maiky amin'zao raha eñy nenteandrozy: aha, reto sabbony
hazo homety atao laka, fa maiva reto. Zay nivanandrozy anio, niasandrozy
laka eo. Lafa amin'zao maiky raha eñy, laha nitery, nihafo. Zey ny
fotorany.'

4 Cf. Malinowski 1922:398ff. on the denial by Trobrianders that magic has
ever been 'invented'; and Firth 1939:84ff. on the lack of traditions on disco-
veries and inventions among the Tikopia. See also Bodenhorn 1989:89 for
the legend about the way Iñupiat 'thought' their first survival skills.

5 'Lafa mandeha mitindroke teña, de lafa vita amin'zay mimpoly teña, ka tsy
moly mañandrefa fa moly mañantinana, ka bakandrano miranga an-tana.'

6 The fact that the open sea, which the Vezo only ever reach by accident, is
called *ankafohe* is consistent with this visual orientation. The term *ankafohe*
implies being in the middle of, and surrounded by the sea, so that one is unable to leave it behind one's back. *Ankafohe* is where a Vezo loses hope of
reaching his village again (*tsy velo fa maty teña*, 'one is not alive but dead').
My data on marine terminology differ from Koechlin's (1975:30).

7 There are local prohibitions, such as speaking Merina words (*teny Am-
baniandro*) in places near Belo where Merina armies fought and were trap-
ped and drowned by the rising tide; some marine creatures may dislike
people who have eaten pork or who have light skin. Especially noteworthy
is the lack of female bans on fishing or on contact with fishing equipment.
Although I never asked if menstruating women can go fishing, I was never
told not to do so myself; a woman I knew travelled on a canoe that was
normally used for fishing during her menstrual period.

8 Other version of this story are in Petit 1930 and Birkeli 1922–3.

9 'Fano, biby tsy matimaty matetiky, ka manan-kaja; fa ny fia maty
isanandro, fa ny fano tsy dia matin'olo isanandro; isam'bola na isan'tao no
mamono fano ny olo.'

10 The contrast between sea-turtles and fish is significant in so far as the 'diffi-

culty' of the former highlights the 'easiness' of the latter. Thus, while sea-turtles may be seen as 'giving themselves up to those who act properly', as animals are believed to do by Iñupiat (Bodenhorn 1989:93), fish must be found and caught by applying one's personal skills.

11 In this respect, the sea is neither a *giving* nor a *reciprocating* environment for the Vezo (cf. Bird-David 1990).

12 Although employers of wage labour are not always white people, they are invariably called *vazaha* because of their position of authority.

13 This statement was endlessly repeated to me and to my visitors, but it was also reiterated in conversations I was not directly involved in. As I explain below, the sentence refers indiscriminately to men, women and children (see below, notes 16 and 17).

14 At times this notion is taken literally to mean that 'there is money inside fish' (*de misy vola añaty fia*). The man who told me this claimed that a very old and knowledgeable man had told him that money was first found inside fish. Most people, however, disagreed with this version, explaining that the expression that money comes from the sea is simply a metaphor for saying that the Vezo earn their income with fish sold on the market.

15 Money is to a large extent kept and controlled by women, who control the sale of fish and decide how money is spent (*ampela Vezo manao decision*, 'Vezo women make the decisions'). Men must ask their wives or mothers for cash to buy liquor, and this sometimes leads to lengthy negotiations and quarrels.

16 See Carsten (1989) for an analysis of the gender-specificity of handling money among the Malay of Langkawi. After receiving cash from the men, who control the marketing of fish, the women 'cook' and 'moralize' the money by removing themselves from the competitive and divisive effects that the market has on the community, and by transforming 'the one kind of community, based on differentiation, exchange and alliance and primarily male, into the other, based on the notion of a collection of similar female-dominated houses' (p. 138). Parry and Bloch suggest that the different use that men and women make of money among Malay is an instance of the 'two related but separate transactional orders: on the one hand transactions concerned with the reproduction of the long-term social or cosmic order; on the other, a 'sphere' of short-term transactions concerned with the arena of individual competition' (pp. 23ff.). Among the Vezo, by contrast, the short-term squandering of money is construed as a non-gender-specific characteristic of Vezo-ness; men and women alike join in the second 'sphere' of short-term transactions. As I explain below, the only occasion in which the Vezo recognize that they *must* save is when they need large sums of money to build tombs for the ancestors. The Vezo thus construct and experience the long-term transactional order through planning and saving for the ancestors, an issue to which I return in chapter 8.

17 'The money is gone; it is food that finishes it off' (*vola fa lany, ka hany io ro mandany azy*).

18 After helping with the shrimp-fishing described in chapter 2 above, Kola, aged fourteen, was rewarded with some cash by his mother, who suggested

that he buy a new pair of shorts since the ones he had were falling apart. Kola instead bought a plastic ball, which was hugely successful with the other children; only one day later, however, the ball hit a large spike and 'died' (*fa maty*). Kola's mother did not lose her chance to berate him for his lack of wisdom; and a few hours later Kola was busy with needle and thread trying to patch his old shorts together.

19 Firth (1946:26–7, 293–4) provides a more general analysis of saving strategies in an 'Oriental peasant economy' based on fishing.

20 Such as petty trade, cooking and selling food snacks, cutting and selling firewood and timber for building houses.

21 The contrast between schooners and canoes can be appreciated by noting that an average schooner loads between 20 and 30 tons, and that a 30 ton schooner is about 15 m long and 3 m high.

22 Around when my oldest informant stated he was born in 1905, schooners already existed in Belo. A manuscript I was shown in Morondava by a local politician, who is also a powerful boat-owner (see below), records that in 1888 Albert Joachim, known as Bebe, arrived in Tulear from Réunion to teach the Vezo how to build schooners. He soon moved to Morombe, where he stayed until 1890. Later he moved to Belo, where he married; finally, in 1904, he settled in Morondava, where he opened a boat yard for building schooners. Men were awarded a diploma after working for three years at the boat yard. Bebe died in Morondava in 1932. Although the title-page of the manuscript was missing, I suspect that it might have been a copy of the report by Couvert and Nockain (1963).

23 A study of the transport industry on the west coast of Madagascar made in the early 1960s (see above, note 22), praised the Vezo for their technical skills in building and sailing *botsy*. By contrast, the Vezo's commercial activities were judged unsatisfactory from the point of view of the traders: 'la pratique commerciale des goélettes . . . relève du *tramping* . . . Cette pratique conduit à voire par fois, sur un port donné, une absence totale de goélette pendant une longue période, puis la présence simultanée de plusieurs bâtiments, et ne permet pas aux chargeurs éventuels de faire confiance aux goélettes quant aux transports de leurs produits. A terre, les capitaines de goélettes doivent rechercher eux-même leur frêt en faisant du porte à porte pour solliciter les clients éventuels. Si d'aventure la présence de plusieurs d'entre eux est simultanée, la recherche de frêt les conduit à essayer de s'arracher celui-ci par tous les moyens, y compris l'abaissement à un prix ridicule des couts de frêt.'

4 Avoiding ties and bonds

1 The term *fomba* can refer to any 'way of doing things' that is recognized to be 'customary' (common rather than uncommon) for either an individual or a larger group of people. For example, if a person likes to drink before her meal rather than after, it is her 'custom' (*fombany*) to do so; the fact that people in Betania are used to selling their fish at the market can be referred to as their 'custom' (*fomban-drozy*). In their idiosyncratic form, *fomba* are not defined by their link with the past.

2 This character of speech is not connected with dialectal differences. People seemed pleased to point out to me that in moving from Betania to Belo I was going to encounter a 'different speech' (*resaky hafa*), namely a different pronunciation of certain phonemes.

3 Koechlin (1975:46) reports that the Masikoro tell their children not to be like Vezo children, who are bad mannered (*ka manao ana-Bezo fa raty*).

4 Softness, however, can also be positively enforced. On one occasion I witnessed a girl being scolded by both her parents to the point of being threatened with a fire-brand to stop screaming and wailing. I watched from a distance, shocked by this demonstration of adults' severity and roughness. By way of explanation, however, I was told that the girl was being treated this way because she had asked to be payed for delousing her mother's hair, something she had demanded many times before. This child was 'hard-headed' (*mahery loha*), her 'customs' (i.e. requesting to be paid for her services) were very bad (*raty mare fombany*), and her screaming and wailing proved that she was 'wild and aggressive' (*masiake anaky io*). This example suggests that learning to be a 'soft' Vezo is more conflictual than the Vezo themselves would admit. At the same time, the fact that people depict the shaping of the character and disposition of children as a smooth, unproblematic production of gentleness out of gentleness is in itself significant, for it merely establishes and confirms the pervasive softness of the character of the Vezo.

5 The term '*faly*' is also often used to indicate a prohibition, without by this implying the existence of a taboo sanctioned by custom; for example, children were warned off my belongings by telling them that they were *faly* for them (*faly anao*).

6 I discuss the marriage ritual in more detail in Astuti 1993.

7 The term *mora* used in the expression *fanambalia amin'ny Vezo mora mare* means both 'easy' and 'cheap' (conversely, the term *sarotsy* means both 'difficult' and 'expensive').

8 The ease of Vezo marriage strikes outsiders as well. When I asked Marofasy, the Antandroy man I referred to in chapter 2, what differences he found between the customs of the Vezo and those of the Antandroy, the first thing that came to his mind were the customs related to marriage. Showing surprise and disbelief, he stressed how easy marriage is among the Vezo and then lectured me on the large number of cattle and goats a young Antandroy man like him has to give his in-laws in order to marry. See Baré 1977:58 and Feeley-Harnik 1991:180 on marriage prestations paid by the Sakalava Bemihisatra.

9 See below, pp. 81, 97, on the claim that women are 'the real source – origin – hence the owners of the children' (*ampela ro tena tompony*).

10 My informants seemed to believe that the 'easiness' with which marriage is contracted, and the resulting marital instability, are peculiar to the Vezo; the studies by Ottino (1965) and Waast (1980) on marriage instability among the Sakalava (see also Baré 1977:57ff.) suggest that this view is not correct. My concern here, however, is not with the sociological grounds for my informants' view, but with the Vezo perception of marriage and their construction of it as a non-binding relationship.

11 The father-in-law shouted: '*zahay ro tompon'asa ty, de zahay avao ro mahavita*

azy, ka tsy mila anao. Arosoa!', 'we are the masters of this work, and only we are going to see it through, so that we do not need you. Go away!'

12 An oft-quoted story is that when a Masikoro man falls in love with a Vezo woman – a frequent occurrence, according to my friends, because Vezo women both are beautiful (*ampela Vezo ampela soa mare*) and have a lot of money (*manam-bola maro ampela Vezo*) – he is forced to go to live with her on the coast because she finds the interior too unhealthy and hot. See Feeley-Harnik 1991:183.

13 Among the Menina, the people who live in the northern part of the central plateau of Madagascar, during the marriage ritual, the groom offers his father-in-law a sum of money which is called 'the backside of a sheep' (*vody ondry*). 'By performing the ceremony the son-in-law puts himself at the beck and call of his father-in-law, he receives ancestral blessing from him, he will contribute to his father-in-law's tomb expenses but he does not just become a new son, he becomes a new *super son* . . . He does not just contribute to the tomb expenses like a son, he contributes even more than a son. He does not just help his father-in-law in agricultural tasks, he 'rushes' to perform them before anything else, before the bidding of his own father. He does not just give *vody akoho*, the backside of a chicken, he gives the *vody aondry*' (Bloch 1978:27).

14 As noted by Feeley-Harnik (1983–4:140), 'brutality (*siaka*) was one of the foremost of royal characteristics'.

15 See Koechlin 1975:46–8, 64, 95 for comments on the mobility of the Vezo as a means of avoiding political control. Similarly, Grandidier and Grandidier (1908–28, I:376 note 4) noted that prior to French colonization the Vezo were frequently pillaged by the Sakalava kings (see also Grandidier 1971:14), and that when they had reason to fear a raid they did not hesitate to migrate. Walen (1881–4:12) wrote that because the Vezo were few and weak they were unable to resist the Masikoro attacks; if conflicts arose between the two, the Vezo took to their canoes and fled.

16 See Fauroux 1975:78.

17 See for example Feeley-Harnik 1982 on the role of slavery in the North.

18 This is insightfully explored by Feeley-Harnik (1978).

19 Also known as *tapasiry*.

6 Kinship in the present and in the future

1 See Astuti 1993 for the problems involved in using this term.

2 See below, note 20 for the meaning of the term *tompo*.

3 His gender is irrelevant as far as his vision is concerned; old women enjoy the same vision.

4 According to the reckoning mentioned above, Sary is Lefo's mother; however, Sary and Lefo can also be considered siblings (the father of the mother of the father of Sary's father was a brother of the father of the mother of the father of Lefo's mother).

5 *Dadilahy's* statement could be interpreted as meaning that marriage is divisive because some people, normally one's daughters, are 'lost' as they move out to follow their spouses (see above, pp. 68–72). Given the context of the conversation, and the fact that daughters or sons who move out at marriage remain with-

in *dadilahy*'s inclusive vision of *filongoa* (see below), I find this interpretation unconvincing.

6 The way in which *dadilahy* seems to regard marriage as an instrument for defining people as non-kin resembles the point made by Huntington (1978 and 1988) with regard to the Bara, a group of pastoralists in southern Madagascar. Huntington argues that the Bara 'maintain the categorical distinction between kin and non-kin' by acknowledging that an act of incest has occurred and by accepting that it needs to be atoned for (1988:100). The Merina are also reported to use marriage instrumentally, in their case to establish kinship links. For the Merina, the ideal marriage between deme members 'does not forge a link of affinity between groups, but it reaffirms a kinship link' by strengthening already existing genealogical ties (Bloch 1971:196). The same principle is made to apply even when the two parties are *not* genealogically related; in this case, the act of marriage becomes a sign of kinship even when this does not actually exist (as with the *havana mpifankatia*) (p. 203).

7 The distinction between close and distant kin (*foko* and *longo*) as defined by Ottino (1963) and employed by Lavondès (1967) and Koechlin (1975) was not used by my informants. The latter also strongly denied that the 'close' relatives of ego's spouse become ego's *longo*, as suggested by Ottino; Koechlin (1975:32–3), by contrast, states that it is not marriage but the birth of offspring that creates kinship ties, and consequently also marriage prohibitions. Cf. Feeley-Harnik 1991:203 for an example of the latter.

8 *Dadilahy*'s descendants draw upwards from themselves many paths of ascendancy, and they do so *simultaneously*; they do *not* select one among the many available. Therefore, the process by which they draw themselves *to* an ascendant (rather than *from* an ancestor) has different implications from those discussed by Errington (1989: 216, 222).

9 More recently, Southall has pointed out that the 'discussion of the social organization of Malagasy people has focused a good deal on whether they are predominantly cognatic or agnatic . . . It now begins to appear that this debate may have been misconceived' (1986:417). In his 'recapitulation' of the social organization of the northern Sakalava, Baré (1986:390) makes a similar point: 'the discussion on whether Malagasy social systems are "cognatic" or not seems to me to be by now devoid of any meaning'. However, whereas Southall (1986:417) suggests an alternative model of 'cumulative kinship', according to which 'what seems to be distinctive about all Malagasy kinship systems is not their qualities of cognation and agnation, but their emphasis on kinship and descent status as something achieved gradually and progressively throughout life, and even after death, rather than ascribed and fixed definitively at birth', Baré (1977) addresses people's membership to a descent group from a static perspective, by stressing that clanic affiliation is 'activated' by an 'optative' choice of residence that is nonetheless fixed in space and time. On the other hand, his analysis suggests the 'cumulative' character of descent for women and women's children (1986:374).

10 Cf. also Baré's work on the Bemihisatra monarchy of northern Madagascar, in which he takes residence as the principle by which 'one dominant clan membership' is established (1977:35ff.). Fauroux (1980:83ff.) and Schlemmer (1983:104) have also commented on people's choice of one clan affiliation among many.

11 Cf. Hecht's analysis (1977) of Pukapuka patrilineal descent as 'cumulative pat-
     rifiliation through burial', and her description of *pö* and *wakavae* (the patrilineal
     units) as 'patrilineal and burial categories'.

12 Bloch (1971) also notes that the Merina consider it tactless to enquire about
     people's *karazana*, although the cause of unease seems to be rather different
     from that of the Vezo. Since, among the Merina, membership of the demes is
     indicative of people's rank (according to the demes' closeness to the monarch),
     asking about a person's *karazana* has embarrassing hierarchical implications.
     By contrast with the Vezo, however, an individual's deme membership is a use-
     ful piece of sociological information, which can be tactfully obtained by asking
     for a person's *tanindrazana* (the land where the ancestors lived). Since 'an ex-
     perienced Merina carries in his head a sociological map of old Imerina', know-
     ing a person's *tanindrazana* amounts to knowing her *karazana* and rank (p. 107).

13 References in this chapter to the paternal/maternal or father's/mother's *raza* are
     to the *raza* the mother or father is expected to become a member of through
     burial; I am not implying that either father or mother 'belongs' to a *raza* as a
     living person.

14 The type of ritual referred to in conversation is quite clear from the context, and
     people normally refer to *soron'anake* as *soro*; I follow the same practice in my
     account.

15 I use *iano*, which means 'so and so' and is ungendered, as a proper name for the
     sake of convenience.

16 If Iano's father is still alive, Iano is buried in the tomb where his father is ex-
     pected to be buried. In turn, Iano's father's place of burial is determined by
     whether Iano's grandfather had performed *soro* or not for his son.

17 I intentionally use the term 'elders' very vaguely here; further detail is provided
     in the section on the *hazomanga* below.

18 See above, note 16.

19 *Soro* might still be performed by Iano *itself* (*misoro vata*, 'to do *soro* for oneself')
     even after Iano's father's death.

20 'Manomboky eto, manan'anaky ny lehilahy. Laha tsy mahavita soro, tsy
     manan'anaky ny lehilahy fa ampela ro tompon'ajà, ampela, neniny niteraky
     azy: ie ro tompon'ajà. Laha mahavita soro, baban'ajà ro tompon'ajà. [pause]
     Hoatsy: maty ny zaza; laha mbo tsy mahavita soro babany, milevy amin'ny
     lolon'neniny. Maty zaza, maty ajà, vita soron'babany, milevy amin'ny
     lolon'babany.' I have rendered the term *tompo* rather awkwardly with 'master'
     and 'mistress' because the term has a wide range of meanings, from simple
     ownership of an object (*tompon-kiraro reto*, 'the owner of these shoes') to a rela-
     tion of authority over things and people (*tompon-trano*, 'the master of the
     house', 'the head of the family'; *tompon'aja*, 'the master of the children', the per-
     son who has control and responsibility over them; *tompon-tany*, 'the masters of
     the land' or autochthons). In many parts of Madagascar *tompoko* ('my master')
     is a term of address equivalent to sir and madam.

21 Although a father need perform *soro* only for the first-born child in order to
     establish burial rights over all the children the mother will subsequently bear
     him, he does not acquire permanent rights over the woman's *fertility* as is in-
     stead common in bridewealth systems. Moreover, if the marriage breaks up *soro*

loses all effect, for the man who has done *soro* is not the 'master' of children had from other men. The fathers of these other children have to perform *soro* in turn; if they do not, the offspring are buried in their mother's tomb. In other words, a father's paternity is neither established nor guaranteed by *soro*, confirming that *soro* does not concern control over procreation but control over dead bodies. A very different interpretation of *soro* among the Masikoro is in Lavondès (1967:63–7); for Schlemmer (1983:101) the ritual concerns 'the production of men [sic] as labour force: of men of working age'.

22 See also Koechlin 1975:133.

23 More seldom, depending on the customs (*fomba*) of the woman's *raza*, the man can be asked to bring bananas or beans.

24 Lavondès (1967:64) reports that for the Masikoro *soron-tsoky* is a ritual 'intended for "lifting" the consequences of the wrongdoings undertaken, knowingly or unknowingly, by the woman's family [*soro ala havoa*]'. It is performed by offering a head of cattle provided by the man's family, which is killed at the woman's elders' place; if the family is poor the ritual can be performed with rice. There is no suggestion that *soron-tsoky* acts as a substitute for the *soro* performed after the child is born; see also Schlemmer 1983:100–1. While Koechlin (1975:134) does not discuss the issue explicitly, he would seem to suggest that the Vezo he worked with in Bevato consider *soron-tsoky* a substitute for *soron'aomby*.

25 *Biby* has a wider range of meanings than the term 'animal'; it designates what is not human, including animals, people who behave inhumanly, ancestors (see p. 106 below), and various creatures of the sea and forest. I have therefore preferred to leave the term untranslated.

26 Although there is some disagreement as to the exact age when a child should be buried in a tomb, the general principle I have stated is upheld unanimously.

27 Another person told me that although 'water babies' have bones, these are still very soft and weak (*taola fa misy avao, fa malemy, tsy henja*).

28 See Beaujard 1983:446ff. for an example of conflict and body snatching among the Tanala of south-eastern Madagascar.

29 The fact that a woman enters her husband's tomb as mother-of-her-children and not as wife-of-her-husband is confirmed by the fact that a barren woman cannot be buried in her husband's tomb. To do so is taboo (*faly*) and is therefore not open to negotiation.

30 When the choice is between the father's or the husband's tomb as in the case mentioned above, it is still formulated in terms of the contrast between fatherhood (the relation between father and daughter) and motherhood (the relation between mother and children).

31 The terms *nenikely*, *babakely* ('little mother', 'little father', a junior female/male sibling of ego's parents) and *nenibe*, *bababe* ('big mother', 'big father', a senior female/male sibling of ego's parents) are seldom used to discriminate between a parent and its siblings.

32 Describing the process of depersonalization that takes place during funerals in Mayotte, Lambek and Breslar (1986:407) report that the dead person is addressed as the offspring of its mother, instead of the father, as occurs during lifetime. They suggest that whereas the attribution of paternity is a social con-

vention that therefore has to be asserted, maternity is a self-evident, 'natural' fact; hence, the use of the matronymic form eclipses the dead person's social identity. Among the Vezo, by contrast, the dead person is not referred to as the offspring either of the father or of the mother. By referring to the dead person in terms of the person who performed *soro* for it, what is stated and is effectively activated for the first time is the dead person's identity as a member of the *raza*.

33 People for whom *soro* has not been performed are referred to accordingly as 'women's children' (*anakan'ampela*), for their only link with the 'singular' *raza* and its tomb is through the woman who gave birth to them.

34 I use the term *hazomanga* to indicate the person who *holds* the *hazomanga* proper (wooden poles where offerings are presented to the ancestors), despite the fact that the literature refers to this person as *mpitan-kazomanga* ('the holder of the *hazomanga*'). As I explain below, in the area where I did fieldwork people make no distinction between the two.

35 Koechlin (1975:129) also comes close to explaining the position of the *hazomanga* in terms of his association with the *raza* as a group of dead people buried in one tomb, rather than in terms of his function as the head of the *raza* defined as a group of living people.

36 Women cannot be *hazomanga*, the reason being that 'a woman follows the man' (*ampela manaraky johary*). Although women follow men in marriage (see above, pp. 68–72), in this context it is probably more significant that they can follow them in death as well when they are buried with their children in their husband's tomb. If women were allowed to be *hazomanga*, therefore, they could be the *hazomanga* for one *raza* during their lifetime and then become a member of a different *raza* through burial.

37 When the *hazomanga* calls the ancestors, he cannot (*fa faly*) call his dead juniors ('junior siblings', *zay*, or 'children', *anaky*) by name; they can only be called collectively together with the other ancestors (*ankapobe*). If an offering has to be made to one of them individually, the *hazomanga* has a younger person make the actual offering.

38 See for example Julien (1925–9); Lavondès (1967); Koechlin (1975); Schlemmer (1983:100 note 25).

39 The *hazomanga* in western Madagascar is supposed to have been imposed originally by the conquering dynasties on the autochthons. See Kent 1970:314 for the Mahafaly; Lavondès 1967:21 note 3 for the Masikoro-Sakalava.

40 'Hazomanga maranitse reñy, aminy Vezo, misy avao kiraikiraiky, fa zay no mahasarotsy azy raha zay, fa tsy dea izy loatsy no tompony, fa raha mandimby olo lavitsy añy ka zay ro tsy anañane añoreñane any raha eo. Fa laha teña tompony, manahaka ao Masikoro mbao reo, reo fa tompony reo, razany eo avao laha teo, tsy nandeha baka lavitsy añy, ehe, ka fa maty raiky fa mandimby azy eo ie, maty raiky fa mandimby azy eo ie, zay. Fa Vezo, olo baka lavitsy ka ny razam-beny, tompon' hazomanga io, tsy raha eo fa tavela añy, añy añy. Fa ñanaky avao, zafy avao, mandeha mañatoy, mañatoy io ka io tsy mahazo manory any hazo maranitsy io atoy io, fa tena tompony mbo añy, mbo lavitsy añy.'

41 Koechlin (1975:126) describes the *hazomanga*-object in Bevato; Millot and Pascal (1952:27) publish a picture of such an *hazomanga* in the area of Morombe.

7 Separating life from death

1 On the meaning of the term *biby*, see above, chapter 6 note 25.

2 People use the formula *sañatsia tany manintsy* more generally each time they mention something associated with death and the cemetery.

3 In fact, if one were to adopt Merina categorization, the Vezo would be 'right' in thinking that their cemeteries are hot. For the Merina, tombs and ancestors are cold because they stand for the positive ideal of regrouping and the resolution of divisions experienced in lifetime; for the Vezo, tombs are hot because they represent the divisions that people ignore during their lives (see above, pp. 89–91).

4 Abinal and Malzac (1987) translate Merina *aina* as 'vie' and *miaina* as 'être en vie, vivre, respirer, se retirer, se dilater'. I render *ay* as 'breath' (rather than 'life') because my informants explained the term to me with a demonstration of breathing, even though they employed the term to mean 'life'.

5 See Feeley-Harnik 1979, 1984, 1986, 1991:40 for the distinction between 'hot work' and 'cold work' in the context of Bemihisatra (northern Sakalava) royal services; work involved in royal funerals is hot, all other services are cold.

6 During my stays in Betania and Belo, I participated in twelve funerals.

7 What Bloch (1971:142) writes about hymn singing during Merina funerals applies equally to the Vezo: 'admittedly the songs are often Church hymns, but they are sung in a boisterous way which contrasts with the way they are sung in church'.

8 This is true in Betania, where people use ready-made planks they buy from a woodyard in Morondava; in Belo, coffin-making is more time consuming and is considered a 'big work', *asa bevata*, because the timber is rougher and harder to plane down.

9 For the Merina it is taboo to add salt to meat cooked at funerals 'in case it is thought too good' (Bloch 1971:142).

10 The man whose house I rented in Betania was obsessed that his job at the local Gas Company prevented him from taking part in funerals in Betania. This was difficult and dangerous (*sarotsy*) and very bad (*raty mare*), since whom could he expect to sing at his wake when *he* died?

11 The 'automatism' of funerals is suggested for the Merina by Bloch (1971:142) and for Malagasy speakers in Mayotte by Lambek and Breslar (1986:404–5); by contrast with the Vezo, however, in both instances people's participation in the routine appears to be unthinking.

12 When the first funeral occurred in Betania, just over a month after my arrival, I had to be extremely insistent in order to attend the wake and communal meals. Everyone in my adoptive family seemed keen to convince me that I should not go; 'it did not matter' (*tsy mañahy*) if I didn't. At the time, I interpreted their behaviour as trying to exclude me from something terribly important, and I felt duty bound to insist on being involved also. Most people appeared to be surprised at seeing me at the communal meal and at the wake, and they went out of their way to make it understood that they approved of my being there; my presence was even referred to in a speech to chide the villagers who had not attended the wake. When the funeral was over, I felt grateful towards those who I thought had generously allowed me to join in. Only later did I understand that the villagers were grateful to *me*, because I had given up my coolness in order to share

with them the disruption caused by death. I also understood that my relatives' insistence that I need not attend the funeral was a way of suggesting that, as an outsider, I was under no obligation to take part and could therefore enjoy a good night's sleep and a proper meal at home.

13 The Vezo I worked with did not follow a codified form of mourning (*misaona*), allegedly because they follow the customs of 'the people of the coast'. Some informants told me what external signs of mourning the Vezo would use, were they prepared to do so. Men shave their hair and beard when they return from the cemetery, and then stop shaving for a whole year; women plait their hair and must keep the same plaits for a whole year. Both men and women wear black clothes, which they also never change for a year. A friend argued that the reason the Vezo wear no signs of mourning is that people die so often, that one would have to have unkempt hair and black clothing year after year and one would look silly (*adaladala*). We can imagine that the reason the Vezo do not want to look silly is that this would undo their previous effort to expel death from the village and restore it to coolness and normality. There is similarly little patience for people whose distress at the death of a relative or friend is considered excessively long drawn, even though reactions to death are expected to differ between people according to their relationship with the deceased and according to the latter's status, especially her age (see below). When a strong, healthy and beautiful young man suddenly died in Betania the whole village was shocked. After the funeral, the man's father fell into a state of deep grief and depression. Since my own house and that of my adoptive mother lay very close to this man's home, we could see him lying idle and staring into space for hours on end. For a while his behaviour was considered normal, but only a couple of days after the funeral my mother began to show unease and to suggest to me and other members of our family that the man should not be left to brood all day, that someone should make him go fishing to take his mind off his son's death, and that I should talk to him and give him some medicine. Although my mother was genuinely worried about the man's physical and mental well-being, she was also visibly disturbed by the sight of him, which reminded her and us of his son's death. Hearing her animated discussions of our neighbour, I felt that the reason she wished and urged the man's father to shake off his sadness was that only thus could the expulsion from village life of his son's 'wasteful' death (see below) be successfully concluded.

14 The fact that Dadikoroko's death followed so closely on Safy's was not seen to be especially significant, people remarking that the two women had been close friends and that they were both very old. It was nonetheless implied that Dadikoroko had waited for her friend's funeral to be over before dying herself, so as to avoid the logistical problems involved with having two funerals going on at the same time.

15 One must stress that it is the dead person who is thought to guide the living into performing the kind of funeral she desires. Since people's tastes differ when they are alive, funerals differ accordingly. I chose to describe Dadikoroko's funeral because she was particularly successful in making the crowd happy.

16 Cf. Feeley-Harnik 1991:35, where she reports a speech delivered at the funeral

of an old Sakalava woman of Analalava, in which the speaker 'began by empha-
sizing Mme. T.'s long life and the great numbers of her descendants: sixteen
children (*zanaka*), of whom thirteen were still living; one hundred and nine
grandchildren (*zafy*); and some twelve "second-grandchildren" (*zafy faharoy*)'.

17 I suggested above, that when the dead person is old the communal meal *should
be* what it must *not* be when the deceased is young. The difference between the
two was explained through analogy with the antinomy of joyfulness and sadness, of the celebration of a long and well-lived life and the pain caused by a
wasted life. The emotional distinction between the two kinds of experience is
obvious and recurs in all the other funeral acts. The meal, however, highlights
the contrast through a particularly distressing image, similar to that discussed in
Bloch's (1985) analysis of the Merina myth which describes how in the past
people used to eat their ancestors, and which plays on the crucial difference between the acceptable image of the young eating the old, and the problematic
image of the old eating the young. In Vezo funerals, the contrast between 'the
young feeding on the old' and 'the old feeding on the young' is construed by
contrasting the grandchildren's enjoyment at being fed by a generous grand-
parent, with the careful avoidance of showing greed when the meal would imply
conviviality with a 'wasteful' (i.e. young) death.

8 Working for the dead

1 When the *hazomanga* talks to the ancestors, informing them that their living descendants are going to build a new tomb for them, he refers to it as the ancestors's house (see below).

2 Writing about the LoDagaa, Goody describes how during funerals 'the surviv-
ors ... "act away" their association with [the deceased's] ghost', in order to 'take
out the dream' (1962:129), or 'expunge the memory of the dead man' (p. 130)
from the activities they undertook with him; doing so will prevent them from
dreaming about the deceased (p. 147). In this case, what must be erased is the
memory of the living; with the Vezo, the emphasis is rather on the memory and
the longing of the dead themselves which, as we shall see, can never be entirely
'acted away'. On the complete loss of memory of the living by the dead, see also
Battaglia 1990:67ff.

3 Women may not know which tomb they will join at death (see above, p. 96). A
married woman will participate in the work her husband organizes for his *raza*,
even if she will not be buried in her husband's tomb; however, she will probably
state that she is not a 'master of the work' but just a person related to the 'masters' by marriage (*olo mpanambaly*). On the other hand, she will act as a 'master
of the work' if the work is organized by her father or a brother.

4 The Malagasy language has two possessive suffixes for the plural possessive ad-
jective 'our', one inclusive (*-ntsika*) and one exclusive (*-nay*). If the term *asantsika* is used, the people addressed are included in the responsibility of organizing and performing the ritual; if the term *asanay* is used, they are excluded.

5 For the significance of fences among the Sakalava, see Feeley-Harnik 1980. See
also Lavondès 1967:69 note 3 for an example of the divisiveness of fences among
the living.

6 As people in Betania remarked, very few such sculptures are left, owing to European thefts. See below, note 23.

7 Although concrete seems to have become readily available and accessible to the Vezo only since the early sixties, my interlocutors were remarkably uninterested in my attempts at reconstructing earlier customs, seemingly because they saw no significant break between the past and the present. People simply learned to use this new medium, concrete, which became available thanks to the Europeans and which allowed them to achieve more successfully what they had always aspired to do, that is to build permanent, lasting tombs for the dead. The durability of concrete seems particularly significant in the context of the importance attached by the Sakalava monarchy to the durability of its own tombs (see Baré 1977; Lombard 1973; Lavondès 1967; Feeley-Harnik 1978, 1991; Bloch 1981).

8 The durability and solidity of the houses of the dead, which often contrasts with the flimsiness of the houses of the living, are a widespread feature in Madagascar. Bloch has remarked on the Merina's 'desire to make a tomb which will last as long as possible'; tombs that last far longer than houses are 'a denial of the fluidity of Merina society and indeed of all the societies of the living' – in this way, tombs are the demonstration of what the Merina feels his society was and ought to be (1971:114). As I mentioned in chapter 6, for the Merina the tomb is the place where 'regrouping' is possible, and where the Merina ideal of being 'one and the same' is finally realized and made permanent. With the Vezo, the durability of the tombs acquires a different connotation, for instead of realizing an ideal state in death, it brings to an end the ideal state which can only exist in life. In this respect, concrete is the appropriate medium to mark the transition between the fluidity and indeterminacy of life and the fixity engendered by death, between *filongoa* and the 'single' *raza*.

9 This applies especially to the cross ritual.

10 The money was spent as follows: concrete 52.870 FMG; metal rods 19.000 FMG; paint 7.750 FMG; bricks 50.000 FMG; rum 230.000 FMG; rice 140.000 FMG; one head of cattle 135.000 FMG; meat bought at the market 30.000 FMG; *tsaka*, tomatoes and onions 3.000 FMG; renting of the *baffle* (tape-recorder and speakers, see below) 40.000 FMG.

11 Nine adults, two young nubile women (*somonjara*) and myself contributed to the *cotisacion*; two young unmarried men (*kidabo*) and one young nubile woman who were expected to contribute failed to do so. Contributions recorded in the notebook varied between 5.000 and 80.000 FMG; additional, unrecorded contributions would be made by everyone in equal shares in short-term *cotisacions* throughout the various stages of the rituals.

12 According to the astrological calendar it is taboo (*faly*) to perform any ritual during the month of November. In one instance the *asa lolo* was performed in December, and many people regarded this as unusual and rather improper (*tsy mety*).

13 When the *hazomanga* bought a new canoe in this period his siblings insinuated that he had paid for it with money from the common fund; in fact half of the money was his own and I had lent him the other half. To dispel these rumours, the *hazomanga* called a family meeting on some excuse and showed that the

money collected for the ritual had not been touched.

14 See Parry and Bloch 1989; above, chapter 3 note 17.

15 Great emphasis is placed on the fact tht the dead should *not* be surprised. As we saw earlier (pp. 59–60), being surprised is a distinctive feature of the living Vezo as they 'keep themselves alive' in Vezo fashion. The lack of surprise in the realm of the dead appears to be another feature distinguishing between life and death.

16 'Faly tokoa rozy nandray an'io, nahazo an'io raha io, io raha electrophone hañañam-bazaha ro natoro[-]areo aze, ka faly, ravo reo, ka izay ro añambara anao, iha raza-be matoe, tsy hotseriky nareo noho la añe hoe-he: "laha zafiko reo, anake reo nahazo raha, ka la tsy misy ty fahatarovan-dreo ahiko". Oho, tsy misy amin'zay, ka izay ro ikaihañanareo añambarañareo io.'

17 Adults teach babies how to do *minotsoky* (a child often learns how to perform this dance before learning to walk) and incite children to dance hard, by sticking out their buttocks, holding their arms up, lowering their bottoms by bending their knees and slowly straightening them again.

18 Cf. Feeley-Harnik 1991:442.

19 Although only one cross is customarily 'begged' for, if it is 'given' the rest follow.

20 The diviner indicates favourable days for the first operation (the moulding of the crosses) and for the ritual's concluding act when the crosses are carried to the cemetery. Within this period, all other operations are undertaken in terms of convenience.

21 Since the woman was buried in her husband's tomb, her father and siblings were unable to build the cross for her and had to wait for her husband's initiative in doing so.

22 Whereas a small heifer can cost as much as 100.000 FMG, a case of beer costs less than 30.000 FMG.

23 The breasts on Nentiko's cross were considered an unusual innovation. While people in my family assured me that they had never seen anything like it before, they volunteered the suggestion that the cross's breasts were somewhat like (*mitovitovy*) the sculptures that were once put on tombs; among other things, these sculptures had also represented big-breasted women. On this, see Astuti 1994.

24 On 'the aspect of sacrilege' involved in the Merina *famadihana*, see Bloch 1971:167ff.

25 Even more significantly, the procession with Dadikoroko's corpse and that with Dadikoroko's cross were identical.

26 It is difficult to translate the term *kisaky* satisfactorily. I have opted for 'playful joke' to render both the fact that it is an act of teasing which is done light-heartedly to have fun *with*, rather than at the expense of, the recipient. Dahl (1968:112) translates *kizake* as 'moquerie'.

27 People were horrified by my description of a Merina *famadihana* I witnessed in Antananarivo, a ritual during which people dance with the corpses of their ancestors (see Bloch 1971, 1982). My friends reacted characteristically, stating that Merina practices are 'difficult' compared to the 'easy' ones of the Vezo (see above, pp. 61–5), and did not apparently recognize the similarities between

famadihana and the Vezo cross ritual.

28 Feeley-Harnik (1991:453–4) notes how among the Sakalava of the Southern Bemihisatra kingdom, the work carried out to replace the fence around the royal
tomb (*menaty* service) repeated 'the royal funeral in a more accessible, think-
able, talkable form'.

References

Abinal, R.P. and Malzac, C.P. 1987. *Dictionnaire malgache-français* (first edn 1888). Fianarantsoa.

Acheson, J.M. 1981. Anthropology of fishing. *Annual Review of Anthropology* 10:275–316.

Alvarez, A.R. n.d. Ethnicity and nation in Madagascar. Paper presented at the Conference on Malagasy cultural identity from the Asian perspective, Leiden University, 28–9 March 1994.

Angot, M. 1961. *Vie et économie des mers tropicales*. Paris: Payot.

Astuti, R. 1991. Learning to be Vezo. The construction of the person among fishing people of western Madagascar. Unpublished PhD thesis, University of London.

1993. Food for pregnancy. Procreation, marriage and images of gender among the Vezo of western Madagascar. *Social Anthropology. The Journal of the European Association of Social Anthropologists* 1, 3:1–14.

in press a. 'The Vezo are not a kind of people'. Identity, difference and 'ethnicity' among a fishing people of western Madagascar. *American Ethnologist*.

1994 'Invisible' objects. Funerary rituals among the Vezo of western Madagascar. *Res. Anthropology and Aesthetics* 25:111–22

Baré, J.-F. 1977. *Pouvoir des vivants, langage des morts: idéo-logiques Sakalave*. Paris: Maspero.

1986. L'organisation sociale Sakalava du Nord: une récapitulation. In Kottak *et al.* 1986 pp. 353–92.

Battaglia, D. 1990. *On the bones of the serpent: person, memory and mortality in Sabarl Island society*. Chicago: The University of Chicago Press.

Battistini, R. 1964. *Géographie humaine de la plaine côtière Mahafaly*. Toulouse: Cujas.

Battistini, R. and Frere, S. 1958. *Population et économie paysanne du Bas-Mangoky*. Paris: ORSTOM.

Beaujard, P. 1983. *Princes et paysans: les Tanala de l'Ikongo*. Paris: L'Harmattan.

Bird-David, N. 1990. The giving environment: another perspective on the economy system of gatherer-hunters. *Current Anthropology* 31:183–96.

1992. Beyond 'the hunting and gathering mode of subsistence': culture-sensitive observations on the Nayaka and other modern hunter-gatherers. *Man* n.s. 27:19–44.

Birkeli, E. 1922–3. Folklore sakalave recuelli dans la région de Morondava. *Bulletin de l'Académie Malgache* 6:185–423.

1926. *Marques de bœufs et traditions de race: documents sur l'ethnographie de la côte occidentale de Madagascar.* Oslo etnografiske museum: Bulletin 2. Oslo.

Bloch, M. 1971. *Placing the dead: tombs, ancestral villages and kinship organization in Madagascar.* London: Seminar Press.

1978. Marriage amongst equals: an analysis of the marriage ceremony of the Merina of Madagascar. *Man* n.s. 13:21–33.

1981. Tombs and states. In S.C. Humphreys and H. King (eds.), *Mortality and immortality.* London: Academic Press, pp. 136–47.

1982. Death, women and power. In M. Bloch and J. Parry (eds.), *Death and the regeneration of life.* Cambridge: Cambridge University Press, pp. 211–30.

1985. Almost eating the ancestors. *Man* n.s. 20:631–46.

1986. *From blessing to violence: history and ideology in the circumcision ritual of the Merina of Madagascar.* Cambridge: Cambridge University Press.

in press. People into places: Zafimaniry concepts of clarity. In E. Hirsch and M. O'Hanlon (eds.), *The anthropology of landscape.* Oxford: Oxford University Press.

unpublished. Seminar paper on knowledge and the person among the Zafimaniry (LSE).

Bloch, M. and Parry, J. 1982. Introduction. In M. Bloch and J. Parry (eds.), *Death and the regeneration of life.* Cambridge: Cambridge University Press, pp. 1–44.

Bodenhorn, B. A. 1989. 'The animals come to me, they know I share'. Iñupiaq kinship, changing economic relations and enduring world views on Alaska's North Slope. Unpublished PhD. Thesis, University of Cambridge.

Borofsky, R. 1987. *Making history: Pukapukan and anthropological constructions of knowledge.* Cambridge: Cambridge University Press.

Carsten, J. 1989. Cooking money: gender and the symbolic transformation of means of exchange in a Malay fishing community. In J. Parry and M. Bloch (eds.), *Money and the morality of exchange.* Cambridge: Cambridge University Press, pp. 117–41.

Comaroff, J.L. 1987. Of totemism and ethnicity: consciousness, practice and the signs of inequality. *Ethnos* 3–4: 301–23.

Condominas, G. 1959. *Perspective et programme de l'étude sociologique du Bas-Mangoky.* Paris: ORSTOM.

Couvert and Nockain 1963. Rapport de la S.A.T.E.C. (sur les goélettes naviguant sur les côtes nord-ouest à sud-ouest de Madagascar). Antananarivo. Mimeo.

Covell, M. 1987. *Madagascar: politics, economics and society.* Marxist Regimes Series. London and New York: Frances Pinter Publishers.

Dahl, O. C. 1968. *Contes malgaches en dialect Sakalava.* Oslo: Universitetsforlaget.

Dandouau, A. and Chapus, G.-S. 1952. *Histoire des populations de Madagascar.* Paris: Larose.

Decary, R. 1964. *Contes et légendes du sud-ouest de Madagascar.* Paris.

Deschamps, H. 1960. *Histoire de Madagascar.* Paris: Berger-Levrault.

Dina, J. 1982. Etrangers et Malgaches dans le Sud-Ouest Sakalava, 1845–1905. Thèse IHPOM, Aix-Marseille I.

Douliot, H. 1893–6. Journal de voyage fait sur la côte de Madagascar (1891–1892). *Bulletin de la Société de Géographie* 1893:329–66; 1895:112–48; 1896:26–64, 233–66, 364–91.

Eggert, K. 1981. Who are the Mahafaly? Cultural and social misidentifications in Southwestern Madagascar. *Omaly sy Anio* 13–14:149–76.

1986. Mahafaly as misnomer. In Kottak *et al.* 1986, pp. 321–35.

Errington, S. 1989. *Meaning and power in a Southeast Asian realm.* Princeton: Princeton University Press.

Fardon, R. (ed.) 1990. *Localizing strategies: regional traditions of ethnographic writing.* Edinburgh, Washington: Scottish Academic Press, Smithsonian Institution Press.

Faublée, J. 1946. *L'ethnographie de Madagascar.* Paris: Maisonneuve et Larose.

1954. *Les esprits de la vie a Madagascar.* Paris: PUF.

Faublée, J. and Faublée, M. 1950. Pirogues et navigation chez les Vezo du sud-ouest de Madagascar. *Anthropologie* 54:432–54.

Fauroux, E. 1975. *La formation sakalava, ou l'histoire d'une articulation ratée.* Paris: ORSTOM.

1980. Les rapports de production Sakalava et leur évolution sous l'influence coloniale (région de Morondava). In R. Waast *et al.* (eds.), *Changements sociaux dans l'Ouest Malgache.* Paris: ORSTOM, pp. 81–107.

Feeley-Harnik, G. 1978. Divine kingship and the meaning of history among the Sakalava (Madagascar). *Man* n.s. 13:402–17.

1979. Construction des monuments funéraires dans la monarchie Bemihisatra. *Taloha* 8:29–40.

1980. The Sakalava house. *Anthropos* 75:559–85.

1982. The king's men in Madagascar: slavery, citizenship and Sakalava monarchy. *Africa* 52:31–50.

1983–4. The significance of kinship in Sakalava monarchy. *Omaly sy Anio* 17–20:135–44.

1984. The political economy of death: communication and change in Malagasy colonial history. *American Ethnologist* 11:1–19.

1986. Ritual and work in Madagascar. In Kottak *et al.* 1986, pp. 157–74.

1991. *A green estate: restoring independence in Madagascar.* Washington and London: Smithsonian Institution Press.

Firth, Raymond 1939. *Primitive Polynesian Economy.* London: George Routledge and Sons.

1946. *Malay fishermen: their peasant economy.* London: Kegan Paul, Trench, Truber.

Firth, Rosemary 1966. *Housekeeping among Malay peasants* (2nd edn). London: Athlone Press.

Fortes, M. 1969. Cognatic systems and the politico-jural domain. In M. Fortes, *Kinship and the social order.* London: Routledge and Kegan Paul, pp. 122–37.

1970. The significance of descent in Tale social structure. In M. Fortes, *Time and social structure and other essays.* London: Athlone Press, pp. 33–66.

1987. The concept of the person. In M. Fortes, *Religion, morality and the person:*

essays on Tallensi religion, ed. J. Goody. Cambridge: Cambridge University Press, pp. 247–86.

Fortune, R. 1963. *Sorcerers of Dobu: the social anthropology of the Dobu Islanders of the Western Pacific*. London: Routledge and Kegan Paul.

Fox, J. 1987. The house as a type of social organization on the island of Roti. In C. Macdonald (ed.), *De la hutte au palais: sociétés 'à maison' en Asie du Sud-Est insulaire*. Paris: CNRS.

Goody, J. 1962. *Death, property and the ancestors*. London: Tavistock.

Grandidier, A. 1971. *Souvenirs de voyages d'Alfred Grandidier 1865–1870 (d'après son manuscrit inédit de 1916)*. Association malgache d'archéologie. Documents anciens sur Madagascar VI. Antananarivo.

Grandidier, A. and Grandidier, G. 1908–28. *Ethnographie de Madagascar*. 4 vols. (part of *Histoire physique, naturelle et politique de Madagascar*). Paris.

Hecht, J. 1977. The culture of gender in Pukapuka: male, female and the *Mayakitanga* 'Sacred Maid'. *Journal of the Polynesian Society* 86:183–206.

Huntington, R. 1973. Religion and social organization of the Bara people of Madagascar. Unpublished PhD thesis, Harvard University.

1978. Bara endogamy and incest prohibition. *Bijdragen Tot de Taal-, Land-, en Volkenkunde* 134:30–62.

1988. *Gender and social structure in Madagascar*. Bloomington: Indiana University Press.

Hurvitz, D. 1986. The 'Anjoaty' and embouchures in Madagascar. In Kottak *et al.* 1986, pp. 107–20.

Julien, G. 1925–9. Notes et observations sur les tribus sud-occidentales de Madagascar. *Revue d'Ethnographie et des Traditions Populaires* 1925:113–23, 237–47; 1926:1–20, 212–26; 1927:4–23; 1928:1–15, 153–75; 1929:2–34.

Kent, R. 1970. *Early kingdoms in Madagascar, 1500–1700*. New York: Holt, Rinehart and Winston.

Koechlin, B. 1975. *Les Vezo du sud-ouest de Madagascar: contribution à l'étude de l'eco-systeme de semi-nomades marins*. Cahiers de l'Homme XV. Paris: Mouton.

Kottak, C.P., Rakotoarisoa, J.A., Southall, A. and Verin, P. (eds.) 1986. *Madagascar: society and history*. Durham: Carolina Academic Press.

Lambek, M. 1983. *Between womb and tomb: notes towards the conceptualization of Malagasy social structure*. Mimeo.

1992. Taboo as cultural practice among Malagasy speakers, *Man* n.s. 27: 245–66.

Lambek, M. and Breslar, J.H. 1986. Funerals and social change in Mayotte. In Kottak *et al.* 1986, pp. 393–410.

Lavondès, H. 1967. *Bekoropoka: quelques aspects de la vie familiale et sociale d'un village malgache*. Cahiers de l'Homme VI. Paris: Mouton.

Lieber, M.D. 1990. Lamarckian definitions of identity on Kapingamarangi and Pohnpei. In Linnekin and Poyer 1990, pp. 71–101.

Linnekin, J. and Poyer, L. (eds.)1990. *Cultural identity and ethnicity in the Pacific*. Honolulu: University of Hawaii.

Lombard, J. 1973. Les Sakalava-Menabe de la côte ouest. In *Malgache qui est tu?* Neuchâtel: Musée d'Ethnographie, pp. 89–99.

1986. Le temps et l'espace dans l'idéologie politique de la royauté sakalava-menabe. In Kottak *et al.* 1990, pp. 143–56.

1988. *Le royaume sakalava du Menabe: essai d'analyse d'un système politique à Madagascar, 17è–20è.* Paris: ORSTOM.

Macintyre, M. 1989. The triumph of the *susu*. Mortuary exchanges on Tubetube. In F.H. Damon and R. Wagner, (eds.) *Death rituals and life in the societies of the Kula ring.* DeKalb: Northern Illinois University Press, pp. 133–52.

Malinowski, B. 1922. *Argonauts of the Western Pacific: an account of native enterprise and adventure in the archipelagoes of Melanesian New Guinea.* London: Routledge and Kegan Paul.

Marcuse, W.D. 1914. *Through Western Madagascar in quest of the golden bean.* London: Hurst.

Marikandia, M. 1991. Contribution à la connaissance des Vezo du Sud-Ouest de Madagascar: histoire et société de l'espace littoral au Fihezena au XVIII et au XIX siècles, Thèse de Troisième cycle, Université de Paris I Pantheon–Sorbonne, Sciences Humaines, UER d'Histoire.

Millot, J. and Pascal, A. 1952. Notes sur la sorcellerie chez les Vezo de la région de Morombe. *Mémoires de l'Institut Scientifique de Madagascar* I, série c:13–28.

Noël, V. 1843–4. Recherches sur les Sakalava. *Bulletin de la Société de Géographie* 1843:40–64, 275–85, 285–306; 1844:385–416.

Ottino, P. 1963. *Les économies paysannes malgaches du Bas-Mangoky.* Paris: Berger-Levrault.

1965. La crise du système familial et matrimonial des Sakalava de Nosy-Be. *Civilisation Malgache* 1:225–48.

Parry, J. and Bloch, M. 1989. Introduction. In J. Parry and M. Bloch (eds.), *Money and the morality of exchange.* Cambridge: Cambridge University Press, pp. 1–32.

Petit, G. 1930. *L'industrie des pêches à Madagascar.* Paris: Société des Editions Maritimes et Coloniales.

Poirier, Ch. 1953. Le damier ethnique du pays côtier Sakalava. *Bulletin de l'Académie Malgache* 31:23–8.

Pomponio, A. 1990. Seagulls don't fly into the bush: cultural identity and the negotiation of development on Mandok Island, Papua New Guinea. In Linnekin and Poyer 1990, pp. 43–69.

Radcliffe-Brown, A.R. 1950. Introduction. In A.R. Radcliffe-Brown and D. Forde (eds.), *African systems of kinship and marriage.* Oxford: Oxford University Press, pp. 1–85.

Sahlins, M. 1987. *Islands of history* (first published in 1985). London and New York: Tavistock Publications.

Schlemmer, B. 1980. Conquête et colonisation du Menabe: une analyse de la politique Gallieni. In R. Waast *et al.* (eds.), *Changements sociaux dans l'Ouest Malgache.* Paris: ORSTOM, pp. 109–31.

1983. *Le Menabe: histoire d'une colonisation.* Paris: ORSTOM.

Southall, A. 1971. Ideology and group composition in Madagascar. *American Anthropologist* 73:144–64.

1986. Common themes in Malagasy culture. In Kottak *et al.* 1986, pp. 411–26.

Strathern, A. 1973. Kinship, descent and locality: some New Guinea examples. In Jack Goody (ed.), *The character of kinship.* Cambridge: Cambridge University

Press, pp. 21–33.

Strathern, M. 1988. *The gender of the gift: problems with women and problems with society in Melanesia*. Berkeley: University of California Press.

1992. Parts and wholes: refiguring relationships in a postplural world. In A. Kuper (ed.), *Conceptualizing societies*. EASA Monograph, London: Routledge and Kegan Paul, pp. 75–104.

Thune, C. 1989. Death and matrilineal reincorporation on Normanby Island. In F.H. Damon and R. Wagner (eds.), *Death rituals and life in the societies of the Kula ring*. DeKalb: Northern Illinois University Press, pp. 153–78.

Waast, R. 1980. Les concubins de Soalola. In R. Waast *et al.* (eds.), *Changements sociaux dans l'Ouest Malgache*. Paris: ORSTOM, pp. 153–88.

Wagner, R. 1977. Analogic kinship: a Daribi example, *American Ethnologist* 4, 4:623–42.

Walen, A. 1881–4. Two years among the Sakalava. *Antananarivo Annual* 5:1–15; 6:14–23; 7:37–48; 8:52–67.

Watson, J.B. 1990. Other people do other things: Lamarckian identities in Kainantu Subdistrict, Papua New Guinea. In Linnekin and Poyer 1990, pp. 17–41.

Index

Cambridge Studies in
Social and Cultural Anthropology

Editors: Ernest Gellner, Jack Goody, Stephen Gudeman, Michael Herzfeld,

Jonathan Parry